PENGUIN MODERN CLASSICS

Israel

Göran Rosenberg was born in a small industrial town outside Stockholm in 1948, the son of two Holocaust survivors. He is the author of the internationally acclaimed *A Brief Stop on the Road from Auschwitz* (2015), which was awarded the August Prize in Sweden and Prix du Meilleur Livre Étranger in France, as well as *Another Zionism, Another Judaism: The Unrequited Love of Rabbi Marcus Ehrenpreis* (2024), which was awarded the Letterstedt Prize for outstanding biography by the Swedish Academy of Science.

GÖRAN ROSENBERG

Israel

A Personal History

PENGUIN BOOKS

PENGUIN CLASSICS

UK | USA | Canada | Ireland | Australia
India | New Zealand | South Africa

Penguin Classics is part of the Penguin Random House group of companies whose addresses can be found at global.penguinrandomhouse.com

Penguin Random House UK
One Embassy Gardens, 8 Viaduct Gardens, London SW11 7BW

penguin.co.uk

First published in the USA by Other Press, 2025
First published in Great Britain in Penguin Classics 2026
001

Copyright © Göran Rosenberg, 2025

An earlier version of this text was published in Swedish as *Det förlorade landet: en personlig historia* by Albert Bonniers Förlag, Stockholm, 1996

The moral right of the author has been asserted

Penguin Random House values and supports copyright.
Copyright fuels creativity, encourages diverse voices, promotes freedom of expression and supports a vibrant culture. Thank you for purchasing an authorized edition of this book and for respecting intellectual property laws by not reproducing, scanning or distributing any part of it by any means without permission. You are supporting authors and enabling Penguin Random House to continue to publish books for everyone. No part of this book may be used or reproduced in any manner for the purpose of training artificial intelligence technologies or systems. In accordance with Article 4(3) of the DSM Directive 2019/790, Penguin Random House expressly reserves this work from the text and data mining exception.

Printed and bound in Great Britain by Clays Ltd, Elcograf S.p.A.

The authorized representative in the EEA is Penguin Random House Ireland, Morrison Chambers, 32 Nassau Street, Dublin D02 YH68

A CIP catalogue record for this book is available from the British Library

ISBN: 978-0-241-79571-2

Penguin Random House is committed to a sustainable future for our business, our readers and our planet. This book is made from Forest Stewardship Council® certified paper.

PREFACE

This book is a about a young man's journey from "specious clarity to obscure groping," to quote Arthur Koestler, the intellectual companion of the young man for most of his life. As Koestler had journeyed from the all-too-clarified springs of communism to "a poisoned river strewn with the wreckage of flooded cities and the corpses of the drowned,"[1] so the young man would travel from the all-captivating promises of the emerging state of Israel in the early 1960s, to the fabricated histories, deceptive myths, and buried villages that he would discover in its wake. And like Koestler (no further comparisons), he would find it necessary to understand what had happened to him, both the enticement and the deception, both the clarity and the obscurity.

The young man is me a lifetime ago, and this book is my attempt later in life at understanding a movement called Zionism, which brought about the creation of a Jewish state called Israel, which would play such a formative role in my life. In this I have endeavored to weave together my own personal journey with an intellectual exploration of the ideas and historical events that came to shape it.

Although this is a book that reflects travels, memories, experiences, encounters, and readings over a longer period of time, the ideas, people, and events that it brings to life remain as central as ever to the understanding of what the State of Israel is and has become. In this, it also remains a book taking its color and tone, and hopefully some of its value, from the time and the atmosphere in which it was conceived.

Nevertheless, the course of events after October 7, 2023, has prompted a revisit of the book, and of people and places of importance to it, in the hope that this will shed some further light on my "obscure groping" with what I see as a turning point not only for Israel, but also for Jewish existence as a whole. In this edition of the book I have thus replaced the original final chapter with two revisits—fully aware that the final chapter of this story is yet to be written.

Göran Rosenberg, March 2025

I

EXODUS

■

Thus says the Lord, the God of Israel:
Let my people go, that they may keep a feast
for me in the wilderness.

—EXODUS 5:1

ASCENT

> The wandering Jew has come to a crossroads,
> and the consequences of his choice will be felt for
> centuries to come.
>
> —ARTHUR KOESTLER, 1950[1]

We ascended to Israel at the end of April 1962, my mother, my sister, and I. Ascension, *aliyah*, is the figurative expression for the emigration of Jews to the Promised Land. In our case, it meant not only that we were heading for a loftier place but also that we were departing from a low point in our life. My father had left us two summers earlier at the age of thirty-seven, overtaken by the disaster he had spent fifteen years trying to survive.[2] On the outside he was handsome and cheerful, with fine features and a warm smile, but inside he was as fragile as glass. Just a few knocks, a disappointment or two, and everything would break. Dad was ill, they said, very ill. He tried hard not to show it, but at night I could hear him calling out unfamiliar names. A few months before he died, during a temporary release from a psychiatric hospital in Strängnäs, we stayed with good friends in a beautifully situated summer cottage on a bay of the Baltic

Sea south of Södertälje. Perhaps the doctors had hoped that a hearty dose of bright spring would dispel the darkness. Early in the morning, while the rest of us were still asleep, he would quietly get up and row out on the bay. I asked to join him, but he never woke me up. After the third or fourth time, he returned with a large pike perch that was left to swim in a bucket all morning—as the rapidly fading memory of a morning's forgetfulness. After lunch the pike perch turned belly-up and a few days later Dad was taken back to the hospital. We never saw each other again.

I was thirteen years old when we left Södertälje, where fragments had begun to heal and roots had begun to search for soil. With desperate determination two survivors had decided to hold on to anything that seemed to give support, and to hold back anything that seemed to open the abyss again. My parents gave me a name they would never learn to pronounce and addressed me in a language neither of them had yet mastered. At the age of two, I was put in one of the first day-care centers of the Swedish welfare state. I learned to cheer for the local ice hockey team and to steal apples from the villa gardens of our white-collar neighbors, and I began to long for the Saint Lucia festival in the assembly hall of the big truck factory, for the midsummer holidays in the small boardinghouse at Näset, and for the walks to the still-fashionable seaside hotel beyond the forest. I saw my father do his military service in a quartermaster's uniform and watched my mother rush off to her job as a seamstress at Tornvalls. Slowly but surely a place that could have been anywhere, and by any realistic calculation should not have been at all, was being twisted and bent and straightened into something that at times was reminiscent of a home.

One summer I found a dead swift in one of the villa gardens, and learned that swifts cannot get off the ground on their own. A cold winter day some kids in the neighborhood threw snowballs at our window and shouted "Jews," wherever they had gotten that word from. Jews were about as common in Södertälje as Blacks, and I was almost as ignorant as they, but my mother's face turned white. For a few years, my parents would sometimes laugh as if the world had begun anew and Södertälje was their home on earth, so how was I to know that what looked like a home was a permanent state of shock?

With my father's death, the fiction dissolved. The footpath through the forest to the seashore, where I knew every blueberry shrub and patch of cowslip like the back of my hand, became a trail of fading memories. The salt- and tar-smelling sea bath, with its ten-meter trampoline and its creaking bridges and its separate pools for naked men and women, was set on fire by Lång-Erik, who used to live at the other end of the rowan-tree alley until they locked him up in an institution for juvenile delinquents a few miles away. By this time the water in the bay was polluted by sewage, and swimming was at own your risk. The dancing pavilion fell into disrepair, the miniature golf course was closed, the beach went silent. For the remainder, the local community had an oil harbor in store, while the forest gave way to warehouses and a large shopping center.

Father was our link to the world, to friends and colleagues, to big dreams and wild plans, but it was a link with the most fragile of attachments. And when the attachment broke, our links broke with it. A few months later, the remainder of the family—my mother, my sister, and I—left Södertälje for Stockholm, and after another year, with our luggage barely unpacked, we moved on.

In the end, it wasn't the low point of departure that made our "ascent" seem so steep. It was the height, after all. We were going to a place flowing not only with milk and honey but with millennial dreams of divine justice and human redemption. To the mother of utopia, the cradle of messianism, the site of redemption, the fulfillment of prophecy. This was the Promised Land, and no other land had ever promised so much, to so many, for so long.

I was of course as ignorant of such promises as I was of the deep disappointments in their wake, but I wasn't wholly unprepared for the mythical dimensions of the journey. Not for nothing had I spent five successive summers at the Jewish summer camp in the archipelago, where glittering bathing shores and lush soccer fields were in constant competition with loftier vistas. In the evenings we would gather to look at photos and listen to stories about the latest and greatest miracle up there—the Jewish State of Israel. I didn't quite understand everything, and it I didn't really see what it had to do with me, but the people portrayed in the photos were all muscular and slender, with their eyes fixated at a point slightly above the horizon. And whether they were carrying a gun or a shovel, it was made perfectly clear that they were on a mission for all of us. Ascending to Israel, we were made to understand, was to assume responsibility for the fate of the Jewish people, to ensure its survival in the face of further persecution, to prevent its final physical and spiritual destruction, and to bring to fruition two thousand years of national and spiritual longing. And if you weren't going to make the journey yourself, which hardly anyone in Sweden seemed willing to do, there was no question that you had an undeniable duty to support those who were. In between pillow fights and athletic tournaments, we learned to dance the hora and to sing the melancholy and stirring songs of the new Zion.

Obviously, the notion of Israel was charged with far greater expectations than I at that age was able to see. Much later, reading books and articles written about Israel in its first decade, I would discover that non-Jews had even higher expectations than Jews. Or rather, that the Jewish expectations were more down-to-earth: Israel as a refuge, an insurance policy, a source of pride and dignity. A blue-and-white collection box with a map of Israel was proudly displayed in most Jewish homes. In most of them also letters and greetings from relatives and friends in the new country. News from Israel was monitored with great intensity and sometimes anxiety. During the Sinai War in October 1956, my father sat glued to the radio, worried not only about what might be happening in Tel Aviv.

For many non-Jews, the State of Israel soon took on a different and more complex meaning. Early Swedish writings on the subject were imbued with mythical overtones, devoid of all criticism and distance, and imbued with an unctuous sentimentality, obviously nourished by the still-unspeakable and taboo significance of the Jewish catastrophe. Soon the survivors went silent and the shocking newsreels were put away, as a new world wanted to forget and carry on as if nothing had happened.

From this perspective, Israel could be seen as a happy ending of sorts, the promise of a new beginning in which Europe would be given a chance to atone for the near-annihilation of its Jews. In July 1957, Herbert Tingsten (the influential editor in chief of *Dagens Nyheter*, who ten years earlier had been critical of the Zionist project) wrote: "My research and recent travels have convinced me that the founding of Israel is one of the great positive developments of our time. I am so absolutely convinced of this that I can't believe that anyone with approximately the same general values and more than a little bit of knowledge of the topic, must not come to the same conclusion."

With almost religious fervor, Tingsten portrayed Israel as nothing less than an earthly utopia, a state whose "learned people" were planning not only for the future of their country but for the future of "humanity" as a whole.

Equally striking during these years was Israel's emerging role as a socialist utopia, not the least in the eyes of Swedish Social Democrats, union leaders, and cooperative activists, whose various delegations enthusiastically reported on the triumph of union-owned enterprises, the large-scale establishment of cooperatives and kibbutzim, agricultural collectives characterized by "a simple, healthy and empowering life without the class distinctions that have caused such deep-seated conflict in Western societies, and without the centralized coercion so inherent in authoritarian states." Israel is portrayed as a vehicle for religious and social salvation, a way out of selfishness, materialism, capitalism, a cure for the social ills of humanity. Its cause is to be the cause of the Western world, and the Jews in their Israeli garb are to be transformed from its pariahs to its social and moral alibi. "It is the absolute duty of Western civilization to give this people all the help it needs for a peaceful and prosperous future in their historic homeland," an envoy from the Swedish cooperative movement concluded in 1957.

What non-Jewish hopes and expectations of the Jewish state had in common was a fascination with the new type of Jew they saw emerging: blond, blue-eyed, stub-nosed, tough, physical, and nonintellectual. Books on Israel were filled with Riefenstahl–inspired portraits of young, muscular men and women with tractors and guns. In a book published 1955 the prominent Swedish journalist Agne Hamrin took great pains to find some biological and environmental explanations for the phenomenon of the un-Jewish Jew or, as he put it, "the anti-Jewish Israeli." He found the "small, pale, bearded East European Jews" appalling, but was nevertheless shocked when he realized that the ideal Israeli Jew looked like an ideal German: "When you keep coming up against this paradoxical observation, you begin to wonder whether it is not the reflection of an unconscious 'antisemitism' among Israeli Jews."

There was a widespread belief that the Jews were about to solve "the Jewish problem" on their own. The Israeli Jew, the resurrected Hebrew, had finally freed himself from his degraded ghetto Jewish past—and his former persecutors from their historical guilt. Israel had opened a way out of a shameful past, to the delight of those who wanted to forget it as quickly as possible. Israel was the mortgage payment, or perhaps the final installment, of the West's debt to the Jews.

Emigration from Sweden to Israel was still an exception. In the summer of 1953, my father traveled to Israel to explore our prospects but was met with food stamps, overcrowded immigrant barracks, and people shaking their heads. Coming now? Are you insane?

So we stayed sane as long as possible. That is, until the earth shook and the move to Israel seemed a safer step than staying put. In Israel lived the remainder of my once numerous family: a surviving brother of my father, a surviving sister of my mother, a surviving sister and brother of my perished maternal grandmother. They were all waiting for us, so what were we waiting for?

On September 23, 1961, on the thirteenth day of the month of Tishri, in the five thousand seven hundred and twenty-second year of creation, I was called upon in the great synagogue of Stockholm to have my trembling voice follow the silver-plated hand's journey across the Torah scroll, and thus become a bar mitzvah, a man ready to fulfill his Jewish duties and honor his covenant with God.

On Easter Sunday, April 22, 1962, we boarded a train to Venice and, as I saw it, never to return.

There are many things that can go wrong on a journey to a lofty goal. The goal can turn out to be a mirage, or the first sight of it might make your heart sink. For a long time, the gate to the Promised Land was the port of Jaffa, where centuries of Ottoman lethargy had left their mark, and where many a feverish fantasy had ended in disappointment and resignation. Not that Jaffa was a particularly desolate city, but certainly it was no Jerusalem. Which even Jerusalem not always appeared to be. In her novel *Jerusalem*, the Swedish Nobel laureate Selma Lagerlöf tells the story of Birger Larsson, a traveler from Nås, who dies of grief and disappointment a few days after arriving in Jerusalem. Where were the walls of gold and the gates of pearls? Where was the city of glory and splendor? Could the Via Dolorosa be a stinking alley? Could the Gates of Zion be lined with rubbish heaps? Could the City of God be inhabited by beggars and lepers?

> Birger Larsson waved Halvor over and solemnly took his hand.
>
> "Now you must tell me something, since you are my kinsman," he said. "Do you really believe that this is the real Jerusalem?"
>
> "Oh yes, this is certainly the real Jerusalem," said Halvor.
>
> "I am sick, and by tomorrow morning I may be dead," said Birger. "You understand that you must not lie to me."
>
> "No one will lie to you," said Halvor.

On our *aliyah*, no one could be suspected of lying, except to themselves. Both the journey and the arrival proved to fulfill even the most unrealistic expectations. I have made many trips to Israel since then, including several by train and boat, but none of them can compare to the journey in the spring of 1962 aboard the white, beautiful *Enotria* of Venice, with its gentle flight across the Adriatic, its magically exact passage through the steeply carved Corinth Canal, its inexhaustible supply of spaghetti and grated cheese, its landings in glittering Dubrovnik, palm-lined Brindisi, noisy Piraeus, sleepy Limassol. It was a journey that in perfect pace and good comfort took us through time and place, away from what increasingly felt like a cold dead end, toward what in my dreams took the form of a warm embrace. There was something definite and irrevocable about this journey, a strong sense of destiny, which no subsequent journey in my life could ever replicate.

Still, the first sight of a mythical goal can ruin it all, but on our journey, the gateway to the Promised Land was Haifa, which on a clear day presents a far more promising sight than Jaffa ever could, and on this bright morning not even Jerusalem could have competed. On the lush slopes of Mount Carmel, the city shimmered chaste, white, and clean. Elegant villas floated weightlessly just below the sparsely populated peak. In the midst of the slope, slightly above the city center, surrounded by slender cypress trees, the marble-white Bahai temple with its golden dome sparkled in the rising morning sun. At the entrance to the harbor a swarm of passenger and cargo ships lay at anchor, while energetic Israeli police and customs boats, with the Star of David proudly flapping from their sterns, kicked up white wakes in the clear blue water. Along the low coastline to the north rose the smoking refineries and overflowing cisterns of economic progress, gradually giving way to the sun-drenched walls of Acre, the green beaches of Nahariya, and the white cliffs of Rosh Hanikra. Everywhere I looked, I saw what I was yearning for: vitality, challenge, purpose. The air was saturated with it, the bustle of the harbor signaled it, the uniformed policemen and customs officers who climbed aboard and made us wait patiently for several hours commanded it with their confident gestures, unbuttoned khaki shirts, and self-assured demeanor.

Even after we had disembarked, and the houses had taken on a more gray hue, and the slightly irritated pulse of the traffic had become noticeable, and the sandy dust was whirling in through the open windows of our little Volkswagen as we drove south toward Tel Aviv, our arrival lost none of its original magic. There was absolutely nothing that did not seem to confirm my view of how things should be.

Thus, for a long time I was convinced that the reason Israelis drove like savages on the roads, as they did even then, was that the country was under divine protection. There were simply no traffic accidents in Israel. Another fantasy, more short-lived, was that in Israel people did not cheat, steal, or murder. Consequently, there were no prisons. I still remember my suppressed amazement as we drove along the coastal road to Haifa past the huge rolls of barbed wire surrounding the large prison in Atlit. Such large prisons in such a small country?

In retrospect, I cannot reconstruct how these childish idealizations came about, except that they must have been the fruit of long-nurtured childhood fantasies. During the months leading up to our *aliyah* I swallowed every argument in favor of breaking up, especially the romantic ones, and carefully pushed away everything that would hold me back—friends, places, memories. I read Leon Uris's newly published blockbuster *Exodus* with a pounding heart, not as a novel but as an ongoing drama. Israel was a heroic epic waiting for my entrance, and I certainly wasn't going to walk onstage with my hands in my pockets. What awaited me was hard work, camaraderie, courage, and sacrifice. And girls of course, but of a very different kind from those at home, tough, modest, and dedicated, more difficult to conquer in the short term, as girls always are in heroic tales, but it was, as I saw it, a temporary sacrifice for long-term rewards. My first Israel was a boy's fantasy, a scout's dream, an endless summer camp.

Departure and arrival, ascent and initiation, longing and belonging, promise and fulfillment were the heavy building blocks of a new Israeli identity rapidly replacing whatever identity had been there before. After a little more than a year, Sweden was a foreign country, Hebrew was my language and my Swedish had an accent. Such a radical change of identity can arguably only happen under very particular circumstances and at a very special age. I was open to becoming someone else and still malleable enough, at least on the surface, to make it happen. It was certainly an identity with rough contours and large gaps, since I still knew very little about my new country, and for a long time there were many things I wouldn't know.

ARRIVAL

For I will bring them into the land which I have sworn to
their fathers, a land flowing with milk and honey,
and they shall eat and be full and fat.

—DEUTERONOMY 31:20

Was my early Israel an innocent society? No, not if innocent means free of guilt and shame, but perhaps yes, if innocence means ignorance. There was enough guilt and shame to go around, but most people seemed ignorant of it. Could they have known? Did they want to know? Did they know after all? I still don't know.

Israel in the early 1960s was a thoroughly ideologized society. This did not mean that everyone lived according to the ideology, or that the ideology did not have shades and cracks, but it did mean that the Israeli society was shaped and permeated by it. It was an ideology that, like all ideologies, created its own reality, shedding light on what should be seen and shrouding in darkness what should be hidden and forgotten. It created a powerful unifying sense of right and wrong, friend and foe. It celebrated simplicity, collectivism, and self-sacrifice. In formal settings the politicians wore unbuttoned white shirts with the collars folded over the lapels of their jackets, the schoolchildren wore light blue shirts and dark blue cotton pants or skirts. On my first day in grade nine at Secondary School Number Nine in Tel Aviv, the teacher kindly asked me to take off the small signet ring I had been given for my bar mitzvah. This was a school where the principal routinely sent girls home for wearing nylon stockings. An untucked shirt, a pair of overly pointed shoes, a hint of color, or a whiff of perfume could draw disapproval. *Tzniut* (modesty) was an early word in my Hebrew vocabulary.

Once a week, we traded our blue school uniforms for khakis and boots to participate in the mandatory exercises of Gadna, Israel's paramilitary youth brigades. We ran cross-country, practiced basic drills, learned to shoot at targets with old Mauser rifles, and sweated our way through a series of multiday marches. What it was all good for, we never discussed or even asked. There were things that every young Israeli knew had to be done, and that we learned to do with enthusiasm and pride. During my first summer vacation, I managed to get into a monthlong training course for Gadna leaders. We were housed in large open tents at the military barracks in Djelil (later hebraized as Glilot) north of Tel Aviv, where we were subjected to willy-nilly commands, hours-long drills, strenuous training sessions, long marches, and realistic night maneuvers (during which one of our group fell into a gravel pit and was seriously injured). I was later told that deaths and serious accidents were not uncommon during this vigorous testing of young people's physical and mental limits. Boys and girls in their early teens, imbued with a sense of destiny and sacrifice, voluntarily faced challenges and dangers that could only be legitimized in a society based on ideological fervor and Spartan ideals of virtue.

I didn't regret a moment of it, of course. The summer at Djelil was a test of manhood and a rite of passage. In a short time I learned what was important and what was not, what was valued and what was not, in the emerging Israeli society. It gave me a strong sense of the bonding and loyalty-building role that the soon-to-come Israeli military service would play in the lives of my friends and classmates. Physical strength, mental stamina, personal sacrifice, and emotional restraint were personal qualities that were highly esteemed, not to say idolized, in a society based on the belief that it must survive as a fortress.

Whatever bourgeois or liberal inclinations many Israelis may have harbored in their hearts, these could not be displayed with impunity in the Israel of the early 1960s. The country's political, military, and spiritual leaders, as well as those of the coming generation, were expected to live simple lives, to embrace the ideal of equality, and to conform to the state-founding principles of Labor Zionism.

Contributing to the ideological uniformity, both figuratively and literally, were the two or three effective and well-supported political youth movements that organized much of the country's young people in those years. They had their respective roots in different, historically more or less warring factions of the Zionist left, but for me the main difference was the color of the cords that tied the necklines of the blue buttonless cotton shirts that formed the common wardrobe of the movements. By sheer coincidence, I became a member of the movement affiliated with Mapai, the ruling Labor Party, tying red cords. The other big movement, Ha'shomer Ha'tzair (the Young Guard), was affiliated with the left-wing Zionist Mapam, and tied white cords. Every Wednesday and Friday night, hordes of young people with color-tied shirts roamed the neighborhoods of Tel Aviv on their way to their *peulot* (activities). I don't remember much of what we discussed there, except that I preferred Friday nights, when Israel was otherwise closed and we sang patriotic songs and danced Israeli folk dances, and many had exchanged their blue shirts for white or black ones decorated with hand-embroidered borders.

In time, both the red and the white cords were expected to form a *garin* (nucleus), an ideologically and personally cohesive group that, after completing basic military training, would serve the remaining one and a half years of their military conscription as a *nahal* (military youth group) on a kibbutz affiliated with their movement, "with the plow in one hand and a sword in the other." Thereafter you were expected to join the kibbutz, perhaps marry someone in your *garin*, and live the rest of your life as a *chalutz* (true pioneer).

An important activity of the youth movements was voluntary work on a kibbutz and organized hikes through the country. Hiking was a central component in a young Israeli's education, serving to forge emotional links to Israel's nature, landscape, and archaeology, to learn to love Eretz

Israel, the Land of Israel. A classic hike in the spring was the *yam el yam* (from sea to sea), which took five days and went from the Mediterranean coast north of Haifa, through the hilly and sparsely populated landscape of Galilee, to Yam Kinneret (the Sea of Galilee). The land was at its most enchanting, the valleys fragrant with flowers and herbs, the hills green from the spring rains, the dry creek beds filled with water, and the nights refreshingly cool.

Another classic hike was the three-day march to Jerusalem, which before 1967 was at the end of a narrow wedge between the armistice lines with Jordan. It was a physically demanding trek with a steep climb. We did it in late fall, in pouring rain, with enemy land sometimes only a stone's throw away. In the no-man's-land of Latrun, through the rainy haze we could glimpse the Trappist monastery with its mysterious silent inhabitants, and in divided Jerusalem we could hear the hustle and bustle of a world that could only be glimpsed through closed gates and walls.

Of course, we also made the obligatory pilgrimage to Masada, which in those days was an arduous several-hour climb up a narrow path carved into a steep mountain wall in the Judean desert. At the top of this seemingly impregnable fortress with its priceless view of the Dead Sea, we were initiated (I can't think of a better word) into the most bizarre and puzzling of archaeological remains within the borders of Israel. This was the place where, after the destruction of Jerusalem in 70 CE, nine hundred Jewish men, women, and children had committed collective suicide rather than surrender to the besieging Roman legions. The contemporary Roman Jewish historian Flavius Josephus categorized them as "sicarii," murderous fanatics impervious to rational argument,[1] but nonetheless recounted with empathy what he could not have known, the last words of the rebel leader Eleazar ben Yair to his men, women, and children—words that were taking on a new meaning and context in a Jewish state that was seeing itself as similarly besieged:

> Since we long ago resolved never to be servants to the Romans, nor to any other than to God Himself, Who alone is the true and just Lord of mankind, the time is now come that obliges us to make that resolution true in practice ... We were the very first that revolted, and we are the last to fight against them; and I cannot but esteem it as a favor that God has granted us, that it is still in our power to die bravely, and in a state of freedom.

We were led around the labyrinthine ruins, where, according to Josephus, huge stores of wine and food had been left by Herod a hundred years earlier, and where over the years large quantities of rainwater had been amassed in underground cisterns. The inhabitants of Masada had not committed suicide for lack of supplies but to "strike fear" into the hearts of the Romans. At night we lit campfires, roasted potatoes in the embers, sang patriotic songs, and watched the sun rise over the Dead Sea.

In the 1950s, Masada was resurrected as the deeply ambiguous symbol of the new Israel by the general, archaeologist, and minister Yigael Yadin—ambiguous because it was so undeniably a symbol of defeat, as well as a violation of Judaism's dictum to preserve life. While Masada was meant to symbolize the historical plight of Israel and the Jewish people, its message was inherently ominous, to say the least. Rabbinic literature, perhaps for this reason, does not mention Masada. The term "Masada complex," the Israeli sense of irredeemable entrapment, was coined out of such a dark reading of Jewish history.

Yadin, on the other hand, wanted to make Masada a symbol of Jewish continuity, a place where a parenthesis of nearly two thousand years had come to an end. Israel was to be a Masada that would never fall again. Accordingly, Masada became a place where Israel's soldiers were brought to swear an oath of allegiance to the nation, accompanied by the words of Yadin himself: "The echo of your oath this night will reverberate in the camps of our enemies. Its meaning is no less powerful than our military defense."

The hikes to Masada and similar sites were an important part of my Israeli education. Archaeology in Israel was a national enterprise with the implicit task of literally uncovering the historical ties between the Jews and the land. Archaeology could also serve to prove the longevity and depth of the Jewish presence in the land, and in the words of the Israeli writer Amos Elon, make sure "that events that had taken place two thousand years ago were grasped more vividly than anything since, until the present."[2]

I cannot recall each and every marching route but the circumstances were similar: carrying heavy backpacks with bread and canned food, sleeping under starry skies, plagued by blisters, chafed feet, and diarrhea, deeply affected by what we saw and experienced. My Israeli years are etched in my memory as one long, intense summer of fearless marching toward big goals—the biggest of which were not on a map.

Etched in my memory are also the images of aging faces with burning eyes. In my early Israel the founding fathers of the state were still in power, exuding ideological energy and certainty. There were also people like the principal of my school, Mr. Fisskopf, a one-man Zionist crusader who took the ideological shortcomings of his pupils personally, who preached, cursed, praised, and sometimes cried. When I finally was to descend again—that is, return to the Swedish exile—Mr. Fisskopf suggested that I be adopted by relatives or friends or, if need be, by himself, so that I could stay in the country and serve it. Our "descent" had purely mundane reasons; life for a single mother with two children proved to be harder in Israel than in Sweden, but I had no doubt that I would return as soon as possible to reassume my proper place in the Zionist adventure.

What the ideology in which we were educated had kept us in the dark about was the existence of alternative movements, ideas, and debates in the history of Zionism and the Jewish colonization of Palestine. It had also kept us in the dark about the people with whom we had virtually no physical and social contact in those years. During my two and a half years in Israel, I never spoke to an Arab (Palestinian was not a common term at the time), saw very few, knew only what I read and heard, and to the extent I thought about it, this seemed to be as much as I needed to know. The Arabs were not a part of our lives except as a threat. During our marches we would imagine them as shadows in the dark, their invisible presence reflected in the Czech Mausers we carried on our shoulders, and in the faint yellow light emanating at night from their poorly electrified villages.

I am not sure that this cartoon image of the Arabs would have been more nuanced if I had lived in Haifa, which had a relatively large Arab population, or in one of the new Jewish settlements in the Arab-dominated Galilee. Traveling from Haifa to Arab Nazareth, or to any of the Arab villages in Wadi Ara, was like traveling to another country and required, at least in those years, a rudimentary knowledge of Arabic, a language that few young Israelis found worth learning. Moreover, the buses that served these places were painted brown, unlike the light blue buses of the Egged cooperative, whose tough drivers with their blue shorts, open cotton shirts, and tanned legs signaled home. The flow of cheap Arab labor into the Israeli economy that would result from the 1967 war, and the kind of Arab-Jewish interaction it would give rise to, did not yet exist. Nor did the territorial frictions and confrontations of the occupation. The principle was still, as in the build-up phase of Jewish Palestine, economic and social separation between Jews and Arabs, and as I would later learn, a high degree of economic and administrative repression.

The sense of physical Arab threat was heightened in those years by the constant military confrontations along the Israeli-Syrian cease-fire line, where the Syrians, from their strategically superior positions in the Golan Heights, carried out seemingly unprovoked attacks on Jewish farmers in the northern Galilee. In Almagor and Tel Katzir, two kibbutzim right under the Syrians' noses, heavily armored tractors had to be used to plow the fields, which did not protect some of the tractor drivers from being attacked, again reinforcing my image of a one-sided and irrational Arab lust for violence.

That the background was somewhat more complicated, that part of the border area was formally demilitarized, that in the early 1950s Israel had begun to cultivate part of the land in violation of the UN Supervisory Commission's interpretation of the cease-fire agreement, and that the antagonism had been exacerbated by Israeli irrigation and drainage plans that affected both demilitarized lands and Syrian water resources was something we did not know or were not told. It was certainly not something that would have excused the Syrians in our eyes, but it would have allowed for a more nuanced image of the "Arabs" to be formed. And not least, a more searching image of ourselves.

Thus, our view of the world was ideologically armored and protected from outside influences. The Ben-Gurion government actively opposed the introduction of television in Israel on moral and ideological grounds (wasteful, corrupt, foreign influence, etc.), which further limited the possibility of seeing "the other." The Arabs remained black-and-white silhouettes, defined by an unreasonable hatred of the Jewish state, historically incapable of constructive compromise, deliberately manipulated by their rulers. In the Israeli children's books at the time, the Arab was almost invariably portrayed as cruel and sneaky, bloodthirsty and cowardly, serving you coffee and stabbing you in the back with the same duplicitous hand.

The feeling of being threatened and vilified by the surrounding world was close at hand. The extermination of Europe's Jews was only eighteen years in the past, and most of my Israeli friends and classmates were the children of survivors. One in five Jewish residents of Israel was a direct or indirect victim of Nazi persecution.

If in retrospect it can be said that the ideological fervor in the Israel of my youth was beginning to wear off, this was not for me to see. What I could see was a state, only a few months older than me, fully absorbed by the ideological challenge of receiving, supporting, and integrating some two hundred thousand Jews who "ascended" between 1961 and 1964, the vast majority of them Oriental Jews from Iran, Morocco, Tunisia, and Algeria. In 1965, the Jewish majority in Israel shifted from Jews of European descent to Oriental Jews, and the ground began to shake under the founding elite. Still, for a decade it would preserve its dominance through grand development projects, impressive economic growth, and the unifying power of external threats and wars. In 1964 there was the inauguration of Ha'movil Ha'artzi, the national water pipeline from the Sea of Galilee to the Negev desert, where water was pumped from two hundred meters below sea level to hundreds of meters above, and then, like an artificial river, gently gravitated to the south via an ingenious system of tunnels, canals, and pumping stations. At one stroke, the irrigated area of Israel increased by a fourth, in the northern parts of the Negev desert by three-fourths. Thirsty desert cities such as Beersheba, Ashkelon, Kiryat

Gat, Arad, and Dimona sprang to life. New large areas were brought under the plow, and collective farms that had once been established along the Gaza Strip for reasons of ideology and security could now live well off the land. New Oriental arrivals were rapidly and unceremoniously brought to new *arei pituah* (development towns), planned and designed by a still-dominant European elite.

We too lived for a year in the rapidly exploding immigrant town of Bat Yam south of Tel Aviv-Jaffa, where new neighborhoods without streets and street numbers were springing up in the sand, and where I soon became disenchanted with the lack of pioneering spirit in our new and mainly Arabic-speaking neighbors. Every morning I rode my bicycle north as fast as I could to our old European neighborhood, to my school, to my youth movement, to my Israel. I returned late in the evening, with angry, half-wild dogs chasing my bike through the narrow streets, and with a strong sense of alienation from the smells and sounds that met me.

What I had experienced was the emerging, multicultural, unruly Israel, with its deepening social and cultural divisions, increasingly impervious to the myths and ideals of its European founders. The Oriental Jews lived worse, had worse jobs, and were largely absent from the country's military and political leadership. They also remained largely outside the ideologically based institutions—parties, cooperatives, and trade unions—that were key to social advancement. In strikingly disproportionate numbers, the political and military elite continued to be recruited from Israel's ideological heartland, the kibbutzim.

Of course, none of this was entirely unavoidable in a society whose population had grown by one-fifth in just a few years, mostly with people from radically different backgrounds than the traditional elites. What could have been mitigated, however, was the clash between ideology and reality. Oriental Jews measured their life in Israel not by the life they had left behind but by the life they had been promised. What were the promises of the new Eretz Israel worth when a Russian-born mother figure like Golda Meir could publicly question whether it was really possible "to raise these immigrants to a reasonable level of civilization"? Or when the Western-educated foreign minister Abba Eban could blithely refer to half of the country's population as coming from places where, "since the decline of Islamic culture, have had no educational history or environment."[3] In school curricula, Jewish history was still synonymous with the history of European Jews, while Oriental Jews were sometimes accused of being unable to fully understand Israel since they had not experienced the Holocaust. In the Israel of my youth, the Oriental or Sephardic Hebrew, with its more guttural and Arabic-sounding pronunciation, was a class marker of the same significance as a Cockney accent in England.

Israel, like the United States, was an ideologically founded state, with its year zero, its act of creation, its mythological big bang, with the difference that in the Israel I came to, the founding was still ongoing. The same people who had come to build a new world, and who therefore did not know what practical politics was, now sat on military staffs, parliaments, and government chancelleries.

Overnight, a myriad of social utopias, messianic dreams, and Jewish rebirth projects were squeezed into the confines of state interest. Existential debates were interrupted mid-sentence, deep conflicts were suppressed, alternative paths remained unexplored. A great amount of ideological energy was now being channeled into the Israeli state-building project.

It was in the waning stages of the founding period that I received my Israeli education.

TRANSFORMATION

> Each and every one must take care to transform the galut Jew within himself into a true emancipated Jew, to mold an unnatural, defective and divided inner personality into a natural and healthy human being in harmony with himself.
>
> —AHARON DAVID GORDON, 1911

In retrospect, it is striking how un-Jewish the modern Israeli pioneer dream was. In terms of its human ideals, its conception of society, its view of religion and faith, and even its view of the Jews of the world, it rather had something anti-Jewish about it. It was a dream for Jews, to be sure, and being Jewish was a ticket of entry, but once used the ticket could be conveniently tucked away and forgotten. From the old Jewish soul disfigured by the Galut (the exile) would then burst forth a shiny new one, with few if any traditional Jewish traits. It would learn to shun what the Jews of the Galut had cherished, and to love what had long been alien or forbidden to Jews.

Life during the Galut had prevented the Jews from knowing themselves, wrote Aharon David Gordon, one of the most influential theorists of state-building Zionism, and it was only through hard physical labor, through literally embracing the "religion of work," that the defective, splintered person within the Jew could be "changed into a natural and sound human being who is true to himself."[1] For Gordon, physical labor was not a means (to prosperity) but an end in itself, a link between man and nature and thus essential for a fully human life.

It was an idea based more on the agrarian romantic utopias of Leo Tolstoy and the spiritual and metaphysical view of labor nurtured by Russian populists than on specifically Jewish ideals. It was rooted not only in a negative view of the Jewish exile but in a contempt for the modern urban human being in general. The renaissance of Zion would be the liberation not only from Jewish misery but from human misery altogether. In the new Palestine, parasitic social groups would disappear, the morality of labor would prevail over the morality of money, the collective would take precedence over the private, and a new type of human would emerge. One might have argued that this was a goal emerging from the sources of Judaism, or that it was the ordained task of Jews to fulfill it, or that Jews had more reason than others to show the way, but in principle the goal was little more than a potent distillation of all the social utopias, romantic dreams, and revolutionary ideals of the late nineteenth century.

Gordon was writing during the Second Aliyah, the radical wave of Eastern Jewish immigration in the decade before World War I, which more than any that followed would shape the founding myths of Israel. It was made up of a distinctively ideological generation, emerging from the political and social turmoil of frustrated Russian revolutions, violent class conflicts, and widespread anti-Jewish pogroms. They also distinguished themselves from other Jews who chose to flee or emigrate, but who overwhelmingly opted for America. Finally, they were the hardened remnants of the altogether thirty-five thousand Jews who left for Palestine in those years, and of whom nearly 80 percent, at the mere sight of the Holy Land, traveled on by return ship to Europe or America. A nineteen-year-old Russian Jewish student who arrived in 1906 contracted malaria, nearly died, and was advised by a physician to go back, which, as his traveling companions pointed out, could hardly be considered a disgrace.[2]

The nineteen-year-old, whose name was David Gruen, chose to stay, and with him some two thousand young Jews who insisted on seeing more than there was to see. They came from every imaginable and unimaginable shade of Russia's revolutionary movements, some having fled conscription to fight in the Russo-Japanese War of 1905; others from their small villages, cramped homes, and murderous surroundings; still others from the social oppression of convention and tradition, most of them convinced that the road to Zion was the road to something greater. They were regarded as fanatics by the Jews from the preceding wave of immigration, the First Aliyah (1881–1904), who were just beginning to adapt to traditional plantation life in colonies such as Petah Tikvah (Gate of Hope) and Rishon Le Zion (First in Zion). Many of the new arrivals were forced to move from colony to colony, starved and downtrodden, but rarely being offered work. Neither their physical condition, nor their agricultural experience, nor their ideas about the dignity of man and work made them particularly competitive in comparison with the Arab labor force that now sustained the Jewish enterprises cheaply and quietly. The Jewish citrus growers' newspaper warned that the newcomers were not only interested in labor and food: "They strive for power, economic and social dictatorship over the agricultural industry and its owners."

Whenever these hardcore puritans and moralists were offered jobs on the Jewish plantations, they rarely missed an opportunity to make a political statement, sometimes by ostentatiously and loudly taking on the simplest and heaviest of tasks, sometimes by refusing to understand the language in which they wore spoken to. One of them, Joshua Altermann, while working at the Rothschild vineyards in Rishon Le Zion, recounted how he was ordered, in Romanian-accented Yiddish, to close the tap on a wine barrel.

> I decided to keep it open . . . He repeated his order. I went on asking him in Hebrew: "What are you saying?" By this time he was furiously screaming in Yiddish: *"Vermach den Kran!"* Again I asked calmly: "What is it that you want me to do?" And all this time the wine was pouring out before our eyes.[3]

Altermann scored an "honorable" victory and was fired. Perhaps he also thought of hebraizing his name like so many others in this rebellious generation of pioneers. To change one's name was to change one's identity, to start one's life anew, to shed the old ghetto suit and put on a new shining armor. Young David Gruen became David Ben-Gurion, the son of a lion.

Among the ideological idiosyncrasies of the Second Aliyah, the cult of manual labor would be the most enduring. Soon there was no other legitimate path to individual and national salvation for the new Jews in Palestine than to personally take on the heaviest and dirtiest tasks, and to do so with a smile and a song on their lips. Gordon was not only the founder of the religion of labor but he also became one of its most devout practitioners. Inspired by Nietzsche and Tolstoy, he came from Russia to Palestine at the age of almost fifty, having decided to break away from a bourgeois life as a financial manager of rural properties. Already an elderly man with a flowing white beard, Gordon demanded to be put to heavy agricultural labor as soon as he arrived. He spent the rest of his life with young immigrants working long days in fields and on plantations and resting short nights in tents and barracks. They were all driven by the ambition to demonstrate the new Jewish man's capacity for hard labor, but for Gordon labor was also a sacrificial cult (the Hebrew word for labor, *avoda*, can also mean just that). In Gordon's writing there is also a suggestive play on the Hebrew words for "people," "man," and "earth"—*am*, *adam*, *adama*—and at times also "blood": *dam*. Only by cultivating the earth (and figuratively shedding their blood for it) could the Jews become a true people, *am adam*.

The widespread influence of Gordonian labor mysticism in the Palestine of the Second Aliyah coincided with the urgent need of the Zionist enterprise for an idea that could motivate new arrivals to engage in the hard, self-sacrificial, low-paying work of settling and cultivating the new lands. The old form of settlement, with Jews owning the land and Arabs working it, had stagnated. The future of the Zionist enterprise required that more Jews be put to hard work for little money. It also required an ideological vision that could mobilize and unite people who had arrived in Palestine from very different backgrounds and for very different reasons. The cult of labor also coincided, as will be seen later, with a new and highly successful policy of purchasing Arab-owned land and leasing it to collectives of Jewish immigrants to settle and cultivate. The cult of labor not only served the economic and social needs of the emerging Jewish society in Palestine but it also symbolized, more than anything else, a break with the past.

The burgeoning cult of labor went hand in hand with the sanctification of Jewish-labored lands. The newly formed Jewish National Fund, which was now buying Arab-owned lands in Palestine on a large scale, stipulated in its statutes that the land should belong to the "Jewish people," and not be used for speculation or for producing profits but for producing a Jewish nation. It also paved the way for a system in which idealism would replace money as a motivating force for young Jewish pioneers. When the old plantation system based on corporate managers and salaried workers began weakening after poor economic results and recurrent labor disputes, the first collective farms were founded in 1911.

Practical, society-building Zionism ultimately promised something very similar to the liberation of Jews from their

Jewish heritage. In Palestine they would free themselves from the historical roles and characteristics forced upon them by a Jew-hating world. In sweat, blood, and soil, the degraded and deformed Jew of the exile would be transformed into a full human being in a nation of his own.

In Zionist writings and documents of this period, it is sometimes hard to draw the line between expressions of Jewish self-liberation and Jewish self-denial. Zionist characterizations of Jews in the Galut were often prone to anti-Jewish stereotyping. The notion of a new and normalized Jew presupposed the notion of an obsolete and dysfunctional one. Zionism wanted to solve a problem that had been defined by antisemitism. Not surprisingly, early non-Jewish friends of Zionism were often people with a negative view of Jews. An illustrative case in point was the Swedish literary critic and author Fredrik Böök.

Early in life, in particular after a visit to wartime Warsaw in 1916, Fredrik Böök came to see the Jews as a problem for the world—and for themselves. If they remained unassimilated, as in the overcrowded ghettos of Eastern Europe, they would be destroyed by their neighbors. If they sought to assimilate, as in the financial and cultural metropolises of Western Europe, they would undermine their host nations. The first scenario, the eternal threat to Jews from their neighbors, was the most potent driving force of Zionism; the second scenario, the growing threat of Jews to their hosts, was a modern antisemitic trope that was nevertheless echoed by some leading Zionists. Neither the path of exile nor the path of assimilation seemed open any longer. What remained was the Zionist path to Palestine.

Exactly what kind of destruction would befall the unassimilated Eastern Jews, Böök could not yet imagine. What he was able conjure up was a combined inferno of pogroms, mass murder, and economic starvation, arguing that only evil could come from the boundless desperation of the Jews. It was the Jews who had instigated the Bolshevik revolution, who had seized power in Béla Kun's Hungary, and who, in every nation where they lived, posed a permanent threat to order, tradition, and national cohesion:

> The Jewish discontent, the savage hatred of state and society, the desire to destroy everything that exists, are of course, in their turn, the fruit of the intolerable conditions in the ghetto . . . Everywhere, destructive and extreme tendencies are supported and nourished by Jewish action. A large part of the discontent which is fermenting in Europe is rooted in the Jewish sense of alienation.[4]

For this historically, to say the least, dubious thesis, Böök claimed, no doubt rightly, to have received support in statements from both the then leader of the Zionist movement, Chaim Weizmann, and from the English benefactor of Zionism, Lord Arthur Balfour. During these decades, a deeply ambivalent relationship developed between the goals of Zionism and the rise of state-sponsored antisemitism in Europe. Palestine was the Jews' salvation from Europe— and Europe's salvation from the Jews.

Böök wrote,

> Zionism has the same roots as antisemitism, the inherent material and moral conflicts that the Jewish existence as a dispersed people in *Goluth*, [*sic*] has created. But it is an attempt to correct what has been distorted, to bring light to the downtrodden, to bestow moral stature on the trampled, to provide a dispossessed people with pure ideals and high tasks. It is the best part of the Jewish soul which, in the form of Zionism, has risen to overcome an overshadowing destiny.[5]

The "overshadowing destiny" of the Jews, according to Böök, was to remain strangers, pariahs, hated, disliked in their host nations. The dream of adaptation and assimilation was a self-deception. Antisemitism was certainly fueled by hatred, cruelty, superstition, inferiority, and envy ("the vulgar movement with which no decent person wants to have anything to do"), but it also had "more legitimate sources." Centuries of exile and dispersion had made the Jews rootless, faithless, untrustworthy, with no sense of loyalty to fatherland and nation. From this perspective, Böök wrote, one must understand

> the indignation at political and moral strivings that is alien to the country or the people, but which enterprising, ruthless Jews are able to advance through skillfully exploited opportunities. Assimilation can be the cover under which Jewish influences seek to oppress and violate a nationality. Finally, antisemitism is fueled by the dislike of the international Jewish jobber, the clearest representative of the cult of Mammon, who, freed from the obligations

of religion, race, and country, can exploit everything and everyone.[6]

With this conspiratorial image of the Jews, Böök found an explanation for the disintegration of national ties and values at the dawn of modernity. The Jews were a social virus that spread nihilism, national weakness, and cosmopolitanism. Wherever Böök searched for Jews, he found them: among radical writers and revolutionary politicians, among restless agitators and nihilist philosophers. In literature, he held an almost unreasonable grudge against the German poet Heinrich Heine and the Danish literary critic Georg Brandes, both of Jewish origin and both evidence of "the national unreliability of the Jews toward their host peoples." The fact that Heine had converted to Christianity and that Brandes was a fierce proponent of secularism only made matters worse. Heine was said to have mocked the national symbols of his fatherland and groveled at its archenemy (France), and Brandes was said to be a "usurper" of Denmark's spiritual property. The fact that Sweden had been spared Jews of Heine's and Brandes's anti-national and cosmopolitan type was an "undeserved grace" due to the low number of Jews. Were the number to increase, Sweden too would experience "the economic and psychological conflicts of interest that give rise to antisemitic movements influenced by many obscure instincts and barbaric prejudices."

How then could Böök emphatically claim that he was not an antisemite? Mainly by emphasizing the similarity between his view of the Jews and that of the Zionists.

"Nowhere are the weaknesses and faults of the Jews judged more fairly, more severely than by the Zionists," he wrote. Hadn't Weizmann himself attributed to "Jewish intelligence and fanatical Jewish ideology . . . a fatal role in the witches' brew of radical movements in Eastern Europe"? What the Zionists had proposed and Böök enthusiastically had supported was a solution to the problem caused by a dysfunctional Jewish presence in Europe. The Jews were not irreparably damaged and harmful. Their "terrible and unhealthy condition" had a historical explanation—and a historical solution.

Whatever one may think of Böök's ambivalence toward Europe's Jews, he was right about one thing: The same ambivalence existed in early Zionism. In the decades leading up to the Nazis' "final solution," there were breathtaking similarities in the view of "the Jewish problem" between ingrained antisemites and leading Zionists. The Jews had become their own disease, which could be cured by emigration and resettlement only.

EMANCIPATION

Give us back our beautiful trees and fields.
Give us back the Universe.

—MICAH JOSEPH BERDYCZEWSKI

What had made the Jewish problem acute? Paradoxically, its purported solution. By the end of the eighteenth century, the walls surrounding Jewish life in Europe were coming down under the pressure from the promises of civic equality and religious freedom offered by the Enlightenment. In less than a century, Europe's Jews moved from separation and isolation to choices and opportunities.

Jews in seventeenth-century France, Germany, or Russia had dressed much the same and led much the same lives, in societies molded by severe external pressures and strong internal discipline. The status of Jews in European societies had been arbitrarily and capriciously regulated by shifting rulers, economic cycles, and popular moods, but their life as Jews had been even more tightly regulated by internalized traditions and regulations. Jews were not only historical victims of sorts, the perennial losers of an endless religious war, but the bearers of a strong, if not always consistent, idea of what it meant to be a Jew. It was not only the historically rooted hostility of the Christian environment that had defined the exclusion of the Jews, but at least as much the ability of the rabbinic tradition to give meaning, stability, and even hope to what from the outside might appear to be hopeless social and human misery. Jewish tradition had positioned itself just outside of time and space, in the tension-filled field between an all-obliging past and an all-promising messianic future. In this way, a remarkably stable balance could be upheld between the divine and the mundane, prayer and destiny, redemption and suffering. The external pressures had made for a permanent state of insecurity; no wealth was protected, no position permanent, no hierarchies enduring. Instead, the stability of Jewish society was upheld and renewed by a living tradition of religious practices and rules of life. Even suffering and persecution were incorporated into this web of purpose and meaning, with Judaism developing its own martyrology, *kiddush ha'shem*, to die for being a Jew was a sanctification of God.

After all, there was also a certain logic to the Christian persecution of Jews. The religions had once been two shoots on the same tree, two Jewish sects competing for the same covenant with God and the same scriptural heritage. The sect that became the mighty Roman Church claimed itself to be the true keeper of the covenant, and Jesus Christ to be the true Messiah. The sect that would become rabbinical Judaism refused to recognize both, prompting the Roman Church to engage in a poisonous theological campaign against the Jews (killers of God, etc.), at times leading to demands for them to be killed. The restrictions and regulations of Jewish life in societies dominated by the Roman Church would henceforth oscillate between paternalistic benevolence (toward the yet unconverted) and religious hatred (toward the God-killers). The freedom of movement of Jews in Europe was severely but irrationally restricted; doors were closed and opened with the same capricious hand. Some districts, towns, and villages had been closed to Jews since the Middle Ages—*non tolerandis Judæorum*—while others, sometimes right next door, harbored thriving Jewish communities. In Fürth, Germany, Jews lived well; in neighboring Nuremberg they were allowed to appear in daytime only, and then only in the company of a Christian resident. In 1743, a hunchbacked fourteen-year-old Jewish boy from Dessau named Moses the son of Mendel was admitted through one of Berlin's city gates after a thorough interrogation, whereafter the sentry noted: "Today six oxen, seven pigs, and one Jew passed the Rosenthaler Thor." Mood swings occurred at short notice. In 1670 the Jews were expelled from Vienna, five years later they were allowed back in. In 1744 they were expelled from Prague, in 1747 they were invited back. In France, an edict of expulsion had been in force since the Middle Ages, capriciously renewed as late as 1613 by Louis XIII, but equally capriciously undermined by thousands of local privileges, exemptions, and professional regulations, sometimes for individual Jews, sometimes for entire communities.

If rabbinical Judaism succeeded, against all odds, to maintain and develop a faith in its universal meaning, it had to do so under anything but universal circumstances. Boundless messianic dreams were kept alive and in check in the most restricted and oppressed of European societies. It was a deep paradox in which European Jewry survived, and at times thrived, until the middle of the eighteenth century.

There were early signs that Judaism harbored an inner restlessness that waited to be released. The expulsion of the Jews from Spain in 1492 had led to strong religious tensions and a wave of mystical and neo-messianic movements. Similar inner turmoil arose among Polish Jews, then the most organized and "learned" in Europe, after they had suffered the bloodiest Jewish pogroms in Europe to date in 1648, instigated by the Ukrainian Cossack leader Bogdan Chmielnicki. Jews throughout Europe began yearning for liberation and escape, for the arrival of the Messiah, for deliverance and redemption. An ecstatic movement for Jewish revival led by Sabbatai Zevi, a self-proclaimed Messiah, almost managed to tear down rabbinical Judaism in Europe and irreparably divide its Jews. Even as Sabbatai Zevi (as so many others) turned out to be a false Messiah (he converted to Islam in 1666), the inner pressures and longings in Jewish life still remained. They would eventually find a lasting expression within the confines of rabbinical Judaism in a movement called Hasidism, with a more experiential and charismatic interpretation of Judaism.

If Jewish life in Europe at the end of the eighteenth century might have looked like a fossil from the past, it nevertheless harbored a vital source of meticulously nurtured and controlled human energy. And when the control rods were taken out, it was released into the non-Jewish world with great force. With Emperor Joseph II's Edict of Tolerance in Austria in 1782 and the French Declaration of the Rights of Man in 1789, the walls of the Jewish quarters began to crumble and new generations of Jews made their way into the non-Jewish world. In 1743, Moses, Mendel's son, had begged to enter Berlin. Thirty years later, Moses Mendelssohn was one of the most famous literary and philosophical figures of the German Enlightenment and the undisputed leader of a movement for Jewish spiritual and social renewal. The question of who was a Jew, and in what way, could no longer be settled at a glance. At first, this may have confused non-Jews more than Jews, but soon the Jewish confusion took hold. If Jews had had problems in the past, they were nothing compared to the problems that civil emancipation would confront them with.

The Jewish movement that Mendelssohn embodied was known as Haskalah, Hebrew for "education" or "enlightenment." It was a natural consequence of the emerging encounter between traditional Jewish learning and Hellenic Christian culture. For an ordinary Jew (though not for the rabbinic scribes), it had long been as foreign and as taboo to read and contemplate, say, Plato, Euclid, Luther, or Newton as it was for a Christian to immerse himself in Hillel's or Rashi's commentaries on the Bible. For a Jew, to go into the world of German learning was to go into exile. In a small circle of like-minded people, Mendelssohn had to penetrate the new world of knowledge on his own, learning

EMANCIPATION

German and Latin by himself, and soon also French and English. Thanks to his position as a tutor in the family of the silk manufacturer Isaac Bernhard, one of Berlin's protected Jews (there were only a few thousand Jews in Berlin at the time), Mendelssohn was provided with the material conditions to complete his spiritual and educational metamorphosis. Within ten years he was writing and performing in stylish German; publishing essays, literary criticism, and drama; being invited to courts and academies; being sought out by kings, bishops, and philosophers.

Jews had entered the Christian world before, but at the cost of leaving Judaism behind. Mendelssohn not only took his Judaism with him but wanted to reshape it, modernize it, adapt it to the more enlightened world he believed was opening its doors to Jews and Judaism. Together with his non-Jewish friend, the author Gotthold Ephraim Lessing, he dreamed of a coming reconciliation between Christians and Jews in a new era of reason and tolerance.

Mendelssohn, who remained an observant Jew throughout his life, imagined that once Jews were allowed to embrace and affirm the cultural heritage of the West, to study in its universities, to acquire its art, literature, and science, and to participate as equals in its economic and social life, the West would learn to respect Judaism as a living and meaningful religion and the Jew as an equal human being.

The weakness of Mendelssohn's program soon became apparent. Once outside the confines of rabbinical Judaism, deprived of its cohesive social and cultural environment, emancipated Jews failed to win the respect not only of Christians but also, to a large extent, of Jews.

Within a few decades, Jews in countries such as Germany and France had left not only the ghetto behind, but in many cases Judaism as well. Of Mendelssohn's own children, all but one were baptized. His daughter Dorothea, who married the philosopher Friedrich Schlegel, converted from Judaism to Protestantism to Catholicism. Most of Mendelssohn's grandchildren were raised as Christians, including the composer Felix Mendelssohn Bartholdy. Jews who personally shied away from taking the step often did it through their children, whom they had baptized at birth. It was not uncommon for the leading families of a Jewish community to convert collectively at the same ceremony. Their children soon knew little about Judaism, and what they thought they knew, they often despised.

In the emerging world of European *Bildung*, Judaism was mostly seen as fossilized, primitive, and obsolete. Hegel wrote of Judaism as a religion marked by unhappiness, ugliness, and a lack of inner harmony, which was a view of Judaism that came to be shared by many converted Jews. "They are a miserable lot," the convert Heinrich Heine reported of the Jews in Hamburg. "What is the secular basis of Judaism?" Karl Marx, the grandson of a rabbi, asked himself and infamously answered: "*Practical* need, *self-interest*. What is the worldly religion of the Jew? *Huckstering*. What is his worldly God? *Money* . . . Emancipation from huckstering and money, consequently from practical, real Judaism, would be the self-emancipation of our time."[1] "The Jews have degenerated beyond redemption," wrote

Ferdinand Lassalle, Marx's comrade in arms, later to become a political rival. The future of the Jews as human beings and citizens lay in the abandonment of Judaism.

For a brief moment such a future seemed possible and attractive. In parts of Western and Central Europe, centuries-old Jewish ways of life were wiped out within a generation. Traditional communities were rapidly dissolving as Jews left the confines of their shtetls and settlement regions. New languages were learned, new occupations taken up, new clothes worn, new religions acquired, and new customs appropriated. In 1839, 40 percent of Berlin's Jewish children studied in Jewish schools; in 1850, only 29 percent did. By 1867, one out every seven students in Berlin's secondary schools was of Jewish descent, four times the proportion of Jews in the population. The progress of Jews in professions and careers previously closed to them was striking. They became lawyers and doctors, founded industries and banks, made success as writers, politicians, philosophers, scientists, journalists, and publishers.

Jews who wanted to hold on to their Jewish faith, and most Jews did after all, soon had very different ideas about what that meant and how it should manifest itself. Some felt compelled to reform and modernize its rituals and traditions to make it more accessible and understandable. There were proposals to reduce the use of Hebrew in the Jewish liturgy and to make synagogues and services more church-like. Many convinced themselves that the ethical and religious core of Judaism had now been incorporated into the European Enlightenment, and that the Jewish emancipation was in fact an event of messianic dimensions. Some went so far as to argue that the Messiah had literally arrived—in the form of an emperor who was tearing down the walls of the ghetto everywhere his armies went. In 1807, when Napoleon resurrected the historic Jewish Council, the Sanhedrin, he presented himself as the new Cyrus, the biblical liberator of the Jews.[2]

Evidently, Jewish emancipation did not produce any distinct new identity, only countless attempts to break free from whatever had been there before. The gap between those who remained on the firm ground of traditional Judaism and those who ventured into the modern quagmire of choices and adaptations grew dramatically. As emancipated Jews lost their relation to traditional Judaism they were prone to see it in the same negative light as the "enlightened" Christian societies to which they were adapting. Where once they had seen wisdom, they now saw superstition; where once they had seen a living tradition, they now saw a fossilized remnant; where once they had seen human beings, they now saw caricatures.

It is not hard to imagine the existential void and social restlessness that leaving the traditional Jewish world behind must have caused in these generations of emancipating Jews, whether they realized it or not. As in the writer and essayist Ludwig Börne (né Lob Baruch), who one day fought against the discrimination of Jews in Frankfurt, only to be baptized the next; who one day tried to break out of "the magic circle" of Jewishness, only to see it close on him the next: "Some accuse me of being a Jew, others forgive me for being a Jew. But all of them reflect on it." Or as in the case of Heinrich Heine, who in a letter to a friend explained that it would have been beneath him to convert to Christianity solely for the right to serve in the Prussian state (which was still a prerequisite for Jews who hoped to do so). A few weeks later, in a letter to the same person, Heine wrote: "I am now hated by Christians as well as Jews; I deeply regret my baptism, only misfortunes have since come my way."

The tragedy of the Jewish emancipation would soon become apparent. As the Enlightenment gave way to nationalism, the intellectual and social climate shifted. The principles and ideals of the Enlightenment had changed most societies in Europe, but perhaps none so irreversibly as the Jewish. While in the societies outside of the Jewish world, these changes could be reversed, no such option remained for the Jews. As the Enlightenment came and went, and European regimes and orders shifted, the Jewish society had unraveled irrevocably.

What distinguished the Enlightenment from previous waves of goodwill toward Jews was not that it promised them civil rights (such had been promised before) but that these rights were given in the name of a new universal creed offering nothing less than the fulfillment of deeply held Jewish beliefs and longings. The Enlightenment promised not only the end of Jewish persecution and alienation but the advent of an era in which ignorance and prejudice would give way to reason, rationality, and human understanding. The Jewish yearnings for messianic redemption had suddenly been provided with a powerful worldly response.

The Enlightenment thus provided arguments both for those who wished to preserve Judaism and for those who believed that it had outlived its purpose. The former saw the Enlightenment as a recognition of Judaism as a religion on a par with Christianity, and of the right of Jews to be "Jews at home and citizens outside." The latter believed that the ethical values of Judaism had been absorbed by the principles of the Enlightenment, and that Jews could now chose to leave Judaism without leaving too much. The radical assimilationists were, in fact, writes Arthur Hertzberg, the truly messianic element in the movement of Jewish emancipation: "The very completeness and unconditionality of their surrender to the dominant values of the majority was a program for the final solution of the Jewish question: let the Jew become like everybody else . . ."[3]

In this sense, the Jews became the most radical product of the Enlightenment, since it soon became apparent that the way out of the traditional Jewish world was fraught with dangers, while the way back was closed. Those who had hoped for the acceptance of Judaism as a respected religion alongside Christianity had relied on ideas and institutions that had now abandoned them.

Emancipation had seemed so close, and yet it now seemed further away than ever.

What most Jews were not yet able to grasp were the inherent pitfalls in their incipient emancipation. It was not only the great universal light that had dawned on humanity, not only reason that had emerged from obscurity and superstition, not only the victory of tolerance over fanaticism. It was also the dissolution of feudal societies into nation-states, and the subsequent demands for national uniformity and cohesion. The ghetto had not only been the result of oppression and confinement but also a place for cultural self-government and self-formation. In a world made up of many small worlds, the Jewish world was, if not loved, at least possible.

In a society striving for uniformity, however, the ghetto was an anomaly. With its own civil laws and courts, its own economic networks and social arrangements, its own religious traditions, the Jewish shtetl was a national affront. The idea of the nation-state simply did not allow for the kind of self-government on which traditional Jewish life had depended.

The French National Assembly's decree of September 27, 1791, on the complete emancipation of the Jews was undoubtedly a historic event, but the message was two-sided. It gave Jews full rights as human beings and citizens, but no rights as Jews. The Jews were not liberated for their own sake but for the sake of the nation. Or to quote Count Stanislas Clermont-Tonnerre's famous statement in the National Assembly in 1789: "Nothing for the Jews as a nation, everything for the Jews as individuals." It was a liberation from above, by an enlightened elite, not a liberation from below, by an enlightened people. This became even more apparent when Jewish liberation was enforced with French arms, as in papal Avignon in 1791, Nice in 1792, and the Rhineland in 1793. In several Italian cities, ghetto walls were literally torn down by Napoleon's troops, supported by young Jews and local revolutionaries.

As one of the first leaders of the Zionist movement, Max Nordau would later point out, the liberation of the Jews by the French Revolution was rooted in abstract and unreal principles, not in real people:

> Just as the French Revolution gave the world the metric and decimal systems, it also created a spiritual system which other countries, more or less voluntarily, accepted as the normal standard of civilization. A country which wished to consider itself highly civilized must thus adhere to a number of institutions created or developed by the Great Revolution, such as representation of the people, freedom of the press, jury system, separation of powers, etc. Jewish emancipation was another of these indispensable accessories of a highly civilized state; just as a piano must not be lacking in the living room of a respectable family, even if not a single member of the family can play it.[4]

The radical Enlightenment had little regard for traditional beliefs, prejudices, and emotions. Overcoming them, however, would take time, which to emancipating Jews seemed a reasonable explanation for the stubborn persistence of anti-Jewish sentiments. Soon, however, they would discover that the anti-Jewish sentiments would not go away with Enlightenment and emancipation, since they were no longer directed against the Jews because of their "unemancipated" religious and cultural distinctiveness, but just the opposite, against their all too rapid adaptation to their non-Jewish surroundings. Already in 1803, Karl Grattenauer, one of the fathers of modern antisemitism, mocked the Jews for eating pork on the Sabbath and indulging in non-Jewish culture. Like his contemporary antisemitic "theoretician" Hartwig Hundt-Radowsky, he lamented that honest Christians could no longer kill Jews with impunity.

Grattenauer's and Hundt-Radowsky's pamphlets foreshadowed a new kind of Jew-hatred, more irreversible and ominous than the old one. Jews, they argued, could never become a full part of the surrounding society, no matter how much they were baptized and no matter how much they adopted Christian practices. Once a Jew always a Jew, always a stranger, always an enemy. Behind the emancipated Jewish facade something treacherous and threatening was hiding.

It would soon become apparent that the Jewish threat, like a chameleon, changed colors with the surroundings. It was a radical and subversive threat in the aristocratic establishment, a threat of backwardness and superstition in the radical salons of the Enlightenment, a finance-capitalist threat in the emerging urban bourgeoisie, an anti-national threat in nationalist circles, a reactionary international among the revolutionaries, and a revolutionary international among the reactionaries.

Sometimes the paradox is unbearable, as in the case of Voltaire, whose perhaps most ardent readers and followers were among emancipated Jews, but who unabashedly used Judaism as a tactical tool in his attacks on religion. Instead of directly attacking Christianity, he attacked it indirectly through Judaism. Christianity's worst self was Judaism. The Hebrew Bible was the original source of Christianity's superstition and stupidity. Judaism (not Christianity) was the proof of religion's enslaving effect on man. The Jews, he wrote, "are an utterly ignorant nation, who for many years have combined the most contemptible misery and the most abominable superstition with a violent hatred of all the nations that have tolerated them . . . The pride of every Jew invites him to believe that it is not his abominable politics, his ignorance of the arts, and his vulgarity that have plunged him into perdition, but the wrath of God in punishing him." And in the great French encyclopedia, Diderot, under the entry *Juifs (philosophie des)*, wrote that the Jews had "all the defects of an ignorant and superstitious nation."

The contributions of Voltaire and Diderot to the Enlightenment and thus, indirectly, to the Jewish emancipation are indisputable. It is also indisputable that they fueled a new secular form of anti-Judaism that would be further developed by their successors and interpreters, as well as by the incipient national romantic reaction against the universal utopia of the Enlightenment. Fichte saw in the Jews "a powerful and hostile state in permanent war with all others"; Goethe argued that the Jews could not be given a full share in a civilization whose very roots they denied; still others saw in the Jews the incarnation of cultural rootlessness and social radicalism. Even a fairly tolerant Romantic thinker like the theologian Friedrich Schleiermacher feared that converted Jews could threaten the Christian character of the Church.[5] The building blocks of the new Europe were no longer the individual and the Enlightenment but the nation and the Christian heritage, neither of which Jews were considered to be a part of.

The tragedy of Jewish emancipation may be foreseen already in Moses Mendelssohn's astonishing journey from the ghetto of Dessau to the literary and scientific elites of Frederick II's Prussia. In the beginning, he opened doors that until now had been firmly shut; he entered the inner circles of German philosophy and literature as a friend and peer of Kant; he gained European fame for a work in German in which, based on a dialogue by Plato, he hoped to prove the immortality of the soul (without the slightest reference to Jewish sources);[6] he became a respected theater and literary critic; he was sought after by princes, statesmen, priests, and philosophers; he was invited to join selective societies and associations, including the Royal Prussian Academy of Sciences in February 1771: "The Academy wishes and hopes that you will accept to become its member. If so, the proposal will be presented to the King tomorrow."

Frederick the Great's rejection a few months later was just one of several blows that hit Mendelssohn on the threshold of liberation. As his name was removed from the academy's list, he found himself involved in a grueling public battle over nothing less than the raison d'être of Judaism. A Swiss deacon named Johann Caspar Lavater dedicated to Mendelssohn the German translation of a book purporting to prove the veracity of Christianity,[7] in which Lavater in a preface challenged Mendelssohn to "publicly refute, unless you find them correct, the *essential* arguments on which the facts of Christianity are supported. But if you find these arguments correct—to do what wisdom, love of truth, honesty invite you to do."

Lavater's insidious challenge shook Mendelssohn's belief in reason and Enlightenment as a path to acceptance and equality. Once again Christianity was pitted against

Judaism, but this time not as dogma against dogma but as truth against lie, science against superstition, Europe against Asia.

Between modern antisemitism's notion of the Jews' inherited incorrigibility and a Christian Enlightenment's demand for the Jews' religious and cultural self-destruction, Mendelssohn's Jewish Enlightenment project was ground to pieces. In his carefully worded reply to Lavater, he maintained that religion was a matter of faith, not a matter of evidence, and that Judaism was not a paleontological precursor to Christianity but a living religion in its own right. "Of the essentials of my religion I am as firmly and irrefutably assured as you or Mr. Bonnet can only be of your own religion . . ."[8]

The trap of emancipation had thus become clearly visible. In an enlightened world steeped in Christian culture, Mendelssohn's continued adherence to Judaism was neither foreseen nor desired.

Moses Mendelssohn's hopes for a new and enlightened future for Judaism were not even embraced by his own children, let alone by Jewish orthodoxy, which saw him as a heretic and a threat. In 1779, Raphael Cohen, the rabbi of Altona-Hamburg, issued a formal excommunication after Mendelssohn had dared to translate the Torah, the five books of Moses, into German.

A parallel path to Jewish emancipation was to explore more worldly ways of expressing the soul of Judaism. Hebrew was being transformed from a language of rabbis and rituals only to a language of writers and literature. In 1783, some of Mendelssohn's like-minded reformers started the

Hebrew-language journal *Ha'measef* as a nursery for a new Hebrew-language generation of poets, scholars, and journalists. After only three years, however, the society behind the journal adopted the quintessentially German name Die Gesellschaft zur Beförderung des Guten und Edlen (the Society for the Promotion of the Good and the Noble). Eventually, *Ha'measef* was to be supplied with a growing number of German texts. In 1806 a German-language competitor, *Sulamith*, was launched, and in 1811 *Ha'measef* ceased publication.

Within a generation, Mendelssohn's reform work had proven futile. He had not succeeded in winning over those who wanted to remain Jews, and those he did win over did not want to remain Jews.

While there was soon to be a nationalist and romantic reaction to the Enlightenment—making it just another pendulum swing in the historical movement by which power is gained, lost, and redistributed—there was no such reaction available to the newly ascendant Jewish middle class. In a Europe where belonging and citizenship were increasingly defined by blood, soil, and nation, the Jews as Jews had literally no place to go.

One option was to push even harder for Enlightenment and universalism.

Another was to affirm the nation as the sine qua non for Jewish existence, and to make the Jews a nation like all others—in a land like all others.

II
THE PROMISED LAND

■

I can't believe it looks like this! I had thought it would be something completely different. I think I have seen this country many times before.

—SELMA LAGERLÖF, *JERUSALEM*

A LAND LIKE ALL OTHERS

The Promised Land; where we can have hooked noses, black or red beards, and bandy legs, without being despised for it . . . So that the derisive cry of "Jew!" may become an honorable appellation, like German, Englishman, Frenchman—in short, like that of all civilized people.

—THEODOR HERZL

To become like everyone else may seem a modest, if not unambitious, ideal, especially for a civilization that has insisted on setting higher standards for itself than for others.

If I were to find a word that would summarize the longing, the joy, the identity that permeated the Israel to which I ascended in 1962, it would be "normalcy." Israel was the country where Jews could be Jews without having to think about it, where the heroes were heroes and the villains were villains without having to point out that they were also Jews. The communists who gathered in the courtyard behind my aunt's house to watch Soviet propaganda films were Jews. The gang of boys who occupied the little park on Shenkin Street were Jews. The rag collector who pulled his cart through the neighborhood and shouted "*Alte sachen*" in Yiddish was Jewish. The school athlete who jumped twenty feet was Jewish. So was the best-looking girl in the class. You could be a good Jew or a bad Jew, where the latter was not necessarily too bad. You could joke about Jews, make fun of Jews, and celebrate Jewish holidays with the same secular casualness as the Swedes celebrated Epiphany or Pentecost.

It was a sense of normalcy that could only be experienced at the edge of the abnormal, as an abnormality in itself, much like a breath of fresh air in an unaired room. Usually the experience is short-lived, as freshness is soon taken for granted, but in Israel the proximity of abnormality was kept alive. From behind lurked the Holocaust, from without lurked the enemy, and from within lurked the Galut Jew. The lightness of being Jewish could only be properly appreciated against the ever-present threat of darkness.

What Israel offered was normalcy—against all odds.

In the early 1960s, the high-minded generation of the Second Aliyah was still dominant. As late as 1957, in the first census of the State of Israel, David Ben-Gurion, now seventy-one, had registered as an "agricultural laborer." The same people who had founded the state were still running it. There was a historically unique continuity between struggle and power, between ideology and practice, between vision and reality. It was as if the first Puritan immigrants to America in 1620 had participated in the Revolution of 1776, led the Constitutional Convention of 1787, and held political power for another fifteen years. The concentration within the Israeli power elite of ideological purists, moral puritans, and settler pioneers was still evident. In the 1948 Constituent Assembly, at least half of the members were socialist veterans of the Second and Third Aliyah, heavily overrepresented in relation to their share of the population but with a hold on the country that had not diminished significantly in the fifteen years that had passed. If nothing else, this could be clearly seen in the dominant role that the sons and daughters of the kibbutz movement still played in public life. They were the undisputed elite, not by virtue of their numbers (4 percent of the population) nor by virtue of money and material status, but by virtue of their embodiment of the country's moral, social, and military ideals. By the mid-1960s, this small segment of Israeli society provided the air force with 30 percent of its pilots, the army with 22 percent of its officers, and the Zionist Labor Party with 25 percent of its representatives in the Knesset.[1]

It was the ideals of this elite that formed the Israel I was absorbed into, and which could easily be brought to life by a week or two of work on a kibbutz, where members still lived and dressed simply, where the size of pocket money and clothing rations could provoke stormy discussions at members' meetings, where collective child-rearing and collective householding were a given, where new members were expected to give up their previous (and any additional) property, where libraries were filled with political newspapers and magazines, philosophical and literary classics as well as modern Hebrew literature. In addition, there were books and magazines on combines, apple varieties, fertilizers, and irrigation techniques. It was an Israel where studying at the agricultural schools of Mikveh Israel and Kadoorie was as highly regarded as studying at the technical college Technion in Haifa. Most of the songs in the youth movement were about farming and labor, about building the country and being built by it. I still remember the early, dewy mornings as sleep was slowly wrenched from our bodies, and the smell of soil rose to our nostrils, and the creaking of the tractor-drawn platform rocked us to the fields and plantations in the twilight of dawn, and the sensuality of idealistic self-torture slowly warmed our cheeks and hands. It was a lifestyle that seemed not only mandatory and necessary but was also attractive and satisfactory.

The idea that the Jews must become a nation like all others was born out of the belief that the nation-state was the normal state of humanity. A people without a state eventually became abnormal. Not only did it deform itself but it deformed the social order of their host countries as well, creating antagonisms and resentments. Giving the Jews a country, a piece of territory anywhere in the world, was the surgical intervention in history that would make the Jewish problem disappear once and for all. As the Jews became a people like all others, the causes for antisemitism would vanish.

Had I read the earliest thinkers of political Zionism without knowing where it all would lead, I would have been struck by the delirious tone, the lurking madness, the personal despair. Only people who had given up on the world could rationalize it so freely. The Russian Jewish physician Leo Pinsker, author of *Auto-Emancipation* (1882), the first pamphlet of political Zionism, ominously compared the plight of the Jews to an individual who, despised and ostracized, sees suicide as the only way out. No one should be surprised if the Jews collectively killed themselves. Pinsker regarded the hatred of Jews as a hereditary and incurable mental illness. "The fight against this hatred, like any fight against inherited dispositions, can only be in vain."[2]

Political Zionism was a cry of doom. It advocated a revolution so radical and uncompromising that it left no room for extenuating circumstances. It was conceived by people who spoke the language of the Enlightenment, indeed who considered themselves to be the truly enlightened, but who no longer believed in reason and knowledge as a means to combat the hatred of Jews. Against a hereditary and incurable disease, reason and knowledge argued in vain. What it required was a physical operation, not a political process. First territory, then cure. First uprooting, then rebirth. First incision, then redemption.

At times, it didn't seem to matter where or how the incision was made. Only a year before the publication of his 1896 pamphlet *Der Judenstaat* ("The Jewish State," or more literally, "The State of the Jews"), Theodor Herzl had proposed to "solve the Jewish problem, at least in Austria," through a mass conversion of the country's Jews to Christianity. The movement would be led by himself and be based on a personal deal with the pope: the commitment of the Catholic Church to fight antisemitism in exchange for newly converted Jewish children. The ceremony would take place in St. Stephen's Cathedral in Vienna at noon on a Sunday, in broad daylight, with a solemn parade and ringing of bells. A whole generation of Jews would lead their children, "with a proud gesture," to the threshold of the Christian Church:

> We, the steadfast leaders, would have constituted the final generation. We would have remained with the faith of our fathers. But we would have made Christians of our children before they reached the age of independent decision—after which conversion looks like an act of cowardice or calculation. As is my custom, I had thought out the plan in finest detail. I saw myself in negotiation with the Archbishop of Vienna, I stood, in imagination, before the Pope—who regretted beyond words that I didn't become a Christian too—and sent the slogan of race-merger flying across the world.[3]

Herzl's idea to create a state for the Jews, which followed soon after, had the same all-redemptive character and basically amounted to the same thing, getting the Jews out of Europe. From one generation to another, as once from Egypt, the Jews would march out of their host countries. From one generation to another, Europe would be rid of its Jewish problem. From one generation to another, the Jews would be cured of their historical deformity.

Herzl's Zionism was as concrete and practical an operation as the ceremony at St. Stephen's Cathedral, though more extensive and in two stages. First, a territory had to be secured through a grant from an imperial power; then, "with money, money and more money," a gigantic transportation and supply apparatus had to be built up ("not merely food and water as in the simple days of Moses"), the Jews had to be mobilized, emigration and transit agreements had to be concluded, attractive housing had to be built (otherwise the middle class would not come), industries had to be established, and a new state government had to be organized.[4]

As the Jews left their host countries, the hatred of Jews would die out. The Jews would no longer be around to stir the resentment of their non-Jewish neighbors. No one would be able to shout "*Hep, hep*" or "*Saujud*" after the famous correspondent and playwright Herzl. There would be no Herzl to shout at.

Read as a line of action, the Zionism of Herzl was unreal and incoherent, as a cry for help it was heartbreaking. It was the fantasy of people whose worldview had collapsed overnight, and who hoped to repair it by dawn. It was the kind of reality-defying utopia that emerges when victory is in sight—but out of reach. The men who formulated the ideas of political Zionism had themselves gone as far as the promises of the Enlightenment would take them, only to discover that they had not come very far and that the promise was false.

The Jewish pogroms in Odessa in 1881 proved Moshe Leib Lilienblum wrong about antisemitism. Odessa was a modern, secularized Russian city, with a pleasant climate, an educated middle class, and an atmosphere of enlightenment and tolerance. Lilienblum belonged to the growing circle of

Russian Jewish intellectuals who had previously advocated reform and integration, but who were now beginning to formulate Zionist colonization programs. If Jews could be killed in Odessa, they could be killed anywhere. After 1881, the question was no longer whether and how Jews would adapt to modern society but whether and how they would survive it. A few years earlier, Lilienblum had regarded antisemitism as a dying remnant of the past, now he saw it as a harbinger of the future. Modern civilization was not only incapable of eradicating antisemitic ideas, it contributed to them: "The drive for national self-determination is the very soil in which antisemitism flourishes . . . Antisemitism is the shadow of our new and fine contemporary civilization; it will no more do away with antisemitism than the light will destroy the shadows it casts."[5] Lilienblum became one of the central figures of Chovevei Tzion (Lovers of Zion), the first modern Zionist movement, not mainly because he saw a new possibility opening up but because he saw all other possibilities closing.

In 1882, the first pioneers of the movement emigrated from Russia to Palestine under the name BILU, after the Hebrew initials of Isaiah 2:5: "Ye of the house of Jacob, come let us walk in the light of the Lord."[6] In their manifesto, they thanked God for awakening the Jews from their slumber and false hopes, but called on the Turkish Sultan for help with the earthly practicalities. In return for the promise of a small state within a state where the Jews could freely manage their internal affairs, they would help the Turkish empire manage its external ones, "so that we may help our brother Ishmael in his time of need."

Zionism was the child of shattered illusions and opening horizons.

On the shattered illusions there was agreement, on the horizons there was not. The messianically inspired thinkers said Jerusalem and meant Jerusalem. The political solvers of the "Jewish problem" may have said Jerusalem but meant a piece of land. The important thing was not to return to the "holy land" but to a land of one's own, wrote Leo Pinsker. First and foremost, the land had to be open to settlement, as well as offering space, security, and livelihood. It could be Palestine, but it could also be "a small territory in North America, or a sovereign pashalik in Asiatic Turkey."[7] In any case, the land had to be acquired with the support of the governments of the world and be politically safeguarded by them. The Jewish problem was a world problem, and it was in the world's interest to solve it. What the Jews had lacked so far was organization, determination—and a Moses.

Fourteen years later, Herzl wrote much the same as Pinsker, bringing little new to the Zionist idea—but its Moses or Messiah. "When I was ten years old," wrote David Ben-Gurion in his memoirs, "the rumor spread through the town that the Messiah had come, that he was in Vienna, that he had a black beard, and that his name was Herzl." Herzl himself was no stranger to the idea. "Moses too was severely tested," he wrote in one of his diary entries. And in another: "Moses needed forty years. We require perhaps twenty or thirty."[8]

It was his personality, not his ideas, that was Herzl's secret, wrote Chaim Weizmann, the leader of the World

Zionist Organization and the first president of the State of Israel. "If he had been content with publishing his pamphlet, we would now remember him only as one of the eccentrics of Jewish history."[9]

Weizmann was fourteen years Herzl's junior, but saw him in action as early as the summer of 1898 at the Second Zionist Congress in Basel, and judged him naive and ignorant, with a tendency toward the pathetic, but "a model of courage and sacrifice." According to Weizmann, Herzl's Zionism was based on a grandiose overestimation of the will and power of emperors and sultans, and an ignorant underestimation of the will and power of Jews and Judaism.

The difference between them could be explained by the fact that Herzl came from a sophisticated, assimilated Jewish milieu in Budapest and Vienna, and Weizmann from a small encircled Jewish shtetl in Belarus. Herzl saw Zionism as an elite-driven diplomatic and political operation, a centralized evacuation and colonization plan, a gigantic philanthropic effort in which the world's rich Jews would use their influence with the world's powerful to solve the Jewish problem in one fell swoop. In contrast, Weizmann and the young Eastern Jewish intellectuals who were drawn into the vortex surrounding the new leader saw Zionism as a long-term mass movement for Jewish renewal and liberation. For them, Herzl's Zionism was an empty barrel, a movement driven more by short-term desperation than by long-term conviction.

Herzl, of course, knew as little of the Eastern Jews as he knew of Jews and Judaism in general. He approached his mission with "the confidence of the uninitiated," wrote his early friend and collaborator Marcus Ehrenpreis, who later became the chief rabbi of Stockholm.[10]

As Eastern Jewish intellectuals began to realize that Herzl was not delivering what he had promised, that, as Weizmann proclaimed, "nothing remained but phrases," they tried to put Zionism on a different, less political and more cultural basis, initially with little success. The World Zionist Congress was Herzl's idea and creation, and as long as he lived it stood behind his ambitions.

After Herzl's death, a more pragmatic view of Zionism emerged. The fantasy of momentary diplomatic redemption dissolved into more mundane visions of gradual colonization and nation-building. The number of active Zionists dropped dramatically; the 1903 level would not be surpassed until 1921 and it became clear that Zionism above all was a safety valve. As the antisemitic pressure increased, members and supporters flocked to it; as the pressure decreased, interest waned. The swings in support were dramatic. Parties with tens of thousands of members in 1906 could count only a few hundred three years later. Zionism increasingly became a movement with a double message: emigration and pioneering for a select few, cultural and national rights for those who stayed behind. In high-pressure Zionism was an evacuation organization, in low-pressure it was a life insurance policy.

Herzl's Zionism required high pressure. The promise of a land like any other was not enough for the Jewish masses to flock to it. It required a continuous dramatization of the Jewish existence. Thus, it lived in symbiosis with antisemitism and aggressive nationalism and flourished in conjunction with them. It was no coincidence that Herzl conceived his vision for the new state to the tune of Richard Wagner's *Tannhäuser*. ("My only recreation was to listen to Wagnerian music in the evenings, especially *Tannhäuser*, an opera which I attended whenever it was performed. Only on evenings when I did not attend the opera did I doubt the correctness of my ideas.") Nor that he came to Zionism duly decorated with mensural scars from his dueling in the German student fraternity Albia in Vienna. In 1883 he left Albia after a tribute to the recently deceased Wagner "had developed into an antisemitic manifestation." Still, there was something Wagnerian about Herzl's visions of a Jewish nation. In his diary on June 5, 1895, after hearing *Tannhäuser* at the Paris Opera, he noted:

> We too, shall have such magnificent lobbies—the men in full dress and the women altogether sumptuous. I must exploit the Jewish love of luxury, as well as everything else.
>
> Again I considered the phenomenon of the crowd. There they sat for hours, tightly packed, motionless, in bodily torture—and for what? For an imponderable, for that which Hirsch [a Jewish philanthropist skeptical of Herzl] doesn't understand. For sounds, tones and pictures!
>
> I shall also encourage the composition of noble marches for great occasions.[11]

In the diary's jumble of unbridled fantasies and bitter rants, Herzl vacillates between acuity and madness. June 7, 1895: "Before the statue of Gambetta in the Tuileries. I hope the Jews will erect a more artistic one over me." June 8: "Dig up and transplant whole communities so that the Jews will feel at home and acclimatize." June 10: "The ship that brings my parents, my wife and my children, should also bring close and distant relatives—the whole family." June 11: "A ship with coffins. We will also bring our dead."

At times he apologized for his whims. "I cannot be bound by sober facts alone. Intoxication is necessary. Artists should understand this. But there are so few artists." Or: "Good God, after this confession, perhaps Lombroso [Cesare, an Italian Jewish psychiatrist] will consider me mad. And my good friend Nordau [Max, Herzl's closest ally in the Zionist movement] will quietly swallow the indignation I cause him. But they are wrong: I know that two and two make four."

More than anyone else, Herzl embodied the inner tension of Western European Jews who suddenly realized that assimilation was not working, that there was something alienating about the very effort itself, that they could never be "pure" Germans or French, that there was no escape from being Jewish. Zionism came to their minds as an unexpected but unavoidable intruder, not as a long-sought liberator. Zionism disrupted Jewish strategies that they had hitherto not only embraced but also actively helped to shape. Zionism meant breaking away from a social order to which they felt deeply attached.

For these Jews, the problem with European nationalism was not that it drew boundaries between peoples but that it drew boundaries that excluded Jews and conjured up identities of which Jews were not allowed to be a part. The nation-state detested cultural, ethnic, and religious ambivalence since it undermined its unifying ambitions. The shaping of the nation-state was characterized by "intolerance to difference and peculiarity," writes Zygmunt Bauman in his study of modernity and ambivalence. Herzl's Zionism was an attempt to do away with the ambivalence of Jewish existence once and for all.[12]

To Herzl, antisemitism was a natural reaction to an unnatural condition, a Darwinian push toward a necessary and healthy mutation. "The effects of one push can only be cancelled out by another push." The line between Jews and non-Jews would be made as sharp as the lines between the other peoples of Europe. What the Germans and French already had, the Jews would also have. Their own Wagner, their own flag, their own parades and marches, their own national literature and propaganda. "Men live and die for a flag; it is in fact the only thing for which they are willing to die in masses, provided one educates them to it," he exclaimed to the skeptical Baron Hirsch. "With a flag you can lead men where you will—even into the Promised Land."[13]

Herzl was very much a child of his time—and in some respects ahead of it.

By the end of the nineteenth century, the assimilating Jewish elites of Central Europe and Germany had begun to embrace the nationalist ideals of the day. Many German Jews now regarded themselves as an inseparable part of the German heritage, the *Volksgeist*. The essays of a young Martin Buber abound with concepts from the emerging Germanic vocabulary—*Blut*, *Boden*, *Volkstum*, *Gemeinschaft*, and

Wurzelhaftigkeit: blood, soil, national character, community, and rootedness.

There were even Jewish anthropologists who sought to place the Jews in a racial-biological context, in order to counter antisemitic claims of Jewish racial inferiority. One of the earliest writers in this field, the Anglo Jewish scholar Joseph Jacobs, argued forcefully that the Jews were indeed a race, exceptionally pure at that, with racial characteristics far superior to their reputation. Samuel Weissenberg, another contemporary Jewish race theorist, devoted his anthropological work to the search for the "original Jew," or the original "Jewish type," primarily through extensive anthropometric studies, such as skull measurements of Jews in southern Russia, but ultimately came to a racial-biological void; the original Jew did not exist, the Jews "do not form one exact anthropological type, but are composed of several types, which are not everywhere the same."[14] Weissenberg had started from the common assumption at the time, that the Jews, like the Germans, were a *Volk* with a common historical and biological destiny, but found through his studies that the assumption was based on false notions.

The emerging Zionism did not deny racial biology, only its antisemitic overtones. Herzl saw the Jews as an originally pure and noble race that had degenerated and withered in exile, and Zionism consequently as a movement for the healing and revitalization of the Jewish *Volkskörper*. It was no accident that concepts such as "disease" and "degeneration" were used by Zionists to describe the state of Jews in the Galut.

Regardless of how far the comparison between German and Jewish nationalism can and should be drawn, the fact remains that the Zionist and antisemitic arguments were fueled in part by the same murky sources. "It is clear," writes John M. Efron, "that for Zionists, race was an important category and mode of Jewish self-definition."[15] It is also clear that a number of Zionist-oriented anthropologists and sociologists went to great lengths to positively distinguish and define the Jewish race. "In a sick Judaism, Zionism is the will to live," declared the German Jewish anthropologist Elias Auerbach after German and Jewish nationalists had clashed at a student conference in 1902. Auerbach went to great lengths to prove the unbroken Jewish racial chain from the Bible to the present, demonstrating an impressive ability to ignore the occasional high rates of intermarriage, migration, and mass conversion.

Because it didn't add up, of course. One could not simultaneously assert the purity and excellence of the Jewish race and the deformed character of the Jewish people. It was not possible to praise the unbroken history of the Jewish people one day and to trivialize or denigrate most of it the next. Jewish racial biology dealt as freely with the facts as racial antisemitism but lacked its aggressive, social Darwinist features. The Jews were out to defend themselves against other "races," not to attack them. Zionism countered antisemitism's image of the Jew, not with a counterimage of the enemy but with the image of another Jew.

Thus, while other national movements of Europe defined themselves by romanticizing the existing customs and character of their respective peoples, Zionism defined itself by denying or diminishing the customs and character that had hitherto distinguished the Jewish people. For Czech or Polish nationalists, national liberation meant giving real Czechs or Poles the chance to show who they were. For Zionism, national liberation meant transforming existing Jews into something else.

Herzl was deeply obsessed with the transformation, but since it was the nation that would mold the new Jew, he sought the building blocks of a nation, not the building blocks of Jewish culture and history. He attached so little importance to the latter that he didn't believe in the new nation's ability to create a common language, even less in the revival of Hebrew: "Who among us knows enough Hebrew to ask for a train ticket in that language? It is not possible." No, in Herzl's state for the Jews, everyone would be allowed to speak as he wished. German Jews would speak German, French Jews French. "Each retains his own language, the beloved abode of his thoughts. Switzerland is the ultimate example of the possibility of linguistic federalism."[16] The lingua franca in which most people communicated would eventually reveal itself, in a Darwinian process of elimination.

As diverse as the linguistic base of Herzl's state was to be, its political features were equally eclectic. He wanted to realize all that he considered good in European societies, and exclude all that he considered evil. He tried "to salvage the Jews from the collapse of European liberalism, and to salvage liberalism from the consequences of its collapse in Europe," notes Zygmunt Bauman.[17] The result was a strange and contradictory mix of aristocratic rule, socialist economics, and liberal culture.

Aristocracy was preferable to democracy because democracy required more political virtue than could be expected of the people. In this respect, the Jews were no different than other Europeans. They too would become "insolent in liberty." They too would be tempted to follow whoever shouted the loudest.

Unfettered capitalism had to be rejected because it did not allow for the rational planning and scientific approach to state-building to which Herzl attached great importance. Settlement and subsistence must be regulated in advance and in detail. The state must have the right to control both the management of enterprises and the conditions of the labor market. The seven-hour workday was a social symbol of the new state and was represented by seven golden stars on Herzl's proposed white national flag: "The white field means the new, pure life; the stars are the seven golden hours of our working day. For it is under the banner of work that the Jews will enter the Promised Land." In the "seven-hour country" no old people would be put in old people's homes, "one of the cruelest acts of kindness invented by our simple-minded good-heartedness." The flawed charitable institutions of the old society would be replaced by a new and all-encompassing welfare state, "founded on the basis of all modern experience in social policy."[18]

In Herzl's futuristic novel *Altneuland* (written in 1902, set in 1923), the elements of utopian socialism are even more pronounced, the social structure is *gemeinschaftlich* (communal), and the economy has strong cooperative elements. Neudorf, the novel's fictional village, is explicitly modeled on American, French, and German experimental societies. Free schools and childcare are a matter of course, as is a two-year compulsory education program for all men and women. Unlike the aristocratic republic outlined in *Der Judenstaat*, *Altneuland* presents a radical democracy with universal suffrage and a high degree of female participation in public life. *Altneuland* is the society that Europe had the chance to realize at the turn of the century, but in its embrace of nationalism and capitalism had failed to do so.

Consequently, Herzl makes his new state embody a world of religious tolerance, cultural freedom, and a vibrant creativity reminiscent of Vienna or Paris; a cosmopolitan oasis in a world of nationalist deserts. Religious freedom is a given in *Altneuland*, with all religions effectively expressing the same enlightened moral values. Good and gentle Jews compete with good and gentle Christians. An American Jewess, Mrs. Gothland, has a face "radiant with goodness under the gray hair." An Anglican priest, William H. Hopkins, "minister of the English church in Jerusalem," has "beautiful, dreamy blue eyes" and rejoices when he is mistaken for a Jew. The Arab characters are polite, intelligent, and good. All conflicts, including those between Jews and Arabs, are sublimated in an atmosphere of economic prosperity, cultural curiosity, and political equality. The Arab hero, a European-educated chemist named Reschid Bey, has plenty of wise things to say about salt production, human coexistence, and economic development.

There is even an anticipated conflict with nationalist religious Jews; a rabbi, Dr. Geyer, wants to restrict citizenship to Jews, while the Jewish protagonist, David Littwak, advocates equal rights for Jews and non-Jews. Public opinion sides with Littwak, and Geyer's party is soundly defeated.

It is sometimes touching to see how Herzl tries to provide his state with some Jewish features. He writes of the importance of "establishing places of pilgrimage for the deep religious needs of our people," but the places of pilgrimage he sees as models are Mecca and Lourdes, and he quickly adds that everyone will be blessed in their own way. Nevertheless, Herzl also seems to toy with the idea of a specific Jewish mission in the world. The state of the Jews must not, after all, be like every other state but a model state of sorts, more enlightened, more tolerant, more liberal, better planned, indeed more European than Europe itself: "The world will be liberated by our liberation, enriched by our wealth, and gain greatness by our greatness."

After Herzl's death in 1904, one faction of Zionism broke with all nostalgic regards for Palestine and opted for whatever territory possible, while another faction, soon to be the mainstream of Zionism, took a different course. While Herzl's ideological heirs in the West clung to Zionism as a political evacuation operation in immediate need of a colonial charter, if need be anywhere, the predominantly Russian and Eastern European core of the Zionist movement advocated a more gradual colonization of Palestine only. Zionist ideology, if you will, was adapting to reality. Herzl's grand schemes had all failed; there was no colonial charter in sight, no major diplomatic breakthrough to anticipate. The movement had also lost its main tool for negotiating with kings and sultans: Herzl himself. Within a few years, Zionism became a movement for organizing what was already underway—a Jewish settler society in Palestine.

Still, there remained a faction that wanted to push Herzl's Zionism to the limit, that wanted to put all its energies into finding a territory and founding a state as soon as possible, that looked forward to a "final solution" of the Jewish problem, and that would therefore in time inspire a radical, sometimes rebellious, and eventually violent opposition of impatience and disappointment within the Zionist movement. Pinsker's and Herzl's Zionism required a constantly sounding alarm bell, a permanent state of alert among the Jews of the world, a sense of acute distress and impending salvation—an ongoing drama. Not for nothing had Herzl been a playwright, and not surprisingly, it was another playwright, Israel Zangwill, who most consistently sought to fulfill his project.

The son of Eastern European Jewish immigrants in London's East End, Zangwill had a liberal and freethinking upbringing, first at the Jews' Free School, then at London University. In his plays, he put a Dickensian touch to the characters and settings of London's Jewish immigrant ghettos, and eventually wrote a play set in the United States entitled *The Melting Pot*, which would give name to the vision of a society in which different races and nations would merge. In 1896, Zangwill met Herzl and became a committed Zionist. Like Herzl, he believed that a separate state was the only way to normalize and assimilate the Jews, but he had even less feelings about Judaism itself (though he knew it far better than Herzl).

At the 1905 Zionist Congress in Basel, the first after Herzl's death, Zangwill was the most forceful advocate of a purely Herzlian policy: diplomatic efforts to gain access to a Jewish territory as soon as possible, and thus a continued skeptical attitude toward a small-scale colonization of Palestine dependent on charities. Incidentally, the "territorialists" had their eyes on Uganda, not Palestine.

After having been defeated by the majority at the Zionist Congress, Zangwill formed a new association, the Jewish Territorial Organization, initially supported by a number of prominent Jewish leaders since it so obviously followed the logic of Herzl's program. When Zangwill's diplomatic failure soon became as obvious as Herzl's, he brought the whole territorialist idea down with him.

Another loser was Herzl's friend and chief comrade-in-arms Max Nordau, a well-known cultural figure in the German-speaking avant-garde circles of the Austro-Hungarian Dual Monarchy, recognized for his journalism and social criticism. Like Herzl, he had not considered himself primarily Jewish and almost as strongly as Herzl he had been affected by the realization that he was still seen as a Jew first and foremost. "If you are insane, then I am too," Nordau, whose hair had turned white at forty-seven, told Herzl. The course of Nordau's life, from his childhood in a rabbinical home in Budapest to the pinnacle of European cultural life, had been long and glorious, but now he saw himself brought back to the starting point. The tight-knit Jewish community from which the young Nordau had escaped, and which he had rejected for most of his life, suddenly became a utopia to be aspired to. A territorial state for the Jews would heal what modernity and emancipation had broken. The task of Zionism was to create a new collective Jewish identity to replace the one that had been irrevocably lost, an identity based not on old religious, messianic, or mystical notions but on European-style nationalism: "The principle of nationality has awakened a sense of their own in all the peoples; it has taught them to regard their unique qualities as values, and has given them a passionate desire for independence," wrote Nordau in 1902.[19]

At the 1905 Zionist Congress, Nordau warned the movement against returning to the futile methods of "small-scale colonization" and called for intensified negotiations with the major international powers for the immediate creation of a national home for "the entire Jewish people." To that end, even Uganda must be discussed, at least as a temporary refuge, pending a more definitive destination.

As he realized that the majority was against him, Nordau retreated offstage and barely showed himself during the rest of the proceedings. After a few years, he left the Zionist stage altogether. During the First World War, he declared himself a pacifist and went into Spanish exile. In 1917 he came out to criticize the Balfour Declaration, the British government's promise to give the Jews a "national home" in Palestine, for not going far enough. What the Jews needed, Nordau wrote, was not a vague promise of a future national home but the immediate establishment of a Jewish state. The war had led to a catastrophic deterioration in the situation of the Jews, with displacements and pogroms on a wholly new scale. In 1903, the murder of a few dozen Jews in Kishinev had raised a storm of protest and provided Herzl's Zionists with a strong case for immediate action. From 1918 to 1920, more than fifteen thousand Jews were murdered without so much as a raised eyebrow from a war-weary world.

Which in 1919 was reason enough for Nordau to put forward a plan for the immediate evacuation of millions of Jews from Eastern Europe to Palestine. The plan was ignored by the Zionist leadership at the time, but was later embraced by Nordau's and Herzl's logical successor, the right-wing nationalist leader Vladimir Jabotinsky. The Nordau plan once again articulated the dream of a rapid and definitive solution to the Jewish problem, a dream that would remain alive in Zionism.

From a historical perspective, the main difference between one Zionism and another was impatience. A tactical difference, if you will, between a nationalism that saw the acquisition of territory as the overriding condition for creating a nation, and a nationalism that sought to acquire the territory in accordance with the actual power of an emerging nation. The latter required the patient mobilization of a self-sacrificing elite, the former the impatient mobilization of the material and political resources of the larger Jewish world.

The strategy of patience meant attaching more importance to the means than to the end, or at least keeping quiet about the end before the means were in place. It was a strategy that soon would take on radical socialist, and even revolutionary, overtones, but it was still based on the idea of a self-sacrificing Zionist avant-garde settling the land dunam by dunam. It was a proudly pragmatic strategy that established collective farms when collective farms were deemed appropriate for Jewish colonization; created the Histadrut, a monopolistic Jewish trade union movement, when it was deemed necessary for the formation of a Jewish society; and forbade the "exploitation" of Arab labor when Arab labor was deemed a threat to a national Jewish economy.

Patient Zionism postulated that Jewish control of the land was the precondition for a Jewish state, but unlike Herzl and the territorialists, it didn't believe that control of the land could be granted from outside. Control of the land could only be achieved by owning, working, and protecting it. Patient Zionism was a land-buying, land-draining, and land-expanding enterprise.

To the generation that founded the State of Israel, becoming a nation like all others meant building a land where the nation was more important than the individual, the map of the past more valid than the landscape of the present, the creation of a new people more important than the creation of a new social order, the dunam-by-dunam conquest of the land more important than diplomatic treaties and promises.

The State of Israel was not primarily, as many would come to believe, the miraculous outcome of a Jewish disaster but the determined result of an ideological ambition to make the Jews into a cohesive nation, the Jewish exile into a historical parenthesis, and Jewish Palestine into a nation like all others.

A BETTER LAND

> I will make you a light to the nations,
> that my salvation may reach the ends of the earth.
>
> —ISAIAH 49:6

In the aftermath of World War II and the Holocaust, the idea of a Jewish state as the solution to the Jewish problem went from being a minority view among the Jews of the world to becoming a dominant creed. Even Jewish groups and individuals who had no intention of emigrating had come to see a Jewish nation-state as a life insurance policy of sorts. In Sweden, where Zionism had previously had little influence and whose Jews had been spared, the catastrophe of the war marked a turning point. Zionism was seen as a guarantor for Jewish existence everywhere, not only in a Jewish state in Palestine.

From the very beginning there had been Zionists who saw things exactly this way: The aim was not to create a state for all Jews but a Jewish spiritual and cultural center for a still-existing Diaspora. Before Herzl's territorial dreams, few Jews could imagine a Jewish state, let alone one that could accommodate and sustain the Jews of the world. Even the early theorists of Labor Zionism did not seriously imagine that a Jewish settlement in Palestine would literally solve the Jewish problem.

Yet, curiously, this was an interpretation of Zionism that early on acquired an "oppositional" character, notably through its most prominent exponent, a Russian Jewish intellectual from Odessa named Asher Zvi Ginzberg, later known by his nom de plume, Ahad Ha'am, Hebrew for "one of the people." Ahad Ha'am contrasted the Zionist idea of Palestine as a spiritual and cultural center for the Jews of the world with Theodor Herzl's Zionist idea of a state for the Jews of the world, and argued that the two Zionisms were incompatible with each other.

What did Ahad Ha'am mean? In his debates with Herzl, it seemed simple. Herzl wanted to solve the Jewish problem through mass emigration of Jews to a nation of their own, preferably but not necessarily in Palestine. Ahad Ha'am wanted to strengthen Jewish national life everywhere by establishing a Jewish spiritual and cultural center in Palestine, nowhere else. His main argument against Herzl was that a state for Jews in Palestine—physically small, geographically exposed, and dependent on great powers—would not solve the problems facing the Jewish existence, but instead would be adopting "the dangerous doctrine of the impossibility of Jewish life in the Diaspora." Against this, the task of Zionism must be to create "a single permanent center which can [. . .] transform the scattered [Jewish] atoms into a single entity with a definite and self-subsistent character of its own."[1]

What Ahad Ha'am feared was a Zionism for which the state itself would become the overarching goal, making for a state that would be Jewish in name only, like Palestine under Herod in which "the national culture was despised and persecuted."[2] Nor could such a state be anything other than a Jewish Serbia or Montenegro, another shard in the mosaic of new nation-states.

Did Ahad Ha'am want a state at all? Well, maybe later. But a state built on a specifically Jewish basis, a spiritual and moral model, not a state like all others. His version of Zionism, Chibat Tzion (Love of Zion), advocated the creation of a Jewish center in Palestine, from which

> the spirit of Judaism will radiate to great circumference, to all communities of the Diaspora, to inspire them with new life and to preserve the over-all unity of our people. When our national culture in Palestine has attained that level, we may be confident that it will produce men in the Land of Israel itself who will be able, at a favorable moment, to establish a State there—one which will be not merely a State of Jews but truly a Jewish State.[3]

It is not hard to see parallels between Ahad Ha'am's spiritually guided Jewish center and Plato's philosopher-ruled republic. In Ahad Ha'am's society, as in Plato's, the wise and the morally educated were set to rule. To this Ahad Ha'am added the thesis that the Jews, having for millennia imposed on themselves heavier moral obligations than others, had developed a stronger sense of morality. "It is admitted by almost everybody—not excluding Nietzsche—that the Jewish people is preeminent in its genius for morality," he wrote.[4]

Not surprisingly, Nietzsche was a major source of inspiration for Ahad Ha'am. In an 1898 essay on Judaism and Nietzsche, he certainly polemicized against Nietzsche associating his ideal of the Übermensch with an "Aryan" ideal of physical strength and beauty. He could just as easily, Ahad Ha'am argued, have postulated a "Hebrew" ideal of "highly developed moral strength, the subordination of the animal instincts, the pursuit of justice in thought and deed, eternal war against falsehood and wickedness—in a word, the moral ideal of Judaism."[5]

The central task of a Jewish center in Palestine was to create the conditions under which Jews could perfect their moral fiber. "[T]here must be one nation whose inherent characteristics make it better fitted than others for moral development, and whose scheme of life is governed by a moral law superior to the common type of morality, so that it may provide the ideal conditions for the growth of the superman we want."[6]

Ahad Ha'am's Zionism was predicated on the assumption that the specific Jewish potential for morality would be released when the Jewish people would be "free to order its life in its own way." A Jewish moral mission that had failed in exile would be made possible by a spiritual center in Palestine. "And possibly," Ahad Ha'am wrote, "it is the sense of this contrast between what is and what might be that has unconsciously made Zionists of many who scoff at the idea of the 'chosen people' and the moral mission, and express their Zionism in purely economic and political terms."[7]

Ahad Ha'am was soon to be disillusioned by the moral practices of Jewish settlers "free to order their lives in their own way," and his brand of cultural Zionism would become an increasingly elusive alternative to an ethnic-national Zionism that in his lifetime went from vision to reality.

Already in 1891, long before most other Zionists, a tour of Palestine had awakened Ahad Ha'am to the moral challenge of the indigenous Arab presence on the land. In an essay entitled "The Truth from the Land of Israel," he painted a highly critical and unsentimental picture of the behavior of the new colonizers and their ideas about the land and the people. Above all, he wrote, no one should go there in the belief that Palestine was a land without people for a people without a land:

> We tend to believe abroad, that Palestine is nowadays almost completely deserted, a noncultivated wilderness, and anyone can come there and buy as much land as his heart desires. But in reality this is not the case. It is difficult to find anywhere in the country Arab land which lay fallow; the only areas which are not cultivated are sand dunes or stony mountains, which can be only planted with trees, and even this only after much labor and capital would be invested in clearance and preparation.[8]

The Palestinian Arabs, he emphasized, were not a passive and picturesque background to the Zionist project but people with their own national feelings and aspirations, and above all with their own culture, who did not deserve Zionism's nonchalant and superior attitude:

> We tend to think abroad that all Arabs are desert barbarians, an asinine people who does not see or understand

what is going on around them. This is a cardinal mistake [. . .] The Arabs, and especially the city dwellers, understand very well what we want and what we do in the country; but they behave as if they do not notice it because at present they do not see any danger for themselves and their future [. . .] But when the day will come in which the life of our people in the Land of Israel will develop to such a degree that they will push aside the local population by little or much, then it will not easily give up its place.[9]

Even now, therefore, the Jews must learn to treat the Palestinian Arabs with respect, not to use violence to resolve disputes over land and water, and to prevent what would otherwise lead to hatred and revenge:

One thing we certainly should have learned from our past and present history, and that is not to create anger among the local population against us [. . .] We have to treat the local population with love and respect, justly and rightly. And what do our brothers in the Land of Israel do? Exactly the opposite! Slaves they were in their country of exile, and suddenly they find themselves in a boundless and anarchic freedom, as is always the case with a slave that has become king; and they behave toward the Arabs with hostility and cruelty, infringe upon their boundaries, hit them shamefully without reason, and even brag about it. Our brethren are right when they say that the Arab honors only those who show valor and fortitude, but this is the case only when he feels that the other side has justice on its side. It is very different in a case when [the Arab] thinks that his opponent's actions are iniquitous and unlawful; in that case he may keep his anger for a long time, but it will dwell in his heart and in the long run he will prove himself to be vengeful and full of retribution.[10]

The suspicion that the morality of Zionism was neither better nor worse than that of any other national movement led Ahad Ha'am to question the whole project. When it was reported that an Arab boy had been murdered by Jewish settlers, he began to question the very foundations of his Zionism: "And if these were to collapse, what would I have to show in my old age after a lifetime of toil? Except, that is, for an empty heart and a despairing soul?"[11]

Ahad Ha'am's prophetic clarity on the problems of Zionism did not prevent his own vision from remaining abstract and somewhat obscure. He noted with a keen eye and a sharp pen what was wrong but never formulated a proposal for how a rapidly emerging Jewish society in Palestine could be made to conform to the higher Jewish morality he had taken for a given. After his move to Palestine and Tel Aviv in 1921, Ahad Ha'am became an increasingly symbolic slave on the Labor Zionist bandwagon, an officially respected and celebrated testimony to the movement's high moral and cultural ambitions, a reminder of sorts that the Land of Israel, once the dust of state-building had settled, would not be a land like all others.

In the spring of 1907, a thirty-year-old German Jewish lawyer and economist named Arthur Ruppin traveled to Palestine. He had already written an acclaimed book on

Darwinism and social science and another on "Jews today" and had now been commissioned by the Jewish Colonization Association in Vienna to investigate the economic conditions for increased Jewish immigration to Palestine. After six months of travel, Ruppin delivered a report based on careful observations and precise details of land and property relations, of the economic and cultural viability of different population groups, with concrete proposals for new methods of settlement, cultivation, and organization in the Jewish colonization policy.

Ruppin believed in Rationality as other people believed in God or Fate. Just as humans had come to understand the general conditions for the evolution of species, they would now be able to understand and influence the conditions of their own existence. Increased Jewish colonization in Palestine was quite possible if only the Zionist movement would understand how to correctly assess and calculate the external and internal conditions for its colonial enterprise. Ruppin's Zionism was all about funds and credit, acquisition and investment, markets and returns, motivation and organization. He could not see a problem without proposing a solution, often in the form of a calculation or a budget.

Ruppin soon became one of the most important organizers of the early Zionist settlement project. He was involved in several large and strategic land purchases, commissioned the first loans for the construction of Tel Aviv, calculated the costs and principles of immigration policy. In 1909 he was instrumental in the establishment of Degania, the first agricultural collective in Palestine on the southern shore of the Sea of Galilee, more a result of calculation than of vision.

The form of settlement that would later come to symbolize the ideology of Labor Zionism was in fact a pragmatic solution to a practical problem.

The problem was how to get young, idealistic, inexperienced immigrants from Russia to work for starvation wages on large farms owned by Zionist funds and institutions, and run by top-down appointed managers educated in the administration of private European estates. In 1909, their high-handed way of running things had triggered a strike among agricultural workers in the Zionist colony of Kinneret. Ruppin's solution was to give a core group among the strikers a piece of land of their own and a share of the profits—for half the pay. A year later, the Degania agricultural cooperative was founded on social and economic principles that would set an example for the entire kibbutz movement.

Once again, Ruppin had made the right calculation. The external conditions for colonization and immigration were centralized land purchases, large-scale farming, and little material reward; the internal conditions were strong ideological commitments and deep longings for community and identity. The colonization project needed an institution that could farm the land efficiently, to train inexperienced immigrant groups in agricultural work, to create new bonds and traditions, to sap the power of idealism and self-sacrifice, and to sort the wheat from the chaff (Ruppin's Darwinian hobbyhorse). A kibbutz, or as it was still called a kvutzah, is "a magnificent school for the recognition of the able and the elimination of the unable individual . . . If the ability of our land workers is today immeasurably higher than it was ten or fifteen years ago the credit must be given primarily to the process of selection which went on in our kvutzot."[12]

I am convinced that it was this seemingly cold, calculated rationality in analyzing the conditions and prospects of Zionism that eventually turned Ruppin into a cautious dissident. He continued to hold senior positions in the Zionist movement, his energy and enthusiasm for building the institutions of Zionism seemed undiminished, but he had calculated and calculated, and concluded that a purely Jewish state in Palestine was a mathematical, or at least a moral, impossibility. In 1926 he founded Brit Shalom (the Peace League), a small oppositional movement calling for negotiations and settlement with the local Arabs on the basis of "absolute political equality between two culturally autonomous peoples."

Three years later, in the summer of 1929, Ruppin addressed the World Zionist Congress in Zurich (where he was reelected to the executive committee):

> We must avoid the erroneous view that prevailed in Europe for an entire century and which led to the catastrophe of the World War—the view that only one nationality can be sovereign in one state. Under the aegis of the League of Nations, Palestine must become a political entity in which Jews and Arabs live side by side as two distinct nationalities enjoying equal rights and privileges. Neither is to rule—neither is to be enslaved. The right of the Jews to come to Palestine is as great as the right of the Arabs

to remain there [. . .] We abominate chauvinism in other nations; we must combat it in our own.[13]

What had been Ruppin's calculation? Well, first of all he had calculated like Ahad Ha'am, namely that Palestine could not possibly accommodate all the Jews of the world. Partly because there was not enough land, and partly because the land was mostly owned and used by others. As early as 1913, he cautiously reported that "every inch of cultivable land is [for the time being] in the hands of private owners and is in fact cultivated, even if only extensively rather than intensively."[14] He advocated the utmost tact in the acquisition of land and the greatest possible consideration for the existing population.

Ten years later, Ruppin had refined his estimates and was now able to show that additional agricultural land for colonization in Palestine would be expensive and difficult to obtain. For one thing, Arab-owned land was rarely for sale, regardless of price. Second, two-thirds of the arable land consisted of already cultivated small plots that were unusable for colonization purposes. Finally, it was politically and morally unacceptable to deprive Arab farmers of their land. One-third of the arable land and one-sixth of the total area of Palestine was available for Jewish land acquisition.[15]

For Ruppin, therefore, there was only one rational and defensible goal for Zionism: to build a spiritual and cultural center in Palestine for all the Jews of the world, not a physical bunker for a few. The land acquisitions, the collective farms, the cooperative industries, the Hebrew schools, the social institutions were Zionism's means, not its ends. For those interpreters of Ahad Ha'am who only wanted to build schools and teach Hebrew in the belief that they were building a cultural center, the Darwinist and realist Ruppin had no sympathy. A strong culture required well-tended orange groves.

The passion and sense of doom that can be read between the lines of Ruppin's calculations and spreadsheets, indeed his entire commitment to Zionism, was most likely rooted in a single overriding and fundamentally pessimistic calculation about the survival of the Jewish people. In a synthesis of social Darwinism and statistics on the development of Jewish life in the world, the two fields he had carefully studied, he became convinced that the Jews of the world were threatened with "final annihilation." Not by physical extermination (he could not imagine Auschwitz) but by accelerating cultural and religious decay. The energy of traditional Jewish life had been spent. The "destructive forces" of assimilation were rapidly eating away at the communal foundations of Judaism.

For Ruppin, the evolutionary disappearance of the Jews was an unbearable thought, a terrible Darwinian error that had to be stopped in time. Assimilation was a devastating poison from which the Jews in the Diaspora could not protect themselves. The antidote had to come from the outside:

> A Jewish life vigorous enough to overcome the influence of alien cultures and to infuse the Diaspora with a living Jewish spirit can arise only in a land far off the highway of Christian culture—the land to which we feel historically bound and which revives all the Jewish sentiments that

have sunk down in our sub-consciousness, the land where the language of the Bible is the speech of our children and the molder of their minds. [. . .] No serious Zionist has ever thought that Palestine can absorb all the Jews of the world. Even in the days of the ancient Jewish State many more Jews lived in other countries than in Palestine itself; and we shall have to resign ourselves to the fact of a large Jewish Diaspora in the future also. But Palestine can cure the ill from which this Diaspora is now suffering. Today the Jewries of the various countries are but scattered members that lack a central organ, a heart. Palestine can become their heart, the spiritual motive agent which will bring forth new and vital values from the well of Jewish community life in Palestine.[16]

In founding Brit Shalom, Ruppin actively opposed a "Montenegro or Lithuania solution" to the Jewish problem. A Jewish ministate established by force and expulsion could never meet the ethical demands of the situation. The means of colonization must be proportionate to its ends. "Some may believe that in Palestine a higher type of humanity will evolve of itself. I do not share that belief. We shall reap in Palestine what we sow today."[17]

Despite Ruppin's central position in the Zionist movement and the participation of intellectual luminaries such as Hugo Bergmann, Hans Kohn, Gershom Scholem, and Martin Buber, Brit Shalom remained a movement on the political margins. The incipient armed Arab uprising of 1929 strengthened the nationalist currents within Zionism and undermined the support for a binational state. Brit Shalom also suffered from the lack of response from authoritative Arab leaders, or rather the lack of sustainable Arab authorities. A hesitant interest from people in the Zionist leadership turned into disinterest and open criticism when it became clear that Brit Shalom's contacts and initiatives failed to establish a credible political alternative. Some members began to question the realism in its positions, while others tried to push it in an even more radical direction. "What's the point of trying to unite internally," complained a disappointed Ruppin in a letter to Judah Leon Magnes, the rector of the Hebrew University of Jerusalem, "if there is no one on the other side?"

In 1929, Ruppin resigned as president of Brit Shalom. His calculations had failed.

Magnes, a Jewish reform theologian and community leader from the United States who had settled in Palestine with his family in 1922 at the age of forty-five, was one of the few among the Palestinian Jewish elite who was not deterred. From his central intellectual position, and with the support of influential American Jewish leaders, he pursued the idea of a two-nation state with even greater fervor. For Magnes, Zionism must be a movement with the highest ethical ideals and aspirations, and Palestine not a land like all others.

> We are told that when we become the majority we shall then show how just and generous a people in power can be. That is like the man who says that he will do anything and everything, so that he may do good with

money thus accumulated. Sometimes he never grows rich—he fails. And if he does grow rich under those circumstances his power of doing good has been atrophied from long lack of use. In other words, it is not only the end which for Israel must be desirable, but what is of equal importance, the means must be conceived and brought forth in cleanliness. If as a minority we insist on keeping the other man from achieving just aims, and if we do so with the aid of bayonets, we must not be surprised if we are attacked and, what is worse, a moral degradation sets in among us.[18]

The orgies of violence of the First World War had made Magnes a committed pacifist and anti-imperialist. He detested and distrusted the colonial power intrigues leading up to the British Mandate for Palestine, and he criticized Zionism for mixing religious and political motives. While most Zionists cheered, Magnes warned. The Balfour Declaration and the mandate were not steps toward redemption from exile but crass maneuvers "conceived and born in impurity." The very idea that the holy city of Jerusalem had been taken by British force was "a paradox worthy of a smile of derision."[19] The Jews' "historic right" to Palestine was not the right to impose themselves on other peoples, only the right to "settle freely and unhindered in the land, with their laborers, their peasants, their physical, spiritual and human capital, to become, if possible, in due course, a dominant element in the population." The same right, however, must also be granted to Arabs, Syrians, Muslims, and Christians.

In such a spirit, Magnes wanted to lead the Hebrew University, which was inaugurated with pomp and ceremony on Mount Scopus in Jerusalem on April 1, 1925. Ahad Ha'am's vision of a spiritual Jewish center in Palestine would here be rendered concrete substance and meaning. This was the very place from which Judaism would draw new strength and inspiration. The Hebrew University was the concern of the entire Jewish world, not just the Zionists in Palestine, and must therefore be independent of the Zionist establishment.

Consequently, Magnes's leadership of the university was not based on Zionist support but on support from Jewish American benefactors, especially the banker and philanthropist Felix Warburg, a non-Zionist who shared Magnes's criticism of the Zionist policy toward the Arabs. In fact, the Zionist leadership made repeated attempts to remove Magnes. A few years after the inauguration, no less than Albert Einstein, now a member of the university board, was mobilized in the effort. Chaim Weizmann, the chairman of the board, succeeded in giving Einstein the impression that Magnes was a scientific "dilettante," a mere theologian, a puppet in the hands of his American donors, incapable of guaranteeing the university's scientific independence and reputation. However, with 70 percent of the university's income coming from Magnes's American donors, all arguments for dismissal, contrived or real, fell to the ground.

The conflict with official Zionism was not only over Magnes's oppositional political ideas but also over his stated desire to prioritize the humanities over the natural sciences. The primary task of the Hebrew University, he thought, was to explore and bring forth a Jewish perspective in the studies of history, literature, and philosophy, "in the hope that a Jewish university will give to Judaism, as much as to the Jews, new and fresh values. [. . .] If the various faculties of the university are but nothing else than Palestinian replicas of European and American schools, they will, of course, have their immediate practical value, but they will not be serving Judaism as much as they might."[20]

Weizmann was equally adamant that what Palestine needed above all were faculties of science and medicine. The university was to be a practical means of Jewish nation-building and as much as possible cater to the needs of Zionist institutions. "Must the influence of a great organization which has constantly to render accounts of its doings to its adherents and to the public at large be necessarily worse than those of a few men of finance who make big contributions?" Weizmann asked sarcastically in a letter to Magnes.[21]

It was an illustrative discussion about essentially anything but academic preferences and needs, between two concepts of Zionism that were diverging from each other. Magnes's fierce critique of any attempt to build a Jewish community over the heads of the Palestinian Arabs made him an increasingly isolated dissident, even among people who had previously been close to him. To Ruppin, the founder of Brit Shalom, who after the Arab violence of 1929 had declared the idea of a two-nation state dead, Magnes wrote an angry letter in which he accused Ruppin of echoing what the right-wing nationalist revisionists had long been preaching.[22] He wrote to Weizmann that the choice was now between a Jewish Palestine founded on militarism and imperialism, and the development of a Jewish spiritual center. The basic condition for the latter was a settlement with the Arabs based on moral principles:

> I do not say that this is easy of achievement nor do I absolutely know that it is possible [. . .] But this policy of co-operation is certainly more possible and more hopeful of achievement than building up a Jewish Home (National or otherwise) on bayonets and oppression. Moreover, a Jewish Home in Palestine built upon bayonets and oppression is not worth having, even though it succeed, whereas the attempt to build it up peacefully, cooperatively, with understanding, education, and good will, is worth a great deal—even though the attempt should fail.[23]

From the perspective of realpolitik Magnes's position must have seemed wholly utopian. He resented military power, and therefore did not reckon with it. He resented traditional diplomacy, and therefore acted undiplomatically. He believed that divisions could be overcome by negotiation, and therefore underestimated divisions that were hard to negotiate, most obviously that between the Zionist interest in increased Jewish immigration and the Palestinian Arab interest in the opposite. Not that he ignored the issue—Jewish immigration was central to Magnes—but his proposals seemed increasingly detached from the political realities on the ground.

However, Magnes's perspective was not that of realpolitik but that of Judaism as a moral commitment which a

Jewish community in Palestine must live up to. Not just for the sake of Palestinian Jews, not even for the sake of Jews in general, but for the sake of the world: "Eretz Israel will have to be judged by whether or not it can help the Jewish people to do its work and determine its function in this larger world," he said in a speech in Jerusalem in 1923.[24] The Land of Israel was a potential strengthening of Judaism, not a condition for Jewish survival. Jewish Palestine had to be built decently, or not be built at all.

Even as Arab resistance escalated in the 1930s, and even as Hitler's rise to power in Germany created an acute threat to millions of European Jews, Magnes did not waver from his call for cooperation and accommodation with the Arabs. He argued that a greatly increased Jewish immigration required Arab acceptance; he pushed for a Palestinian democratic legislature, knowing full well that it would have an Arab majority for the time being; he threw himself into a whirlwind of personal diplomatic initiatives, in which neither he nor those with whom he negotiated represented a majority opinion. When the first proposal for the partition of Palestine, calling for a transfer of populations, was put forward in 1937 by the British Peel Commission, he sounded the alarm in a *New York Times* article: "With Arab consent we could settle many hundreds of thousands of persecuted Jews in various Arab lands. That is worth a real price. Without Arab consent, even our four hundred thousand in Palestine remain in jeopardy, despite the momentary protection of British bayonets."[25] Partition would create a new Balkan where unruly ethnic armies would be played by one government or another, and at best bring about a Jewish ministate with little prospect for spiritual and material development.

With the outbreak of war, the extermination of the Jews of Europe, and the growing sectarian violence in Palestine, Magnes's vision finally collapsed. In the eyes of the Zionist leadership, his actions bordered on treason. David Ben-Gurion, with whom Magnes had enjoyed good relations, informed him accusingly that his "honest striving for peace [was] being exploited to undermine our position."[26]

Magnes himself eventually realized that a voluntarily negotiated Arab-Jewish agreement had become a political impossibility. In an article in the American journal *Foreign Affairs* in January 1943, he therefore proposed a joint British-American intervention to prevent partition and to actively promote the establishment of a union between Jews and Arabs within the framework of a binational Palestine. This union would be incorporated into a newly created economic and political federation with the neighboring Arab states, which in turn would be part of a comprehensive union of free nations "to be born out of the ruins of the decaying world."[27] At the same time, he founded Ihud (unity), a political organization that was invited to argue for a federative solution to the Palestine problem before the Anglo-American Committee of Inquiry in 1946 and the UN Special Committee on Palestine in 1947.

With the UN partition resolution in November 1947, the proclamation of the Jewish state in May 1948, and the ensuing Arab-Israeli war, the efforts of Magnes came to nothing. In the end, he probably felt more at home in his native America, with its ethnic diversity and relative tolerance, than within the contested borders of the emerging Jewish state. A final trip to New York in April 1948, at the behest of leading Jewish non-Zionists and the US State Department circles that disapproved of the partition decision, yielded no results. On May 5 and 6, with Palestine in a full state of war, he was able to present his case to Secretary of State George Marshall, where he found sympathy and understanding, but no willingness or ability to intervene.

With the two-nation solution out of the equation, Magnes spent the summer promoting the idea of a confederation between the new Jewish state and a future Palestinian Arab state. He was too ill to return to Jerusalem, but the point he wanted to make could be made more effectively in the United States. As early as June, he presented a plan entitled "United States of Palestine—A Confederation of Two Independent States." The confederation would give the two states great autonomy, but it would also establish common federal institutions for foreign policy, military defense, international finance, federal legislation, protection of holy sites, and immigration. Jerusalem, the common capital of the confederation, would become a *corpus separatum*, an international, demilitarized, and neutralized zone. If necessary, the United Nations would be given a supervisory and decisive role in the federal institutions.[28]

In Count Folke Bernadotte, the Swedish UN mediator for Palestine, Magnes saw a good-hearted man and a political ally. Bernadotte's proposal in July 1948 for a Palestinian confederation was very much in line with Magnes's ideas.

He described as "reasonable" Bernadotte's suggestion that after a two-year transitional period the questions of immigration and land acquisition be referred to a joint confederal body or, in the worst case, to the United Nations. Although opposed to the idea of making Jerusalem the capital of the Palestinian Arab state, he gave Bernadotte his moral support in what was increasingly looking like a suicide mission: "I gather from the morning's papers that despite all discouragements and difficulties you are still of stout heart and dogged in your determination to see things through. That is great."[29] In a public statement shortly afterward, he claimed that Bernadotte "had done more to advance the cause of peace and reconciliation in Palestine than all other persons put together."[30]

The murder of Bernadotte in September 1948 by the Jewish Stern Gang was a severe blow to Magnes. Despite a lifetime of defeats, his faith and confidence had rarely wavered. Together with his temporary American assistant, a young German Jewish philosopher named Hannah Arendt, he was still working on new peace plans to replace the failed ones, but with Bernadotte's death the tragedy seemed irreversible. When shortly afterward Arendt published an article warning of the consequences of the failure of the Bernadotte plan, Magnes wrote to her: "Your article has depressed me and I am asking myself, is there really no way out?"[31]

Still, he refused to give up. His diary entry for October 22, 1948, begins: "Marshall Plan for the Middle East. I should discuss this with Landis [US State Department official]."[32]

Five days later he was dead, and with him the vision of a Palestine without partition, war, refugees, and ethnic cleansing. In the official Israeli historiography, he is reduced to a footnote: a good-hearted man with the best of intentions, but oh so naive, with no sense of the political realities in Palestine.

After the establishment of the state, few people still advocated a binational solution of some kind. Among the exceptions was the philosopher Martin Buber, who had stood by Magnes until the end. In the 1950s and '60s, he became another link in the line of moral voices drowned out by war, settlement, and immigration, but who nevertheless embodied the notion of Eretz Israel as a spiritual and moral project. A Jewish state in Palestine "must not become just another of the numberless small states that are devoid of spiritual substance, a place like any other in today's Western world where spirit and people are separated, with both languishing."[33]

In 1942, Buber sharply attacked "the Jewish nationalism that . . . recognizes no task for Israel save that of preserving and asserting itself."[34] Where was the sense in replacing foreign idols with homemade ones? Judaism was threatened not by those who would let us serve the true God in an alien land, "but by those who would readily approve any idol-worship in our homeland if only the idols bear Jewish names!"[35] He regarded Zionists who sought to elevate the nation or the Jewish community in Palestine to absolute values in themselves as traitors to the religion of Israel.

For Buber, Zionism was meaningless without the connection to God, to the destiny of the Jewish people, to the commands of justice and righteousness. Zionism must be part of Judaism's historical endeavor to eliminate the duality between spirit and matter, morality and politics.

"Unity" is a key word in Buber's Zionism, not the unity of the nation or the ethnic group or even the religious faith but the unity of ethical action: "The Jew can truly fulfill his vocation among the nations only when he begins anew, and, with his whole, undiminished, purified original strength, translates into reality what his religion taught him in antiquity."[36] As a Jewish plow prepares the fields of Palestine, so must a Jewish morality prepare the fields of politics.

Thus, there was a double meaning to Ihud, the name of the organization that Buber came to represent after the death of Magnes. It certainly expressed the hope for political reconciliation between the two peoples of Palestine, but it also reflected Buber's spiritual dream of a new humanity. Like other proponents of a spiritual and cultural Zionism, he regarded the relationship with the Palestinian Arabs as a moral touchstone for the Zionist project as a whole.

A STRONGER LAND

> From the pit of decay and dust
> With blood and sweat
> Shall arise a race
> Genius, generous, and cruel
> Shall arise again in all its strength and glory.
>
> —VLADIMIR JABOTINSKY, "THE BETAR SONG" (1932)

My history teacher in Secondary School Number Nine in Tel Aviv had nicotine-yellow fingers, heavy eyelids, and a high, liver-spotted forehead deeply wrinkled by a long-standing dissatisfaction with the times in general and its youth in particular. He must have been in his late fifties and, unlike the other teachers, wore a suit and tie, even if the suit was shabby and the tie had breakfasted on eggs. There was something dark and unredeemed about Dr. Israel Zvi Kanner. Or was it just something I imagined after hearing some of my classmates, the ones with the white cords in their blue shirts, whisper that Dr. Kanner was a fascist. Eventually I learned that "fascist" denoted something as seemingly innocent as being a member of Herut (Freedom), Israel's main opposition party. I also learned that perhaps it wasn't so innocent after all.

In retrospect, I cannot recall that Dr. Kanner's teaching differed in any significant way from that of other teachers. He corrected our exams with an angry red pen and repeated question marks, but usually for minor things. On the other hand, history was a subject in which a potential fascist agenda could easily be hidden. The curriculum was heavily structured around the role of the Jewish people in history. The explicit purpose was to strengthen our understanding of the unique role and character of the Jewish nation, and of the State of Israel as the historical fulfillment of its destiny, which was a history that happened to suit the alleged political affiliation of Dr. Kanner well.

Otherwise, the party that Dr. Kanner allegedly belonged to was a shunned outsider in the Israeli society of my youth. It was sustained by traditions and ideas largely alien, or even hostile, to the state-building ideals of Labor Zionism. It had little reverence for the emblematic kibbutz movement, regarded the all-pervasive trade union movement Histadrut as an enemy, and portrayed itself as the victim of a historical injustice inflicted by Labor Zionism. Herut was not just a losing party in Israeli politics; it was a party of losers. It was a party with a defeated view of Zionism and the role of the Jewish state. It was a party nurturing the myth that Israel owed its existence to the losers, not the winners. The Herut Party had its roots in Irgun, the armed nationalist movement, which in the 1930s and '40s had declared war not only on the Arabs and the British but also periodically on the Zionist leadership in Palestine. In the losers' mythology, it was the armed terror that had paved the way for the founding of the state, not the colonization, institution-building, and diplomacy of the Labor Zionists. By force of arms Israel had been created, and by force of arms Israel would in due course expand to its biblical borders, which in some versions stretched from the Nile to the Euphrates.

On the history of Zionism and the State of Israel, Dr. Kanner might have had a thing or two to add to what was in the official textbooks, but he never got the chance as I recall, since Zionism was a topic of its own, with a special teacher who rightly taught us that Dr. Kanner was a loser.

In 1963, few could imagine that the fascists would ever come to power. Their members, organizations, and institutions were carefully kept outside the political establishment, and thus outside large sectors of Israeli economic and social life. Throughout the 1950s and '60s, Herut never received more than 13 to 16 percent in the general elections, but persisted with cultlike contempt to pursue its expansionist view of the proper borders of Israel. There was an air of unreality about the former guerrilla leader, later party leader, Menachem Begin's fixation on the wrongs of the past, his rhetorical refighting of battles lost, his melodramatic struggle against the German reparations to Holocaust survivors, his lilting exhortations in Polish-broken Hebrew to "complete" Eretz Israel—that is, to conquer the West Bank (which was still ruled by Jordan).

This was a party that had cultivated a historical countermyth inspired more by interwar European notions of national honor and identity than by the political realities of modern Israel. It was a myth whose historical founder, Vladimir Jabotinsky, had instructed his movement's young recruits to eat "quietly and slowly," not to slurp their soup, and generally to behave like English gentlemen: "If all Jews could behave properly, the antisemites would probably hate us anyway, but it would be hatred mixed with respect, and our position in the world would be quite different from what it is today."[1]

To Jabotinsky, the Hebrew word *hadar*—honor, splendor, glory—represented everything that the oppressed Jew in the Diaspora lacked: "dignified beauty and harmony of manner, gesture, speech and attitude." *Hadar* was a reversal of the antisemitic Jewish caricature (and thus, to some extent, an acceptance of its premises). *Hadar* was the centerpiece of a myth in which the nation became the highest expression of morality, virtue, and pride.

It was a myth that certainly did not lack affinities with official Labor Zionism, but which, with the formation of the State of Israel, became encapsulated in the historical bitterness and rhetorical self-pity of the loser.

It would take the war of 1967 for the losers to commence their march from the periphery of Israeli society to its center.

Zionist right-wing nationalism or revisionism, like Labor Zionism, was to an astonishing degree the work of a single generation of young people and their conception of the world. While the ragtag socialists of the Second Aliyah who created Labor Zionism were molded in the wake of the revolutionary uprisings in early twentieth-century Russia, by nineteen-year-olds like David Ben-Gurion, the uniformed activists who created Revisionist Zionism were molded in the antisemitic nationalism of interwar Poland, by nineteen-year-olds like Menachem Begin. Whereas nationalism in the ethnically homogeneous nations of the West had promoted liberal and democratic values, nationalism in the ethnically and politically complex societies of Central Europe was based on honor, cohesion, and strength, and eventually on expansion and racism. It was a nationalism born from a long-lasting suppression and humiliation of ethnic minorities by dominant and self-confident ethnic majorities. Poland was characterized by centuries of occupation and national humiliation, with almost a third of its population belonging to ethnic minorities. Poland's young nationalism was from the outset vindictive, self-righteous, and authoritarian.

A key figure in the formative world of the founder of Revisionist Zionism, Vladimir Jabotinsky, was the Polish marshal and national hero Józef Piłsudski. At the outbreak of World War I, Piłsudski, with the support of Austria-Hungary, launched a guerrilla war against the country's Russian rulers and succeeded in expanding Poland's borders beyond what the victorious war powers had envisaged. As the undisputed leader of the newly formed Polish state, he strived to restore Poland's territory to the pre-partition borders of 1772 and establish a militarily strong nation between Russia and Germany. The country's ethnic and religious minorities would be offered limited autonomy under Polish national and cultural sovereignty. Jabotinsky characterized Piłsudski as a benevolent and enlightened leader, keen to see his Poland "clean, punctual, efficient and decent."

In opposition to Piłsudski's modernizing nationalism rose a more xenophobic variety led by Roman Dmowski. After Piłsudski's death in 1935, Dmowski's blatantly antisemitic movement became increasingly influential, which undoubtedly contributed to Piłsudski becoming a role model for Jabotinsky. Piłsudski's patriotism was, in Jabotinsky's appreciative words, "an austere and ascetic religion, scornful of all emotionalism."[2] Piłsudski may not have loved Jews, but he did not hate them either. It was only in the nature of things for Polish nationalists to be concerned about Poles and for Jewish nationalists to be concerned about Jews. "One cannot help suspecting," wrote Jabotinsky, "that he [Piłsudski] would not have thought it regrettable had Poland only had 1% of Jews instead of 10%; and as there were never enough jobs to go around, one may imagine (though he never mentioned it) that he wanted them to go to Poles and not to the Jews."[3] Piłsudski and his colonels were men of honor who were only doing for the Poles what Jabotinsky and the Revisionists wanted to do for the Jews. Nationalism was an overarching value and its hallmark was not necessarily ethnic brotherhood. A nation could not expect love from other nations, only respect for its power. In a 1910 publication entitled "Homo Homini Lupus" (Man is a wolf to man), Jabotinsky (whose Hebrew first name, Ze'ev, means "wolf") wrote:

> Stupid is the person who believes in his neighbor, good and loving as the neighbor may be; stupid is the person who relies on justice. Justice exists only for those whose

fists and stubbornness make it possible for them to realize it. [. . .] Do not believe anyone, be always on your guard, carry your stick always with you—this is the only way of surviving in this wolfish battle of all against all.[4]

Jabotinsky's nationalism aimed for the Jewish nation to be a wolf among wolves, always suspicious, always ready to strike, always commanding the respect of its neighbors. Jabotinsky's Jewish state was not a means to fulfill certain political, religious, or social ideals but an end in itself; the mystical embodiment of a preexisting Jewish nation—cleansed of its ills, freed of its shackles, fortified against its enemies.

The worldview that gave rise to Revisionist Zionism cannot be understood separately from the Polish and Central European nationalist maelstrom from which it emerged. It was a worldview fueled by the incipient fear and resentment of social and ethnic groups that had hoped for a place in a new Europe, but now saw the abyss opening up. These included the hundreds of thousands of Jewish small businessmen, civil servants, and artisans who had belatedly emerged from the Jewish communities and begun to carve out a position for themselves in Piłsudski's Poland, but who in the 1930s were pushed back, persecuted, humiliated, and proletarianized as they competed with millions of Poles for jobs and income in a harsh economic environment. Jewish right-wing nationalism in Poland, like its Polish role model, thus developed in an increasingly radical and activist direction. The members of the Betar youth organization wore brown uniforms, were drilled in marches and parades, trained in self-defense, and, with the open support of the Polish government, organized military training camps for Jewish youth ready to leave for Palestine.[5]

Within a few years, Betar grew into a mass movement among Poland's young Jews and became the core of the Revisionist organization. It promised to make the Jews a respected group in Polish society by becoming a trained and disciplined force of its own, and to rid Europe of its Jewish problem through the "evacuation" of Jews to a Jewish state established by the force of Jewish arms. The evacuation idea was entirely in line with what Polish nationalist parties were advocating at the time.

When in the mid-1930s Irgun was formed in Palestine to launch offensive operations against the Palestinian Arabs and to organize illegal Jewish immigration, it retained its main base of support in Poland. Indeed, Irgun's operations in Palestine would probably have been impossible without the support of the Polish government. The name Irgun Zvai Leumi (National Military Organization) was directly copied from its Polish counterpart, Piłsudski's Organizacja Bojowa (military organization). Its terror tactics were clearly inspired by Piłsudski's hit-and-run warfare during the early Polish liberation struggle. While most other Jewish organizations in Poland, Zionist and non-Zionist alike, distanced themselves from Poland's nationalist and antisemitic parties, Betar had no hesitations whatsoever in this regard. On the contrary. "These ties with the Polish establishment were forged precisely in the years of heightened antisemitism and the growing influence of the radical right in the Polish ruling elite," notes the Israeli historian Yonathan Shapiro. "A bizarre identity was forged between an antisemitic and nationalist radical right and a Jewish national movement."[6]

This was the movement that formed the generational unit of Begin, and eventually the party he some forty years later would bring to power in the State of Israel. Begin himself soon became one of Betar's senior leaders in Poland, and in the spring of 1939 the most senior. Already responsible for Irgun's Polish activities, he now sought to coordinate Betar with Irgun. Recruitment to Betar in Poland would also be recruitment to Irgun's armed struggle in Eretz Israel.

After Hitler's rise to power in Germany, Jabotinsky had gradually begun to distance himself from organized fascism in Europe. He emphasized the need for help from European states, especially Britain, to establish the Jewish state and bring about the "evacuation" of Europe's Jews. In Palestine, he sought a political settlement with Ben-Gurion and a coordination of their respective military organizations, the Haganah and the Irgun.

In blatant opposition to Jabotinsky, Begin argued for a full militarization of Zionism, an immediate armed conquest of Eretz Israel, and a possible armed struggle in countries other than Palestine (following the pattern of the Irish nationalists in England). It was a course of action that excluded all diplomacy and any attempt to win external support for the Jewish cause. In Palestine, it resulted in an armed rebellion against the British and an uncompromising fight against Ben-Gurion's policy of *havlagah* (restraint). At the Betar Congress in Warsaw in September 1938, the following exchange took place between the still-revered but increasingly circumscribed Jabotinsky and the increasingly powerful Begin:

> Jabotinsky: Would the gentleman please tell me how he will get the Betari soldiers into the country [Palestine] without the support of foreigners?
> Begin: If the force is created, help will also come from the Diaspora.
> Jabotinsky: Has the gentleman taken note of the proportions of the Jewish military force and the Arab force in Eretz Israel?
> Begin: We will win by virtue of our own moral strength.[7]

Then the pleasantries ended. Jabotinsky likened Begin's speech to "the squeaking of a door," called his conquest plans absurd, and argued that until there was a Jewish majority in Palestine, the Jews were dependent on the conscience of the world: "someone must hold the doors open for us." Begin's policy was tantamount to suicide. "If there is no more conscience in the world, the only alternative is jumping into the Wisła [River] or [joining] communism."

Jabotinsky made strong efforts to prevent Begin's election as the leader of Betar, but in vain. Despite his undisputed formal leadership, he had been politically outmaneuvered. The movement in Poland was radicalized by the developments in Palestine, while the movement in Palestine seemed to ignore the developments in Europe. The result was a politically reckless and chauvinistic Zionist faction, which until the very end, as late as April and May 1939, published articles in the Yiddish newspaper *Die Tat*, in which Western democracies were equated with Hitler and Nazism, Hitler's views on the racial question were commented on with sympathy (apart from the objection that the anti-Jewish policy "in practice" prevented the Jews from establishing their own state), and antisemitism was not necessarily an integral part of Nazism, which in the final analysis was a version of fascism and therefore a good thing.[8]

Could European Jews become fascists? Before 1933, indeed even before 1939, the answer was not complicated. Of course Jews could become fascists, and right-wing nationalists too, for that matter. In the Italian fascist movement, which was not programmatically racist or antisemitic, the proportion of Jewish activists was for a long time far greater than the proportion of Jews in the population.

It was not entirely uncomplicated, of course, since Jewish nationalism did not have a nation, but in the high-strung political climate in which a belligerent Jewish nationalism nevertheless emerged, this mattered little. Uniforms, military drills, and dreams of national redemption gave hope and meaning to a young Jewish generation that no longer had a foothold in Jewish society, and who were now being deprived of their new-won foothold in Polish society. More problematic, indeed paradoxical and eventually tragic, was that the Revisionist movement came to accept antisemitism in both theory and practice as a fully legitimate expression of the national aspirations of other peoples. "[The] Jewish people is a very nasty people, and its neighbors hate it, and they are right," Jabotinsky recalled saying at one of the first Zionist meetings of his youth. "Its end in the Diaspora will be a general Bartholomew night, and the only rescue is general immigration to Palestine."[9]

This understanding of the "objective" causes of antisemitism would become a recurring theme in Jabotinsky's work. Shortly before his death in 1940, he was still trying to distinguish between a rational and manageable antisemitism, the "antisemitism of things," and a more pathological and difficult-to-reach type, the "antisemitism of people." The first and in Poland predominant variant was, he argued, due to factual circumstances that must necessarily lead to conflict—there were too many Jews in a country with too few jobs and too little food: "Apart from the hooligan element, there was little actual hatred of the Jews in Polish society. Often enough, those who were ready to sign a petition for anti-Jewish legislation would swear that they were honestly sorry for the harm which their action was bound to cause the Jews—but there was no other way out: 'it's either my son or the Jew's son, for there is only one loaf.'"[10] The Polish nationalist leaders, including Piłsudski, who for most of the 1920s and '30s had turned a blind eye to antisemitism, and when appropriate used it for their own purposes, had acted out of national self-interest. In a kind of tragic echo of Nazi propaganda, Jabotinsky was convinced that "the Jewish curse" was the ubiquitous cause of the war. Its origin was not so much Jew-hatred as a sympathy with "one's own people," a basic and primordial instinct "which cannot be criticized because, after all, it is as natural as preferring one's own children to one's neighbor's offspring."[11]

The early association of Revisionist Zionism with fascist ideas and rites was no aberration. Its notions of a common destiny and mission of the Jewish people, of the Jewish state as the embodiment of that destiny, and of Eretz Israel as the sacred living space of the Jewish state, could be given a fascist framing with very little shift in perspective. In addition, Jabotinsky's early assertion of the importance of race to the character of a society was not that there were entirely pure races or that some races were necessarily superior to others, only that race was "a fundamental factor of all civilisation and all history," that each nation had a distinct racial psychology, and that a nation's institutions, even its economic life, were profoundly shaped by racial factors.[12] Although Jabotinsky's racial thinking was not premised on intolerance—he advocated broad ethnic and cultural autonomy within the framework of a dominant nation (which became revisionism's "solution" to the "Arab problem"—it led him to a fascist-like view of the nation as a distinct organic personality to which individual members must accommodate themselves.

The Jewish state that Jabotinsky dreamed of establishing in Palestine arguably had some fascist features: autocratic and charismatic leadership instead of parliamentarism and democracy, state-organized professional corporations instead of parties and trade unions, state regulation of the labor market instead of free bargaining and the right to strike. Moreover, in the early 1930s the Revisionist movement in Palestine reached a strong enough position to try to put its ideas into practice. One of the main targets was Histadrut, the powerful Labor Zionism trade union movement that had succeeded in negotiating a system that often made union membership a condition for employment. The system was condemned by Jabotinsky as a blow to the national cause in general and to the supporters of the nationalist movement in particular. The latter were now forced, like everyone else, to seek their jobs through the local Histadrut offices and not directly from employers. In 1930, some plantation owners tried to break the power of the Histadrut by directly recruiting workers from Betar. The move triggered physical clashes between protesting Histadrut workers and Betar activists and put in motion a violent spiral of strikes and strikebreaking over the next three years. In fiery articles, Jabotinsky urged his followers to "break" the Histadrut and establish a new workers' organization that would put the interests of the nation above those of the class. The Jews of Palestine would see themselves not as workers or proletarians but as "volunteers" willing to sacrifice their futile personal and material interests for something greater than themselves.

During these years, parts of the Revisionist movement in Palestine developed in an explicitly fascist direction. One of Betar's central figures, the journalist Abba Ahimeir, a former member of a left-wing Zionist organization, now titled his newspaper columns "From the Diary of a Fascist" and called for a Jewish Mussolini. In 1936, he enthusiastically supported Franco in Spain, hoping for a "Zionist Alcázar," a symbol of fascist loyalty and sacrifice.[13]

A circle of other former left-wing intellectuals formed around Ahimeir, among them the poet Uri Zvi Greenberg[14] and the writer Heschel Yevin, who, formerly from the left and now from the right, called for a relentless struggle against "corrupt" democracy and for the establishment of a "spiritual dictatorship." In response to what they perceived as Jabotinsky's leaning toward appeasement and compromise, they formed *Brit Ha'birjonim,* the pugilists' union, which advocated violence not only against the external enemies, the Arabs and the British, but also against the traitors and appeasers of the Zionist establishment. Its members liked to compare themselves to the Sicarii, a sect of knife-wielding assassins who did not hesitate to liquidate suspected collaborators during the Jewish revolt against the Romans (67–70 CE). The assassins were the true heroes of history, Ahimeir wrote. A murder was justified when the motive was just.[15] This made for a political culture steeped in secrecy and suspicion, loyalty and betrayal, sacrifice and submission, which was the culture that formed the man who fifty years later would lead the State of Israel.

Betar member Yitzhak Shamir (né Yesernitsky) had arrived in Palestine from Poland in 1935 at the age of twenty, and was immediately drawn to the circles that in 1941 would form the most extreme and uncompromising of the underground terrorist groups of Jewish Palestine, Lochamei Herut Israel, known as Lehi (Freedom Fighters of Israel). Its leader, the poet Avraham Stern, initially promoted the thesis that Hitler and Churchill were equally bad, that the world war was a fight between evil and evil, and that Germany could very well be made an ally of the Zionist cause. By deporting Europe's Jews to Palestine, Hitler could kill two birds with one stone: get rid of the hated Jews and undermine British power in the Middle East. Confident that Hitler would see it their way, Lehi called for immediate and unrestricted military actions against the British in Palestine—and against anyone else hoping to hinder the establishment of a Jewish state "from the Nile to the Euphrates."[16]

Out of this deranged political fantasy grew a ruthless terrorist organization. It was no coincidence that Stern adopted Yair as his nom de guerre, after Eleazar ben Yair, the suicide leader of Masada. Nor was it a coincidence that Lehi member Shamir single-handedly and without much ado executed his fellow combatant Eliahu Giladi on the grounds that he had become "dangerous to the movement." "It is my belief that I had no alternative," Shamir wrote fifty years later in his memoirs. He also wrote that in 1940 and 1941 "it was reasonable to feel that there was little for Jews to choose from between the Germans and the British."

The Shamir who killed Giladi, and who regarded Churchill as as great an enemy as Hitler, carried his dark and vengeful world with him through his career in Israeli intelligence, his rise to the top of Herut, and eventually his years as Israel's foreign minister and prime minister. Behind an increasingly polished facade of officialdom and politics lingered the thoughts of an extremist and the feelings of a terrorist. It was not a modern, democratic statesman who summarized his life in 1994, but a suspicious and bitter fighter who lamented the injustice of history, the evil of the world, and the weakness of humanity. No, not even Begin, his predecessor and mentor, had understood that murder was sometimes a necessary political measure: "He wanted courtrooms, trials, validation; cautious legal procedures that were impossible in the underground [. . .] 'Do you really think you can create a state with pistols?' he asked me once before he became commander of the Irgun."[17]

Shamir's answer is implicit.

Essentially, Shamir's and Lehi's political fantasies did not differ much from those of Jabotinsky and Begin. In principle, the Revisionist movement was in favor of an immediate military confrontation with the Arabs and, if necessary, with the British in order to conquer all of the Land of Israel. The Jewish state must come first, the Jewish majority later. Their minimum territorial demand was the entire British Mandate for Palestine, including Transjordan, or, as they preferred to put it, the former Hebrew kingdoms on both sides of the Jordan River. Geographical size and territorial expansion were central ideological tenets in the Revisionist concept of the Jewish nation, not a matter of political and pragmatic considerations. What could seem impractical, unrealistic, or even inhumane was nevertheless necessary. Ultimately, the leader decided what was necessary and what was not, which in practice meant that there was plenty of room for unprincipled considerations. Jabotinsky saw principles as a mobilizing and inspiring factor, not necessarily as a program of action.

Another principled idea of revisionism was the formative role of violence in nation-building. Violence was not only a means to achieve national goals but also a way to restore national honor, respect, and dignity. The hero of the nation was the soldier, not the farmer. For Jabotinsky, however, the symbolic significance of armed forces remained more important than their military usefulness. The army was a source of loyalty, discipline, and pride, but not necessarily a substitute for politics. In practice, a Jewish state in Palestine could only be realized through a combination of military strength and a political alliance with the West, not through an isolated Jewish war of conquest.

The dramatic events of the 1930s gradually increased the tension between the ideological principles of revisionism and the pressures of realpolitik. Jabotinsky's faith in diplomacy and alliances was inevitably coming into conflict with the radical elements in Betar who opted for terror and guerrilla warfare. "We must shoot, the hit is not important," Begin wrote from Poland,[18] and in Palestine Brit Ha'birjonim staged a series of spectacular actions to provoke confrontations with the Arabs, the British, and the Labor Zionism establishment. Initially this tactic enjoyed certain public support among Palestine's Jewish settlers in the face of growing Arab resistance, but in June 1933, when one of Brit Ha'birjonim's main objects of hatred, the socialist mayor of Tel Aviv, Chaim Arlosoroff, was murdered while walking along the beach with his wife, the movement lost its legitimacy. Arlosoroff had been involved in attempts to negotiate with Nazi Germany to bring about Jewish emigration and the transfer of Jewish assets to Palestine, if need be in the form of German-made products. For this and other things, he had been labeled a traitor and became the subject of harsh personal attacks. It was Arlosoroff that Ahimeir had referred to in an article on the day of the murder when he wrote: "Jews have always known how to deal with those who trade on the honor and beliefs of their people."[19] And it was Ahimeir and some of his followers who were arrested, prosecuted, and convicted for the murder (only to be acquitted by a higher court a few years later).

The murder of Arlosoroff was a turning point in the history of the Revisionist movement. Until then it had been a politically dynamic and partly successful competitor to socialist Labor Zionism. Toward the end of the 1920s, at a time of growing Arab resistance (symbolized by a massacre of Jews in Hebron in 1929) and with signs of a negative shift in the British view of the Jewish national movement, its influence grew dramatically within the Zionist movement; from 4 percent of the vote at the 1927 World Zionist Congress to 25 percent at the 1931 congress. There was a corresponding increase in support for the Revisionist demand for a Jewish state on both sides of the Jordan River. Some believed that Jabotinsky missed the opportunity to get a majority at the 1931 congress and to wrest power from Ben-Gurion's Labor Zionists. Or as one of the participants summarized: "They were in sight of the 'Promised Land'—the capture of the Zionist leadership—which they hoped to achieve at one stroke, and they were laying down impossible conditions."[20]

Two years later, at the 1933 congress, the tide had turned. Hitler was in power, Arlosoroff had been assassinated, and the Revisionists' fascist-inspired rhetoric had taken on increasingly dark undertones. Their share of the votes now plunged from 25 to 14 percent, while Ben-Gurion's Labor Zionist party, Mapai, soared from 29 percent to 44 (71 percent among the delegates from Palestine), taking a decisive step toward half a century of ideological hegemony.

Revisionism, on the other hand, became increasingly alienated from the Zionist mainstream. A last-ditch attempt to heal the rift through direct and secret negotiations between Jabotinsky and Ben-Gurion failed. Not because the leaders were far apart, in fact they managed to reach an agreement, but because they could no longer control their own highly polarized constituencies. The agreed compromise was emphatically rejected by Mapai and weakened Jabotinsky's authority within the Revisionist movement. Shortly thereafter, the Revisionists left the World Zionist Organization. Doors were slammed shut, rifts were widened, plots were hatched, weapons were loaded.

In retrospect, it is hard to understand how the Revisionist movement so effectively managed to put itself out in the cold. The Labor Zionists wanted a Jewish state as much as the Revisionist Zionists, but by different means and, above all, based on a different understanding of what was achievable. What Labor Zionists preferred to do in silence, the zealous Revisionist Zionists wanted to shout out loud and do in the open. Their fascist-inspired ideology had them worship physical action, muscular strength, theatrical heroism, and subversive provocations, fostering a deep disregard for tactical considerations and political compromises.

Considering the nature of its Zionism however, Revisionism was little more than the political and logical extension of Theodor Herzl's feverish fantasy of a Jewish state in one fell swoop. Like Herzl, Jabotinsky believed that the Jewish state must be the instantaneous outcome of an alliance between Zionism and a European imperial power. On top of everything else, Jabotinsky was an inveterate Anglophile and to the very last he hoped it would be England. Herzl may have been unaware or naive about the conflict with the Palestinian Arabs. Jabotinsky was not.

Like Herzl, Revisionists regarded the Jewish problem as insoluble and acute, and Zionism as a rescue operation. Just as Herzl was discussing Uganda as an alternative venue, Jabotinsky was considering Jewish statehood in British Guiana or Western Australia as late as 1940. It was also Jabotinsky who brought to life Herzl's confidant Max Nordau's 1919 plan for the immediate transport of 1.5 million Jews to Palestine from Eastern Europe, a project that would certainly "reduce the tension in Eastern and Central Europe" but at the same time put an end to the Labor Zionists' dream of a farmers' and workers' state. At a stroke, the Jewish state would have a majority of small businessmen and craftsmen, an economy based on manufacturing rather than agriculture, and a growing social base for nationalist rather than socialist policies.

It seems more than an irony of fate that Herzl and Jabotinsky, the emblematic founder of the Zionist movement and its enfant terrible, are officially and solemnly buried a stone's throw from each other on Mount Herzl in Jerusalem.

Tragedy has long shrouded the history of revisionism in gracious silence. The fact that Jews had allowed themselves to be carried away by the same thoughts and visions as their would-be executioners was for a time hard to bear. Other aspects of the intellectually brilliant Jabotinsky were brought forth to show that some part of his contradictory personality was also democratic and liberal. Nor was Menachem Begin's central role in Betar in those fateful years allowed to color the image of either him or the party he later would bring to power in Israel.

But nothing was forgotten, of course. And nothing was regretted. Very soon after his metamorphosis from underground, fascist-inspired guerrilla leader to the leader of a political party in a parliamentary democracy, Begin introduced into Israeli politics the historical themes of revisionism: the demand for territorial expansion, the glorification of the army, the sanctification of the Jewish state, the distrust of the non-Jewish world, the justification and glorification of the actions of the Revisionist underground in the creation of Israel. Or as Begin would put it in his melodramatic fashion: "If there had not been found in a section of Jewry, the strength and the spirit to rise in revolt, the sun would have set on our people. [. . .] We should not today have a Jewish state. We should have had a ghetto with our enemies trying to turn it into a graveyard."[21]

The Revisionist version of Zionist history also came with its own stab-in-the-back myth, based on an event in June 1948. During a temporary cease-fire in the war between Israel and the surrounding Arab states, David Ben-Gurion, the provisional leader of Israel, ordered the newly created Israel Defense Forces (Tsahal) to open fire on a ship loaded with weapons and volunteers for the Irgun, which no longer officially existed as an independent army. The leaders of Irgun had not yet fully grasped the power-political consequences of Israeli statehood but insisted, in breach of a UN embargo on bringing weapons into the combat zone, that the cargo be landed openly just north of Tel Aviv, and that 20 percent of the weapons be distributed to the remaining Irgun units in Jerusalem. There is reason to believe that Ben-Gurion was driven to his drastic action not only by respect for the UN embargo or by concern for the cohesion of the Israeli army but also by fear of a right-wing military coup.

From this act of "fratricide" (several Irgun members were killed in the battle), Menachem Begin would spin an intensely propagated myth that the "War of Independence" had been undermined by Ben-Gurion, that true Jewish patriots had been shot in the back, that military battles that could have been won were lost, that Israel's borders could have been extended if Irgun had been allowed to dislodge its weapons and carry out its planned military operations.[22]

What had been lost through betrayals and injustices, the revisionists would make up for in due course. The struggle for a Greater Israel on both sides of the Jordan River became the central theme of the revisionist Herut Party for nearly two decades. "Our right to all parts of the homeland is unassailable," wrote *Herut*, the party newspaper, in 1949. The 1949 armistice lines were described as "grotesque," befitting a state "in a Levantine operetta." Israel was no more than a ghetto surrounded by Arabs, "if we do not eliminate the borders, the borders will eliminate us." Israeli raids into Arab territory were glorified, while Arab raids into Israel were consistently labeled as pogroms. In 1951, Begin accused the Israeli leadership of failing to use the assassination of King Abdullah of Jordan to "complete" the territory. In 1954, with the military coup by Nasser in Egypt, it should have similarly "seized the opportunity" to take Gaza.

Throughout the 1950s, the Israeli electorate showed a striking indifference to this vociferously expansionist foreign policy. Even after the Sinai War in October 1956 and the subsequent return of war-conquered Sinai and Gaza to Egypt, Begin failed to gain popular support for his territorial demands. Until 1965 (when Herut formed part of a new right-wing coalition, Likud) the party never received more than 14 percent of the vote in general elections. The politics and culture of the revisionist world failed to capture the ideological imagination of most Israelis. Not necessarily because the revisionists were the only ones dreaming of more territory or celebrating military strength but because there were too many wrongs to avenge, too many unfinished battles to fight, too little joy, confidence, and contentment.

Begin came from a world of bygone symbols and myths, from a generational unit whose carefully constructed reality had capsized and which would probably have dissolved and perished in any other society. Only in the ideologically charged Jewish state was there enough mythmaking energy to keep even the most obsolete myths alive.

Paradoxically, it was the fixation on past wrongs, nourished by the bitterness and frustration of exclusion, that in the late 1960s would become the key to Herut's electoral breakthrough in Israeli politics by offering a language and a worldview to another excluded segment of the Israeli population—the Oriental Jews.

With the territorial conquests of 1967 the ideological isolation of Begin and his revisionist party finally broke. Positions that had seemed far-fetched, to say the least, were now literally taken up by the Israeli army. Suppressed historical myths were suddenly reinforced by current events. It was not the "unrealistic" revisionists that had succumbed to the realpolitik of Labor Zionism but realpolitik that had succumbed to Revisionist Zionism. Entrenched Herut slogans about the historical right of the Jews "to the whole Land of Israel," *Eretz Israel Ha'schlema*, were gaining public support. The ideological gap between Herut and Mapai on foreign policy and defense was significantly narrowed. Within Labor Zionism there were now factions who saw the establishment of Jewish settlements in the newly conquered territories as a fulfillment of their own ideological ambitions. These were the same factions that in the 1930s and '40s had opposed the partition of Palestine and advocated a Jewish "socialist commonwealth" throughout the whole territory of the British Mandate. There was, if you will, a dormant left-wing expansionist tradition that was now coming to life again. The first demands for new Jewish settlements came from within the ranks of Labor Zionism.[23]

It became suddenly apparent that the line between the two competing Zionist ideologies, Revisionism and Labor, was being drawn in the sand. Gradually, Labor Zionism had incorporated select but important elements of

Revisionist thought. The state had become more important than class and the army had become the emblematic national institution.

The war of 1967 marked the ascendance of a new generation of Israeli-born leaders. Their legitimacy and authority did not come not from sustaining and managing the ideological myths of Labor Zionism but from their capacity to run the state and win its wars. While Revisionism radiated ideological certainty, Labor radiated administrative competence and military-strategic genius. That image was severely shattered in the disastrous war of October 1973, and in the postponed elections in December of that year, Mapai lost 7 percentage points to the Herut-dominated Likud coalition. One election later, in 1977, the ideological shift was an electoral fact.

In the early 1960s in Secondary School Number Nine in Tel Aviv, there were no myths, only truths and lies. We were all encapsulated in the same certainty that must have characterized the young state's oft-invoked historical hero Judas Maccabeus in his fight against the Hellenization of Jewish Palestine in the 160s BCE. In a world of indifferent gods, unprincipled compromises, and moral confusion, the rebellious Maccabees drew strength from deeply rooted Jewish notions of good and evil, and clear-cut distinctions between right and wrong.

With a mixture of wonder and estrangement, I look at the neat Hebrew handwriting of a fourteen-year-old newly ascended Jewish boy who, on May 13, 1963, writes: "The

Hasmonean uprising was a natural step in the course of events in Judea, part of the struggle for liberation from foreign power, against the extermination order of Antony Epiphanes, and for the introduction of religious freedom for all."

"Antony??? No, Antiochus!" Dr. Kanner has added in his angry red pen. Otherwise, no objections. *Tov*, good, it says at the top.

He would have to wait exactly fourteen more years, Dr. Kanner.

Fourteen more years on the outside.

A LAND AT THE END OF TIME

Then wolves shall dwell with lambs, and panthers shall lie down with kittens; and calves and young lions and cattle shall be gathered together, and a little boy shall feed them. Cows and bears shall graze, and their young ones shall lie down together; and lions shall eat straw like oxen. A baby spinster shall play by the hole of a viper, and a weaned child shall stretch out his hand to the eye of the basilisk. Nowhere on my holy mountain shall one do what is evil and perverse, for the land shall be full of the knowledge of the Lord, as the depths of the sea are full of water.

—ISAIAH 11: 6–9

"Jesus is coming soon, are you ready?" used to be painted in white on rocks and bridges alongside Swedish roads. Less now than before. Perhaps the painting sect has dissolved, perhaps it has begun to question the idea that a Messiah who has come once must come again.

More logically, but equally unexpectedly, similar prophecies and exhortations appeared on walls, posters, banners, and billboards all over Israel in the early 1990s.

More logical since Judaism is still waiting for the Messiah. Equally unexpected, since Judaism does not expect the Messiah to announce his arrival on electronic billboards, or to be a Hasidic rabbi from Crown Heights, Brooklyn, or even to literally appear.

When Menachem Mendel Schneerson, the seventh Lubavitcher rabbi, died on June 12, 1994, at the age of ninety-two, he nonetheless was at the head of a movement that claimed to have 200,000 followers and $250 million in annual revenues, and which was based on the belief that Schneerson himself was the Messiah. Three thousand rabbis were dispatched around the world to proclaim and prepare for the imminent arrival of the Messiah, establish Torah schools, print Jewish calendars with ritual instructions, and distribute images of Rabbi Schneerson in front of Solomon's restored Temple. Jews were urged to fulfill their *mitzvot*, the divine commandments of the Torah; non-Jews to follow God's laws for the "sons of Noah." In the United States, France, England, Australia, and Israel, the movement's mitzvah tanks, camper vans converted into mission centers, were painted with the message "The Messiah is coming." Men on the street were stopped and asked if they were Jewish and, if so, whether they had put on their tefillin in the morning. If not, they were offered free prayer straps and a lesson on how to use them. Jewish women were admonished to light Sabbath candles. Outside Rabbi Schneerson's house in Brooklyn, people queued for days and nights to receive his advice or blessing.

The messianic frenzy reached its first peak in 1991 when Rabbi Schneerson first hinted that the Messiah was within his own circle: "The coming of the Messiah is no longer a distant dream of the future, but a present reality, which will very soon be proclaimed." He saw the collapse of the Soviet Union as a messianic sign, as well as the rescue of Israel's Jews from Saddam Hussein's Scud missiles over Tel Aviv during the Gulf War.

To his followers the signs were clear enough, the Messiah had arrived, and it was Rabbi Schneerson himself. Hadn't he at the age of nine saved a child from drowning? Hadn't he healed thousands of people with his blessings? Hadn't he predicted Israel's victory in the Six-Day War? Didn't numerical mysticism show that the rabbi's address, 770 Eastern Parkway, could be read as Beit Maschiach, the house of the Messiah? In Kfar Chabad, the movement's village in Israel, an exact replica of the Brooklyn house was erected, to stand ready for the Master at his entry into the Holy Land. Out of the traditionally non-proselytizing Judaism, a meticulously well-organized Jewish missionary movement had unexpectedly emerged, fully dedicated to preparing the world for the coming of the Messiah.

Or was it so surprising?

By all accounts, Schneerson was not entirely unprepared for the role, and in any case he was fully at home with the idea that the coming of the Messiah was a matter of time. As the seventh in the line of rabbis from an influential and respected Hasidic dynasty, Chabad (from the initial letters of the Hebrew words *Chochma*, *Bina*, *Da'at*—wisdom, understanding, knowledge), he had absorbed the waiting for the Messiah with his mother's milk. In the Hasidic tradition, the coming of the Messiah was not a theological abstraction but the anticipated consequence of Jews living a righteous life, indeed the very reason to live as a Jew, to live every day as if the Messiah was at the door. It was a world in which recurring self-proclaimed Messiahs were as natural as their equally recurring expulsion and banishment from Jewish society.

Consequently, Jewish history is characterized by messianic outbursts, the first and most extensive at the time of the Jewish revolt against the Romans and the destruction of the Jewish Temple. Jesus was a typical messianic figure of his time, and not the only one, as the contemporary Roman Jewish historian Flavius Josephus attests: "These [false messiahs were] seducers and deceivers, who, under the pretense of divine zeal for subversion and rebellion, worked upon the people, and seduced them into a swarming madness, so that they went out with them into the desert, to see signs from God [that] he would deliver them." An even worse affliction for the Jews, according to Josephus, was "the false prophet from Egypt" who with thirty thousand followers came from the desert to the Mount of Olives, "from where he intended to enter Jerusalem by force, seize the Roman garrison, and make himself ruler of the people."[1] Among rebels with messianic claims, Josephus mentions the Galilean Menahem, son of Judah (also mentioned in the Talmud), who managed to take a fortress in Jerusalem and proclaim himself king before being killed by a rival. He was followed by Bar Kochba, whose revolt against the Romans in 132 CE triggered the final destruction of the

Jewish community in Palestine, but who was nevertheless considered to be the Messiah by none other than the greatest Jewish authority of his time, Rabbi Akiva.

The false Messiahs appear periodically in Jewish history. Around 470, a Moses in Crete promised to take his followers across the sea to the Holy Land without getting wet, but he failed and people drowned. In 1280, Abraham Abulafia, a self-proclaimed Messiah, traveled from Spain to Rome to convert Pope Nicholas III to Judaism. In 1502, Ascher Lämmlein, a German Jewish Messiah, promised that the pious and righteous would be transported to the Holy Land on a pillar of smoke. Twenty years later, David Reubeni presented himself to Pope Clement VII as the brother of King Joseph of Chaibar in Arabia, the alleged ruler of three hundred thousand members of the lost Israelite tribes of Reuben, Gad, and Manasseh, and offered to drive the Muslims out of the Holy Land if granted papal armed support. Reubeni was handed a papal letter of recommendation to King João of Portugal, where he was about to obtain eight ships and four thousand muskets. Reubeni's stately appearance made him a Messiah figure in the eyes of those expelled in 1492 or forcibly converted Spanish and Portuguese Jews, which sealed his fate. Large numbers of recently baptized Jews, Marranos, abandoned all caution and reclaimed their Jewish identities. The Marrano Diogo Pires, one of Portugal's most senior judges, took the name of Solomon Molcho (from the Hebrew *melech*, king), circumcised himself, and nearly bled to death. As the messianic fever spread, the Inquisition started to take an interest in Reubeni, who implored Molcho to leave the country, and soon afterward fled himself. Molcho was burned at the stake in 1532 while Reubeni died in oblivion and misery.

This is by no means the end of the list, but it goes to show the very real and at times upsetting role that the figure of Messiah played in Jewish life. This was not only an abstract tenet of faith to be contemplated but a pounding promise to be fulfilled.

The passages in the Hebrew Bible that establish and develop the expectations of a personal redeemer are suggestive, symbolic, and contradictory. They are clearly rooted in a local political and religious reality, but gradually acquire universal dimensions. The Messiah, the anointed king, is elevated from the physical restorer of King David's house after the Babylonian captivity to the spiritual redeemer of all humanity at the end of time. In Judaism, the idea of the Messiah becomes the core of an apocalyptic eschatology, the belief in a coming and final intervention of God in the Creation. *Apocalypse* is Greek for "uncovering the hidden," *eschatology* means "the doctrine of the end." The biblical texts contain the seeds of the idea that worldly time has an end, and that at the end of time the Messiah will come and a new world will arise. Christianity is in its origins a product of this idea.

The concept of the Messiah originates in Leviticus 4:3, with the custom of anointing priests (and eventually kings) with oil. The term is derived from *ha'mashiach*, the anointed one, and originally denotes a quality, not a person. In the era following the Babylonian captivity, the figure of the Messiah is developed in the still-living tension between the longing for the house of David's restored kingdom and God's demands on his people for this to happen. Sometimes the Messiah is a prince at the gate of an earthly realm, sometimes a prophet at the threshold of a heavenly paradise. Sometimes his coming is heralded by terrible events, as in Ezekiel's prophecy of God's victory over the dark prince Gog of Magog; sometimes by a scene of modesty, as in Zechariah 9:9: "Behold your king comes to you; righteous and victorious is he. He comes poor, riding on a donkey, on a donkey's colt." The coming of the Messiah marks the end of war and the advent of eternal peace and brotherhood. In Isaiah: "So shall the dominion be great and peace without end upon the throne of David and upon his kingdom." In Micah and Isaiah: "Then they will make their swords into plowshares and their spears into vineyard knives." In Zechariah: "And I will cut off chariots from Ephraim, and horses from Jerusalem; and the bows of battle shall be cut off, and he shall speak peace to the nations."

In the postbiblical rabbinical tradition, the universal aspect of the messianic idea was further developed, its spiritual and moral significance was emphasized, and the redemption of Israel became linked to the redemption of all humanity. Waiting for the Messiah was gradually incorporated into the institutions and traditions of halachic Judaism and thus into the tasks and duties of daily Jewish life. It was a precarious balancing act vulnerable to recurrent outbursts of messianic activism and attempts to hasten the coming of the Messiah by human intervention.

A central task of the rabbinic authorities was thus to keep the messianic energy under control, to balance faith and hope, to make room for messianic longings without making room for messianic upheavals. Rabbi Moses Ben Maimon, better known as Maimonides, the most influential thinker and interpreter of postbiblical Judaism, devoted much effort to defuse the apocalyptic impulse within Judaism, well aware of its potential destructiveness, but also of its indispensability in Jewish thought and practice. He affirmed the belief in a coming Messiah, but greatly tempered expectations of what would follow:

> Let no one think that in the days of the Messiah anything will be changed in the natural course of the world, or that anything new will be introduced into Creation. No, the world order remains what it has been . . .
>
> The scholars and prophets did not seek the Messianic era to rule the world, or to bring the Gentiles under their power, or to be hailed by the peoples, or to enjoy food and drink, but to have time to study the Torah and its commentaries without being hindered by enemies [. . .] The Messiah comes solely to make peace to the world [. . .] How all this will happen, no one knows until it happens.[2]

Maimonides sought to combine messianism with contemplation and patience. By striving for righteousness in thought and action, by living according to the commandments of the halacha, a Jew should await the coming of the Messiah every single day. Maimonides's twelfth principle of faith reads: "I fully believe in the coming of the Messiah and, even if he is delayed, I will still wait for him every day so that he may come."[3] The difficult-to-translate subtext can be (and has been) interpreted to mean that the Messiah may come any day, but also that to the righteous he is coming every day, in all days. The coming of the Messiah is not an event in time but a condition of life. History does not end, nor does the need to prepare for the coming of the Messiah, as in the Talmudic story related in Psalm 97:8 of how Rabbi Joshua ben Levi meets the Messiah as a wounded beggar at the gates of Rome and asks him when he is coming. "Today," says the Messiah to the astonishment of Rabbi Joshua, and then adds: "Today, if you all hear his voice." The conditions for the coming of the Messiah are fulfilled when the kingdom of the Messiah is at hand. The wait for the Messiah is over when the wolves sleep with the lambs.

From this perspective, the prophecies of the Bible are not about what *will* happen but about what *should* happen; they express God's demands on humanity, not God's plans for the future. For Maimonides, the waiting for the Messiah was about approaching God in the world "as it is," about the daily and mundane striving to be in the image of God, the patient improvement of the never fully attainable conditions of the final redemption. Maimonides's messianism was a potentially explosive source of apocalyptic energy with firmly inserted control rods, a fortress of faith on the edge of despair.

Defusing the tensions between faith and promise without depriving Judaism of its spiritual vitality was an equation that even Maimonides could not resolve indefinitely. When expectations of messianic redemption could be socialized within the framework of rabbinic Judaism, patience and calm prevailed; when social distress and disaster sowed doubt and despair, the potential for messianic eruptions increased.

That the dangers Maimonides sought to avert were real and potentially disastrous was made abundantly clear in 1665 when a messianic movement took hold of large parts of European Jewry. It was led by a Jew from Smyrna, Sabbatai Zevi, who in 1648, at the age of twenty-two, proclaimed himself to be the Messiah. That same year the Ukrainian nationalist leader Bogdan Chmielnicki had orchestrated the largest massacre of Jews in European history and the messianic pressures grew overnight.

Leaving aside the miracle stories that were propagated to boost Sabbatai's messianic credentials, he seems to have been a highly charismatic figure, excelling in dramatic shifts between states of melancholy and ecstasy, asceticism and depravity. For the longest time he was considered a madman, notorious for his provocative and blasphemous behavior.

The turning point in his messianic "career" was a meeting in Jerusalem with Nathan of Gaza, a young Kabbalist who became his itinerant "prophet," or as Gershom Scholem notes, "the John and Paul of the new messianism all in one."[4] Nathan's stroke of genius was to provide an evocative messianic explanation to Sabbatai's bizarre behavior and personality. His followers soon spoke not of madness but of divine signs. One moment God was speaking through his mouth, the next God was subjecting him to severe trials and temptations. The Christian concept of a suffering Messiah was naturally incorporated into Sabbateanism. In other ways too the movement had similarities with Christianity.

The strongest impulse in Sabbateanism, however, came from the Kabbalistic idea of tikkun, the healing of the cosmos, which under the pressure of dire events became prone to political and historical interpretations. The Kabbalists had indeed stressed the spiritual nature of redemption but had concretized it in details that could easily be incorporated into a worldly program of human action. The Sabbatean fever reached its peak in 1666, which Nathan and Sabbatai had proclaimed to be the year of redemption, which also happened to be a year that resonated with Christian visions of the apocalypse from the book of Revelation 13:18: "And its number is six hundred and sixty-six."

As the magical year approached, there were reports of uncontrollable ecstasy, of men, women, and children with froth on their lips, of whole villages where everyday life had come to a halt. Even Christians were said to have been seized by the messianic fever and converted to Judaism.[5]

A record from the Jewish community in Hamburg testifies to the influence of the Sabbatean movement: "If the redemption takes place before Hanukkah in the year 5427 the community in Hamburg will pay the community in Altona 50 Reichstaler to be used for the dedication of the Temple. However, if the redemption takes place between Hanukkah 5427 and Rosh Hashanah 5428, only 25 of the 50 Reichstaler shall be used for the dedication of the Temple." The Sabbateans also gained great influence in the Jewish communities of Berlin, Mannheim, Fürth, and Dresden. In London, the English writer Samuel Pepys noted in his diary that the Jews were betting a hundred to ten that Sabbatai Zevi would declare himself king of Jerusalem within six months. From the same London, the German Heinrich Oldenburg wrote to his friend Baruch Spinoza: "Everyone here speaks of the rumor that the Israelites, who have been dispossessed for two thousand years, will return to their country . . . If the rumor is true, it should lead to great upheaval."[6] In many communities, Jews sold their belongings to be ready when the Messiah sounded the horn. "It is impossible to describe the expressions of joy that erupted when new intelligence about the Messiah arrived," wrote a contemporary Jewish witness, Glückel of Hameln, in her memoirs:

> The Sephardi received the most letters [from Turkey where Sabbatai was] and immediately rushed them to their synagogue [in Hamburg] where they were read aloud; young and old, even Germans, rushed to the Sephardic synagogue. The young Portuguese put on their finest clothes and wore green silk ribbons—the colors of Sabbatai Zvi. Thus, with song and dance, everyone went to the synagogue.

Glückel's in-laws sent two large trunks to Hamburg, one filled with food, the other with linen and clothes, where they would be kept until the departure signal was given and the journey to Jerusalem could begin.

Sabbateanism gained a strong foothold in the Jewish communities of the Balkans, Italy, Lithuania, and the southern provinces of Poland under Turkish rule. It also took root in Bohemia and Moravia, where it gained some of its most influential adherents. Not only were ordinary people converted but also learned rabbis, wealthy businessmen, and reform-minded Jews. The latter would carry the legacy of Sabbateanism into modern times in unexpected ways.

As the year of delivery approached, Sabbatai Zevi was compelled to act. On December 30, 1665, he sailed from Smyrna to Constantinople to consult with the Sultan but was arrested upon landing and banished to a castle-like house in a village on the Dardanelles, where he was allowed to hold court and keep the messianic tension alive. As rumors of miracles and great deeds continued to spread even pious Christians took notice. In Hamburg they anxiously turned to their local priest: "We have received fairly reliable information, not only from the Jews but also by letter from Christian communities in Smyrna, Aleppo, Constantinople, and other cities in Turkey, that this new Jewish Messiah is working many miracles and gathering the Jews of the whole world to himself. What then remains of the Christian doctrine and faith in our Messiah?"[7]

The news about Sabbatai Zevi's continued activities eventually reached the Sultan, who had him brought to Constantinople and given the choice of being burned at the stake or converting to Islam. Sabbatai Zevi chose the latter, took the name Mahmed Effendi, and urged his followers to convert with him. This sent shock waves through the Jewish world and seemed to signify the end of Sabbateanism. But far from everyone was able to accept the events at face value, and many were easily convinced that the apostasy of Sabbatai Zevi was just another stage in the messianic process, a final dark deed that the Messiah had to commit in order to fulfill the tikkun. A new and self-destructive element was thus added to the Sabbatean doctrine. If even apostasy could be considered "holy," what other transgressions could not be considered holy? Or rather, could anything be holy?

Sabbatai Zevi's apostasy led to a wave of "holy" conversions to Islam, most notably in 1683 in Salonika where a Sabbatean Islamic sect, the Dönmeh (Turkish for "apostates"), introduced an annual fertility festival in which two or more married couples engaged in sexual intercourse after a communal meal of baby lamb, which was believed to produce holy children.

The apostasy of Sabbatai Zevi also prepared the ground for an even more antinomian and nihilistic messianic movement. Jacob Frank was born Jankiew Leibowicz in 1726 in the Polish province of Galicia to poor Jewish parents, entered the service of a Polish Jewish businessman at the age of twelve, and came into early contact with the Dönmeh on journeys to Salonika and Constantinople. In Smyrna and Salonika, he studied Kabbalah with Berachia, the sect's leading theorist, and after Berachia's death in 1740 succeeded not only in assuming his leadership role but also in convincing a growing number of followers that he, Jacob Frank, was the Messiah. Back in Poland, Frank's message was that evil could only be overcome by evil itself. Just as the seed in the ground had to be destroyed in order to sprout and bear fruit, so the Torah had to be destroyed in order for it to reappear in its true form. All the laws and rules of the Torah were thus to be abolished, not least those concerning sexual relations. The deeper a person sank morally, the more light he would see. In Frankism, "the characteristic confluence of primitive savagery and a morality rotting from within became eerily clear," wrote Scholem.

In retrospect, it is easy to see the existential circumstances that gave rise to both Sabbateanism and Frankism. The external and internal pressures on traditional Judaism had been mounting ever since the traumatic expulsion of the Jews from Spain and Portugal in 1492. The ideas and ideals of the Renaissance, the Protestant revolts within Christianity, and the social upheavals outside the ghetto all fueled expectations of change and renewal among Jews as well— and they grasped for the only change and renewal available to them, the coming of the Messiah. Beneath Sabbateanism and Frankism reverberated the same Jewish sufferings and yearnings that in due time would give rise to Zionism.

III

THE LAND IN THE SHADOWS

■

Listen, friend, a people that let itself be slaughtered and destroyed, a people that let its children be made into soap and its women into lampshades, is a worse criminal than its tormentors. Worse than the Nazis. To live without fists, without fangs and claws, in a world of wolves is a crime worse than murder.

—Z., IN AMOS OZ, *IN THE LAND OF ISRAEL*

THE CHILDREN OF THE HOLOCAUST

Time and again we discover that, although we don't want it, almost every one of us is a messenger of the Holocaust.

—DAVID GROSSMAN

I have two class photos from Secondary School Number Nine in Tel Aviv. In the one from 1963, we are dressed in the light and dark blue school uniform. In the other, from 1964, we are wearing the khaki of our weekly Gadna premilitary training. The photos are taken at the same spot on the inner schoolyard, bordered by an amphitheater-like connection to the upper level on one side and by columned walkways between classrooms on the others. The photographer has placed us in the shade between the columns to take advantage of the mildly reflecting sunlight from the amphitheater, highlighting how different we are. Moshe Rubin from Libya is dark brown, red-haired Alex Danzig is freckled white. Ester Shafreisen's curly blond hair stands out against Gili Ben Baruch's finely chiseled Yemenite features and warm peppercorn eyes. A class photo from Secondary School Number Nine in the early 1960s had good use for every shade and contrast that could be squeezed out of a roll of black-and-white film. I am somewhere in the middle of the gray scale, neatly integrated into the whole.

And yet for nearly thirty years I thought I was the only stranger, the only outsider, in the pictures. All the others were so Israeli, so at home, so secure in their language and culture, so familiar with the country's unspoken and spoken codes, that I took it for granted that they were native Israelis. I knew that their parents usually came from somewhere else, but not that there was sometimes only a five- or ten-year gap between my classmates' *aliyah* and my own.

We never talked about it. Why should we? There was no advantage in having come from somewhere else, quite the opposite. Nor was there much to say about it. What we could have said, if we'd had the slightest reason to do so, was that the State of Israel was not only the happy beginning of something new, as we had been repeatedly told, but also the complicated continuation of something old. It was only when we met again half a lifetime later that I learned that the "super-sabras" Ester, Miriam, Alex, and Ronit had come to Israel from Poland in the 1950s, and that many of my unmistakably "native" classmates were in fact, like myself, children of the Holocaust, or in Hebrew the Shoah, the Catastrophe. The new State of Israel was in fact largely populated by what the Israeli historian Tom Segev had coined "the seventh million." In 1962, a fifth of Israel's Jewish population was made up of Holocaust survivors. Tel Aviv was a neighbor of Auschwitz.

It was not meant to be that way. The calculations of political Zionism did not include the Holocaust. The aim of Zionism was to prevent and anticipate the spiritual and national annihilation of the Jews, not to scrape together the remains of a physical mass extermination. Even those who suspected the worst and urged for a mass evacuation of Europe's Jews, never suspected this. The imagination of Western civilization before 1940 included brutal persecutions, pogroms, mass murders, even massacres of entire peoples, but "never before has a State, with the authority of its responsible leaders, decided and announced the total killing of a certain group of people, including the old, the women, the children, the infants, and turned this decision into fact with the use of all the possible instruments of power available to the State."[1]

Consequently this was not a perspective that characterized the prewar Jewish community in Palestine, the Yishuv. It was established to accommodate an ideologically and physically prepared Jewish elite, not a chaotic onslaught of terrified and partially destitute German and Polish businessmen and academics, not to mention elderly and disabled people. Already a decade before Auschwitz, Jewish Palestine had created most of its social institutions. The recruitment of new pioneers followed well-trodden political lines; the idea of a Jewish state had begun to gain the recognition of major powers, as in the 1937 partition plan of the British Peel Commission.

No one could imagine that the murder of five or six million European Jews would in due course be used as an argument, perhaps the decisive argument, in favor of a Jewish state in Palestine. In fact, when the terrible truth gradually dawned on the Zionist leadership in Palestine, its first reaction was the opposite: How could a Jewish state be justified when its intended population had been wiped out? "The extermination of the European Jews is a disaster for Zionism," David Ben-Gurion said in December 1942, "there will be no one left to build the country."

It did not help that the Zionists in Palestine had long regarded the indiscriminate flow of refugees from Europe as a burden. Now it was not only the ideologically motivated and politically selected who were quickly deployed in the state-building project but a growing number of people who came because they had nowhere else to go and were not considered to be of any immediate benefit to society. Within a few years of Hitler's rise to power, there were calls for better sorting of the "human material" from Germany to Palestine, and for the exclusion of the "sick and unwilling to work." A leading representative of Sochnut, the Jewish Agency for Palestine, demanded that socially overburdening cases be sent back to Nazi Germany. In November 1934, a list of names of people who should not have been allowed to emigrate was sent to the representative of the Jewish Agency in Berlin. In 1935, it was decided that German Jews over the age of thirty-five would be allowed to immigrate only if there was reason to believe that they would not be a "burden on society." Merchants or people "with similar occupations" were not to be allowed to enter other than as Zionist veterans. "Only God knows how many people this little *Eretz Israel* can receive and still maintain a healthy social structure," Chaim Weizmann wrote in a letter in 1935.

The moral dilemma of the Zionists in Palestine was not simple. Immigration permits were limited and choices had to be made, but from the perspective of what happened next, the choices made were morally subversive. For a long time, Europe's Jews were shamefully regarded as a means rather than an end.

Nor would the efforts of Labor Zionism to organize illegal transports of Jews from wartime Europe to Palestine stand scrutiny in the light of Auschwitz. Between March 1941 and March 1944, the official Yishuv failed to get a single refugee boat to Palestine. The reasons were not only technical, writes Segev, but also political. They did not want to take the risk of illegal activities that were too conspicuous. When the head of the Jewish Agency, Moshe Sharett (later Israel's first foreign minister), learned that Vladimir Jabotinsky's rival revisionist underground movement had landed a boat in the middle of the war with "the blind, the crippled and . . . an entire old people's home," he complained about the lack of judgment in the selection of "human material." We must bring the "good" and leave the "rabble," he wrote in his diary in 1940.[2] Sharett would later suffer severe remorse for his and the Zionist leadership's actions during the war.

Whatever may be said about the practical capacity of the Palestinian Zionists to save the Jews of Europe from the Holocaust, the fact remains that only a small number of European Jews were saved through the efforts of the Jewish community in Palestine.

A state is ready to be born, all its organs are already fully formed. In the final week of pregnancy, however, the fetus is transferred from one womb to another. Will it then be the same state?

In the first years of Israel's existence, few of its founders were able or willing to contemplate that the murder of the majority of Europe's Jews had produced a different state than the state they had been planning for. It was as if the child had been unaffected by the brutal operation, as if the genes and features had remained the same. Indeed, as if it had defiantly clung to its original heritage.

The emotional reaction of Palestine's Zionist veterans was to see the Holocaust as the terrible but ultimate confirmation that they were right: If only there had been a Jewish state five or six years earlier. If only the Jews of the Diaspora had listened to us in time. If only . . .

Of course, there could no longer be a discussion of some Jews being more desirable than others. As a matter of course, the Jewish community in Palestine was transformed from an elite colony to an asylum center. Great efforts were made to illegally smuggle survivors from Europe into a closed Palestine. The unimaginable details of what had happened aroused uncontrollable feelings of hatred, disgust, and revenge.

What Ben-Gurion called "a barrier of blood and silence and agony and loneliness" was erected in the midst of Jewish Palestine.[3] In the second half of 1945, ninety thousand survivors arrived from Europe, in the following three years sixty thousand, in the first year of the State of Israel more than two hundred thousand. By the end of 1949, almost one in three Jewish residents of Israel, some three hundred fifty thousand people, were Holocaust survivors. Many were mentally and physically scarred and had difficulty integrating into the daily life of Jewish Palestine. Some had pushed the Holocaust out of their thoughts, while others lived with every second of it etched in their minds. "Of my two years outside the law, I have not forgotten a single thing," wrote Primo Levi forty years after his liberation from Auschwitz.[4] The survivors were people who needed care, attention, and a purpose in life. What they usually encountered was impatience, irritation, and silence.

The silence was largely one of shame—mutual shame. The survivors were ashamed to have survived. A person who is constantly told that you should be dead and who realizes that your survival makes no difference, eventually begins to wonder whether you should have survived. Native Israelis, on the other hand, were ashamed of millions of Jews having "gone like lambs to the slaughter." The shame of the survivors turned into psychological repression, the shame of the native Israelis into contempt. The traditional Zionist view of the Jewish Diaspora as a morally and culturally inferior existence was reinforced by claims that Diaspora Jews had contributed to their own destruction—primarily by not resisting and ultimately by not becoming Zionists in time to go to Palestine. The moral and existential experience of the Holocaust was reduced to a memento for those who had questioned the necessity of the Zionist project.

In the Israeli mythology of the Holocaust, a few heroic Jewish uprisings became the central narrative, while the anonymous mass death in the gas chambers took on a shameful and unspeakable quality. The writer Amos Elon recalled how his Israeli high-school textbook from the late 1950s had annotated the national poet Hayim Nahman Bialik's poem about the 1903 pogrom in Kishinev, "In the City of Death," with the comment: "This poem depicts the mean brutality of the assailants and the disgraceful shame and cowardice of the Jews of the Diaspora shtetl."[5]

I suddenly remembered how we used the Hebrew word *sabon* for "weakling" or "coward." *Sabon* simply means "soap" and its derogatory meaning was derived from the widespread but factually incorrect claim that the Nazis had made soap from murdered Jews. This use of the term may have started during the war of 1948–1949, in which one in three Israeli soldiers was a survivor. These often slightly elderly men and women gained a reputation for being melancholic, unstable, and battle-averse. Many have since testified to the chasm that separated native-born Israelis from the survivors. The former saw themselves as a new Jewish type, physically and morally superior to the ghetto Jew of the exile. The survivors were expected to free themselves from their "Diaspora mentality" as soon as possible and become good Israelis like everyone else.

Perhaps this step was facilitated by the involuntary participation of the survivors in the takeover of Arab property, as they at times were given emptied houses and villages as their first homes. An acute housing problem thus received its not entirely moral solution, and the trauma of the Holocaust was treacherously intertwined with the Palestinian tragedy.

Some became like Ariye Biro, a Hungarian Jewish boy who survived Auschwitz at the age of eighteen weighing thirty-seven kilos and ended his career in the Israeli army with his tongue and jaw shot off. He had received a bullet in the chest, a bullet in the neck, a bullet below the knee. He had injuries to his stomach, legs, and hands. He spoke with an artificial wooden tongue. His name came to public attention with the revelation that Israel had executed hundreds of Egyptian prisoners of war during the 1956 Sinai campaign.[6] Hero or psycho? In a fascinating interview in the newspaper *Maariv*, he spoke openly about the driving force in his life:

> "I settled my accounts with the Germans in April 1945. I killed Germans. Many Germans. I killed until I felt that the German people owed me nothing. I joined the Red Army on January 27, 1945, signed for a Russian PPC machine gun with three magazines, returned one that I couldn't bear to carry."

"Does revenge set people free?"

"Only when revenge is the trigger. I killed some people unnecessarily, for no reason."

"You killed anyone, indiscriminately?"

"Correct. You killed my family. Now I am killing yours."

"Did you kill civilians?"

"Sure, lots of them. I set a target. On what grounds I don't even know myself."

"Hundreds?"

"Many hundreds. It was a great revenge."

"And you feel comfortable with that?"

"I feel very comfortable. My four-year-old brother was not a soldier, nor was my grandfather at that time, nor was my mother's sister. I saw the fear in the eyes of the German soldiers when I stood in front of them with the machine gun, and it was a wonderful feeling. A moment ago the German was a superhuman being, and now he stood there like a *schmuck* in front of the gun, trembling with fear."

"Could the massive killing you witnessed at Auschwitz have contributed to your ability to face death and your ability to kill?"

"Let me put it bluntly. You and I value a human life differently. Death will come anyway, in two days or in twenty years. It is inevitable. I saw people die the strangest deaths in Auschwitz, but as my grandfather used to say, I have never seen anyone die twice. That doesn't mean I devalue human life, I wish everyone to live to a ripe old age as long as it doesn't conflict with my goals. When it does, I will kill him and his family, to the fifth generation."[7]

In the Israel of the early 1960s the Holocaust was still a chapter that had to be closed. It had confirmed what needed to be confirmed and taught the lessons that needed to be learned. The Jewish state was the happy ending of a tortuous journey. What else was there to say? The more emphatically the Jews of Israel turned their backs on their Diaspora past, the less the survivors dwelled on their memories, the faster the wounds would heal and the state would be consolidated. For a few years "the great silence," as Segev called it, settled over the country. The memory of the Holocaust was institutionalized and ritualized. The strength of the Jewish state covered the traces of Jewish weakness. Hundreds of thousands of wandering nightmares were treated with shovels, tractors, and rifles.

When belatedly an Israeli Holocaust Memorial Day, Yom HaShoah, was established in 1951, a date in the Jewish calendar (the twenty-seventh of the month of Nisan) was chosen to precede the memorial day for Israel's fallen soldiers, Yom Ha'zikaron, which was immediately followed by the Israeli Independence Day, Yom Ha'atzmaut. The link between catastrophe, sacrifice, and redemption could hardly have been more effectively put together.

The great silence, which lasted for most of the 1950s, was in fact a state of convulsion, characterized by sudden and uncontrolled outbursts of indignation and anger. The Hebrew press reported briefly and with palpable discomfort on recurring incidents in which survivors recognized a *kapo*, a Jewish tormentor from the camps, and attempted to lynch him in blind rage. The Israeli courts handled with equal discomfort and without much media attention some thirty cases against Israel citizens suspected of having violated a 1950 law criminalizing "Nazis and Nazi collaborators" (usually people having served as Nazi underlings in the camps).[8]

After the war, few Jews in Palestine could imagine having anything to do with Germans or Germany ever again.

The name itself had become a curse of sorts. The slightest association with the murderous nation and its murderers seemed unthinkable for generations to come. Jews who chose to return and settle in Germany were told that they could not come back to Israel. Israeli diplomats were trained in the art of avoiding Germans. Demands for physical revenge were widespread and unrelenting. Suggestions were made in the press to ban contact with German citizens, including those of a temporary or private nature. Israeli passports were stamped as invalid for entry into Germany. German films, books, and magazines were boycotted (but appeared anyway, bearing Swiss or Austrian origin). In 1950, censors intervened against a performance of opera arias by Mozart, Schubert, and Brahms in German. When Martin Buber was awarded the Goethe Prize, criticism in the press and in the Knesset forced him to turn it down. Discussing relations with Germany in terms of realpolitik and national interest was considered beyond the pale.

Nevertheless, in 1951 secret negotiations were initiated between the governments of Israel and West Germany on financial compensation for the victims and survivors of the Holocaust, and thus on the normalization of relations between the two states. The negotiations became official in 1952 and resulted in an agreement that year in which Israel would receive goods and money equivalent to some $10 billion in today's rate over a period of twelve to fourteen years. Hundreds of thousands of survivors were also guaranteed lifelong individual reparations and pensions totaling several hundred million dollars at the time.

The official decision to enter into negotiations with Germany was taken by the Central Committee of the Mapai

Labor Party in December 1951—and caused a storm. In biblically charged and deeply emotional attacks, the decision was described as a shameful sellout of the murdered and a betrayal of the survivors. "What should I say to my loved ones, my burned ones, my murdered ones, when they come to me at night, now and forever," asked the editor in chief of *Maariv*. Many conjured up images of bodies for sale and price tags on the ashes and bones of loved ones. Still others saw the decision as a relapse into the morality and mentality of ghetto Jews. The Jews of Israel could never bend, never forgive, never accept blood money.

One of the anti-negotiation members of the Mapai Central Committee, himself a survivor, recounted how he and the Jewish leaders in the Vilnius ghetto, starving and freezing in the cold of winter, had been offered the bloodstained clothes of their murdered brothers—but refused to accept them, lest they be humiliated and used in Nazi propaganda. Another member with the same background said that the only compensation he could accept was a father for a father and a child for a child. "My soul would be at rest if it knew that there would be six million German dead to match the six million Jews. If we do not have the ability to do that, then at least we have to do a historic thing that will pain them like the pain of blood—to spit in their faces."[9]

It soon became clear that Menachem Begin, the leader of the right-wing opposition, intended to use the issue of negotiations to try to bring down the government. On the eve of the decisive vote in the Knesset on January 7, 1952, he bluntly accused Mapai and Ben-Gurion of having sold the Jews to the Nazis, of having sold the Jews to the British, and of wanting to sell them again. Herut Party posters screamed: "Bones of our parents and martyrs for sale in the Nazi-Mapai blood market!" Supporters of negotiations were labeled as traitors. The decision was referred to in the nationalist party press as "the day of judgment" and people were urged to take matters into their own hands if necessary.

What that meant became clear when the thousands of protesters who had gathered in Jerusalem's Zion Square in the cold and rain on Judgment Day began to move toward the police cordon surrounding the Knesset building. Many wore yellow Stars of David and the mood was excited. In his speech, Begin had called all Germans, "including Adenauer," Nazis and murderers; he had revealed that secret negotiations had taken place behind the back of the Jewish people; he had made the audience swear eternal loyalty to their murdered relatives; he had urged them to "take a stand" and surround the Knesset; and he had warned them that the Israeli police were going to use tear gas *made in Germany*—"the same gas that suffocated our parents to death!"

The revolt ended in a stinging defeat for Begin and the opposition. The Israeli parliament voted in favor of negotiations with Germany by sixty-one votes to fifty, Begin was suspended from the Knesset "for threats of violence," and the Herut Party was close to being outlawed.

It was not only the material blessings of the agreement that silenced the criticism. It was also the unwillingness or inability of Israeli Jews to see the Holocaust as a collective experience. For most of them, the Holocaust was still an unmentionable personal memory, a pain with names and faces, a trauma that could not be generalized. They had no need to turn their lives into playscripts in Begin's drama of fate, nor could they see how a little compensation from the Germans had the power to "compensate" or "forgive" anything.[10]

In retrospect, we can better understand how deeply the Holocaust affected the early Israeli society. How it imperceptibly hardened into phobias of confinement and vulnerability. How it added an extra layer of bitterness and intransigence to attitudes toward the outside world. How it projected its Darwinian us-or-them logic onto the Israeli-Arab conflict and its European nightmares onto the nearest Arab village. How it turned every battle into the last, and every defeat into a Holocaust.

It was sometimes said that Holocaust survivors had been inoculated against racism and intolerance. Those who had once been robbed of their human dignity, indeed their very reason for being, could be expected to react with particular sensitivity to other people being humiliated and degraded.

And many surely did.

But many had been inoculated with something else: a dark microbe that generated fear, suspicion, bitterness, and misanthropy. Humiliation and degradation produced not only humility and humanity but also a desire for revenge, retribution, and power. A military and ideologically encircled Israel fueled such desires more than universal dreams of human brotherhood and dignity.

One might even say that the Holocaust helped to exacerbate the intolerant aspects of Jewish nationalism. The moral debt to the Palestinian Arabs was somehow neutralized by the moral lesson of Auschwitz. Gentleness and conciliation were luxuries that others could afford—not the victims of the Holocaust.

The Holocaust also darkened and distorted the image of the Palestinian Arabs, who would be accused of wishing for another Holocaust (throwing the Jews into the sea). It would also prompt a pragmatic "dove" like Abba Eban to name the 1949 armistice lines "Auschwitz borders." It fostered in Israel a sense of living in a besieged fortress or—why not—in a fenced camp.

One might have imagined that the growing knowledge of the Holocaust would add an element of reverence and respect to the Israeli Zionists' critique of the annihilated Jewish world in Europe, but the ideological contempt for the Diaspora actually increased. In the 1950s, opposition to Yiddish took the form of schools or individual teachers sometimes forbidding their students to read a poem or sing a song in Yiddish. The devaluation of Jewish life in exile remained an integral part of the exaltation of Jewish life in the State of Israel.

The American Jewish theologian Steven Schwarzschild would describe it as a distortion of the morality of the Holocaust. The Jewish lesson of the Holocaust, Schwarzschild wrote, was not necessarily the need for resistance and heroism (the heroic perished too) but the need to remain *Menschen* even under the most inhumane conditions, "to sanctify the name of God while surrounded by a flood of heathenism, to study, preach, and pray in a world in which only murder, rape, and brutality reigned, to squeeze a precious drop of life through the sieve of all-consuming death."[11] A knight might have chosen to resist, but the Jews had chosen to be Jews, not knights.

"The problem for our Jewish generation and our children," Schwarzschild concludes, "is whether we can live with the ethics and politics of the persecuted having, in some ways, ceased to be the persecuted."[12]

I am not sure that the survivors of the Holocaust were ever the natural bearers of the "ethics and politics of the persecuted." The Holocaust did not leave behind morally wholesome, intellectually lucid, and emotionally unproblematic people. The Holocaust left behind people with dark minds, twisted hearts, and anguished eyes, people whose overriding experience in life was total humiliation and contempt. A nation built by and on such people must, whether it is aware of it or not, have that humiliation and contempt deeply ingrained in it. Persecution does not automatically breed tolerance. Annihilation does not automatically breed a zest for life. Annihilation breeds fear, and fear has its own ethics and its own politics. Nazism had taught that a person who did not want to be a victim has to become an executioner. How many victims lived in the belief that on this point Nazism had been right?[13]

When on May 23, 1960, Ben-Gurion announced to the world that the State of Israel had kidnapped former SS Lieutenant Colonel Adolf Eichmann in Buenos Aires and intended to put him on trial in Jerusalem as responsible for "the final solution to the Jewish question," his political objective was explicit. Israel's future generations would learn once and for all what it meant to live as a Jew among non-Jews, and that the State of Israel was the only place on earth where Jews could live in security and freedom. Whatever Eichmann had been guilty of as head of Department IV B 4 of the Reich Security Service for dealing with the "Jewish question," and it was certainly no small matter, it was far more than his own crimes that would be on trial. "We want the nations of the world to know ... and to be ashamed," Ben-Gurion wrote in a series of articles on the eve of the trial, laying out what he thought it should be about. In her book *Eichmann in Jerusalem*, with the subtitle *A Report on the Banality of Evil*, Hannah Arendt gives her account of Ben-Gurion's motives: "The Jews in the Diaspora were to remember how Judaism, 'four thousand years old, with its spiritual creations and ethical strivings, its Messianic aspirations,' had always faced 'a hostile world,' how the Jews had degenerated until they went to their deaths like sheep, and how only the establishment of a Jewish state had enabled Jews to hit back ..."[14]

Arendt's coverage of the trial for *The New Yorker* turned into a scathing critique of what she saw as an attempt to rectify the history of the Holocaust for political purposes, as well as of the judicial procedure itself. A court whose legitimate task was to determine Eichmann's personal responsibility for the specific crimes with which he was charged, was largely transformed into a stage for a dramatic reenactment of the crimes of the Nazis and the world against the Jews. Eichmann became a kind of secondary figure in this context, a means rather than an end. The central figures of the trial, as Ben-Gurion had intended, were the hundred or so witnesses from every crime scene of the Holocaust, summoned by the prosecutor Gideon Hausner to testify. The testimonies, which were broadcast live on Israeli radio and reported in the Israeli press, rarely related to Eichmann's personal role in the Holocaust machinery. Fifty-three witnesses came from Poland and Lithuania "where Eichmann's competence and authority had been almost nil," Arendt noted.[15]

The political effect was largely the desired one. The shadow of the Holocaust deepened over Israel. Israeli youth reportedly lost some of their faith in the outside world. Many became aware of their European heritage for the first time. The death sentence of Eichmann in December 1961 stated "that the terrible slaughter of millions of Jews by Nazi criminals . . . was one of the great causes for the establishment of a state of survivors. The state cannot be disconnected from its roots in the Holocaust of European Jewry."[16]

When I arrived in Israel at the end of April 1962, Eichmann was still on death row in Ramla Prison. The protests against his execution, organized by Martin Buber, Hugo Bergmann, Gershom Scholem, and others, were met with fierce resistance, especially from the survivors. "For their sake, the sentence must be carried out," argued Hausner. In a diary entry, Bergmann wrote: "I am concerned for the soul of Israel. The horrible experience of the Holocaust has already made its impression on us and on our souls. All the complexes that have plagued us these hundreds of years . . . have reawakened."[17]

Five years later, the demons of the Holocaust were unleashed in full. First as ghetto phobias during the Arab buildup in May 1967, then as liberation fantasies after the victory in June. Begin's Herut Party, which for twenty years had sought to harness the memory of the Holocaust to its program for territorial expansion, suddenly had military conquest on its side. The Revisionists thus gained an interpretative edge not only in their view of Israel but also in their view of the Holocaust. When Begin became prime minister of Israel in 1977, he thus purposefully turned the memory of Auschwitz into a nation-building institution.

When Israeli warplanes bombed an Iraqi nuclear reactor in June 1981, he justified it on the grounds that one and a half million Israeli children had been murdered in the Nazi gas chambers. When Israel invaded Lebanon in June 1982, Begin told his government: "Believe me, the alternative is Treblinka." As criticism of the invasion grew, especially after the massacre in the Palestinian refugee camps of Sabra and Shatila, Begin angrily declared that no one had the right to preach morality "to our people." In a letter to President Ronald Reagan, he compared the destruction of Yasser Arafat's headquarters in Beirut to the destruction of Hitler's bunker in Berlin.

Even Israel's secret nuclear weapons program was tacitly legitimized by the threat of another Holocaust. "The capacity grievously to damage or wholly to destroy an adversary is at present, Israel's most credible guarantee of survival," wrote the American Jewish theologian Richard L. Rubenstein.[18]

There were those who feared Israel's instrumentalization of the Holocaust for national purposes, arguing that the notion of the Jews' inherent vulnerability in the world imbued the new state with a trait of paranoia, intransigence, and arrogance. A people who learned that all other peoples hated and persecuted them would eventually feel relieved from any obligation to other peoples. It would allow itself to treat others as it took for granted that others would treat it.

These fears would soon come true. On the fringes of Jewish nationalism emerged movements which believed that Arab lives had less value than Jewish lives, who taught their children that a dead Arab is a good Arab, and who would go on to kill Arabs—and eventually Jews as well. Moshe Zimmermann, a leading Israeli historian and professor of German studies at the Hebrew University of Jerusalem, would eventually compare their ideology with Nazism, thus turning the debate on the Holocaust and the State of Israel on its head:

> It is quite clear that in every respect we have better "reasons" [than the Nazis] for many of our actions. But at the same time a monster is growing within each of us, and if we imagine that we are always right in what we do, the monster will grow. We Jews must therefore always keep the German example in mind. Already today there exists . . . a whole sector of the Jewish population which I would undoubtedly define as a copy of the German Nazis. Look at the children of the Jewish settlers in Hebron; from an early age they learn that all Arabs are evil, and that all non-Jews are against us. They turn into paranoids, they think they belong to a master race, they are exactly like Hitler Jugend.[19]

It was these very movements that would propagate images of Prime Minister Yitzhak Rabin dressed in a Nazi uniform (or in a keffiyeh, a checkered Arab shawl, which for them was the same thing), before one of their zealots shot him dead. The Holocaust rhetoric of eternal threat inspired violence and intransigence rather than peace and reconciliation. Rabin had held out the prospect of normalization, while the "lesson" of the Holocaust precluded normalization. On Holocaust Day 1994, Israel's largest newspaper, *Yedioth Ahronoth*, published an editorial calling for an end to the exploitation of the Holocaust for nationalist purposes, an end to organized school trips to extermination camps and gas chambers, an end to the propaganda of pitting the Jews against the world:

> This deliberate distortion of human history is part of a criminal attempt to train a young generation of Jews to care only about what happened to the Jews of Europe, to accept as a given that all non-Jews are against us, and consequently to be indifferent to any injustice committed against non-Jews.[20]

Now that I know how many of us had a history worth remembering, and remember how little we thought of it, and marvel at how little we knew each other, I can't help but see the old class photos from Secondary School Number Nine in a more ambiguous light. I see life stories not told, contrasts not captured, shadows not visible.

Next to me sits Shimi. His khaki shirt is unbuttoned and hastily tucked inside the trousers, probably at the request of the teacher or the photographer. You can see the freckles on his pale face and take note of his absent-minded smile. An arrogant smile some teachers thought, when Shimi smiled instead of answering the question, but Shimi was never arrogant. He just didn't do his homework. In his worn leather briefcase there were no books or notes, just soggy cream cheese sandwiches. When asked a question he couldn't answer, he looked the teacher in the eye and smiled, at once shy and indulgent. As if to say: Why are you wasting my time with this? It was a smile that never evoked anger, only wonder. Shimi was different, a little off the chart, and I liked him a lot.

How he became a sturdy man with a beard and curled sidelocks, a hat with a brim, a black coat, a wife with chastely covered arms, and eleven children in a newly built ghetto on a Jerusalem hilltop is, as Shimi responded when we finally met again, too long a story to be told in one sitting.

Unsurprisingly, it had everything to do with Holocaust.

UNTO THE THIRD GENERATION

Still, my son, the debt cannot be repaid.
A life for a life is not enough.
Skin must shed skin, toe by toe shed.
Every finger is driven in. Every tooth, every hair.

—NATHAN ALTERMAN,
"SONGS OF THE PLAGUES OF EGYPT" (1944)

Secondary School Number Nine in Tel Aviv didn't look the same anymore. A large sports hall had been added, a high barbed-wire fence surrounded it, armed guards were posted at the gate (was there a gate before?) asking for identification and the purpose of my visit. The sandy path leading up to the school had been paved and widened and there was a parking lot for teachers and students. The school uniforms were gone, as were most traces of the 1964 generation. In stairwells and corridors hung photos of the graduating classes, the earliest in black and white, though none of them early enough to have me in them. The tradition of portraits seemed to have started a few years later, or maybe thirty years was too much for the space on the walls. In the earliest photos I recognized the headmaster and some of the teachers, but they quickly faded away. The sports teacher, Mr. Kormann, had stayed the longest, well into the era of color photos.

On one of the exterior walls, overlooking what used to be a sandy field where we played soccer but which was now a green lawn between the school building and the new sports hall, there was a plaque commemorating students killed in action. At the time of my visit, there were thirty-three names inscribed, arranged chronologically by day of death according to the Jewish calendar. Shamai Shayevitz was number six. He died on the sixth of the month of Iyyar in the year 5728 (May 4, 1968), during a patrol along the border with Jordan, in a skirmish with Palestinian guerrillas. Shamai was tall and lanky and laughed a lot. In the class photo from 1964, he sits in front of me and Shimi, laughing. On the back of the photo, where the class had scribbled farewell messages, Shamai had written: "To Yoram [my hebraized name] with love. Don't let life disappoint you. Good luck with the girls."

When I wanted to get in touch after thirty years, I had to search for contacts. The last letters were exchanged in the early 1970s. One summer Shimi came to visit me in Stockholm, on an excursion from his veterinary studies in Milan, but we had little to say to each other. The world was not the same, and I was not the same.

In the autumn of 1991, I asked the press attaché at the Israeli embassy in Stockholm to help me find some of my old classmates. After six months, I received a list of five names and five telephone numbers, compiled from the school's archives. One name was Ronit, my last mail contact. She had sent a postcard from Jerusalem, where she was studying biology. I had not replied. Twenty years later, I felt embarrassed to get in touch. What did I want? Did I know myself?

Nevertheless, letters and photos were exchanged. The question of who we had become seemed to interest all of us. I, *ha'schvedi*, the Swede, became a time machine of sorts, transporting a small group of Israeli adults to a time that contrasted, in an almost surreal way, with the time in which they now lived.

To some extent the contrast was normal; life as an adult is rarely what you imagine as a teenager. Less normal is coming into adulthood in a tight-knit society where everything had seemed preordained. We were raised to believe that our lives had a collective meaning and a collective purpose. We had our futures mapped out more clearly than most other young people. We carried ideals and dreams that did not belong to modern fifteen-year-olds but to a fifteen-year-old state with fundamentally outdated visions and aspirations. We would not live our lives for the sake of living but for something bigger and higher.

This was not to be the case. Our two years together were the years in which the specifically Israeli sense of collective destiny and identity reached its inevitable peak. They were perhaps the last years of ideological zeal and moral certainty. They were the years before shadows and doubts settled over the Zionist project, the years before Israel became an occupying power, the years before pioneers became settlers, the years before undisputed beliefs were undermined by ambiguity and doubt.

The Israeli generation of my class went straight from school to a war, then to another war, then to an invasion, then to a Palestinian uprising. They had experiences that I would never share or truly understand. They were faced with choices that I was lucky to have escaped.

In June 1992, I traveled to Israel to meet some of my former schoolmates. These were the weeks leading up to the elections that would bring Rabin and the Labor Party to power. I wanted to see if I could better understand what had become of Israel, by seeing what had become of them. I am not sure that they saw it the same way. As it turned out, they wanted to see one another as much as they wanted to see me. I became the catalyst in a process from which imperceptibly I could have stepped out. During a few evenings at Ester's house in the rapidly urbanizing countryside idyll of Yahud outside Tel Aviv, the conversations often went far beyond my horizon.

Shimi deviated from the pattern. I had asked everyone I contacted, but no one knew his whereabouts. Rumors of his vagrant lifestyle had died out in the mid-1980s. It was said that he was living the high life in a hippie colony in Rosh Pina in the northern Galilee, that he ran a veterinary clinic in posh Nof Yam north of Tel Aviv, that he had gone Orthodox. In the early 1980s, Ester had seen him in Yahud with a goat on a string, which seemed to surprise no one. Gili remembered how, during the class archaeological expedition to Ein Gedi (the year after I had left Israel), he had put a live lizard in his mouth and eaten it, which no one had forgotten. Probably not Shimi either because he became seriously ill.

Shimi was the ever-present black hole in our conversations. Was it true that he had become a *baal teshuvah*, a neo-Orthodox? That he lived among "the blacks" in Jerusalem? That he wore a hat and a skullcap? Suddenly we were talking about him as if he were dead. The subject seemed to both fascinate and frighten. Everyone knew one or more people who had walked the same path. In the midst of secularized Israel, an internal exit door had opened through which seemingly rational and modern people just disappeared.

A few days later, Ester called. She had looked in the phone book and found a Shimon Avidov in Jerusalem. It's a "black" neighborhood, she added. Until then, no one had thought that a *baal teshuvah* could be in the phone book.

Nobody called him but me.

Ramot Polin—Poland Heights—must have been designed by a mad architect and approved by a blind building committee. The tightly packed quarters are made up of interlocking pentagon-shaped houses, like pieces in a jigsaw puzzle. Narrow, impenetrable mazes lead between and through the houses. Entering the area requires a map and patience. The inner parts of the labyrinth require you to practically climb in between the gables of the houses. Large numbers in black on the facades indicate which part of the complex you are about to enter, which would otherwise be impossible to know. On the Poland Heights there are Ramot Alef, Ramot Bet, Ramot Gimel, and Ramot Dalet—the A, B, C, and D heights. From a distance the whole area looks like the remains of a space society, or what one might imagine the remains of a space society would look like. Only the covering glass dome is missing. All the heights are "black," that is, almost 100 percent inhabited by ultra-Orthodox Jews.

Ramot Polin is built on the northern border of the former corridor to Jerusalem, just beyond the Green Line, where until 1967 the artillery of the Arab Legion had a good view of the busy road between Tel Aviv and Jerusalem. The road coming here is considered safe, which means that it doesn't pass through Arab-populated areas but provides a direct link, via Prophet Samuel Street, to the Orthodox neighborhoods in central Jerusalem.

I arrive at dusk. Everywhere, little boys in sidelocks and little girls in long-sleeved dresses. The average ultra-Orthodox family in Jerusalem has between seven and ten children. Children are God's blessing and the purpose of marriage. Bearded men with black coats fluttering around their legs hurry with small packages under their arms. Few women are out at this time of day. I park the car below the house with the number 55 and ask for the Avidov family. Everyone knows them. Some follow me all the way to the front and inside and up to apartment number 18.

I had thought about clothing and behavior. What should a visitor wear? What kind of gifts should or could I give? Few secular Westerners would normally come out here. Nor had I made much effort to blend in.

I soon realize that I should have prepared myself better. The lady who opens the door smiles kindly, but when I offer her the flowers I've brought, she doesn't accept them. They are beautiful, she says. After a while I place them on a table. When I eventually extend my hand to say goodbye, she doesn't take it either. Throughout the visit, she remains in the background, methodically engaged in household chores and childcare. She is pregnant with her tenth child, but she does not look old or tired. Her face under the white headscarf is youthful, almost childlike. She wears a long-sleeved purple dress, thick white socks, and low-heeled black shoes.

I recognized Shimi immediately, which surprised me. I had been so excited about this meeting that I had fantasized him beyond recognition. It seemed impossible to reconcile my memory of him with the image of an ultra-Orthodox Jew. Just as I could not possibly imagine an ultra-Orthodox Jew as anything else. The black coats, the heavy sidelocks, and the pale feverish faces belonged to a human species to which I had no point of reference.

In Shimi, I saw for the first time a human being peeking out from behind the Orthodox appearance. The smile was unmistakable, and the eyes bore the same familiar expression of surprised indulgence. The hairline had receded a little, the once slender body had broadened and was covered in wide black pants, a white shirt, and rough-soled black shoes, but otherwise little seemed to have changed. On top of his shirt, Shimon (Shimi, after all, no longer existed) wore a vest with the required four corner tassels (tzitzit), and in the pocket of his trousers I glimpsed a folded prayer shawl, and in his slightly slurred voice I heard a singing tone, as if he were praying. He had just returned home from his daily chores, whatever they were, sighed heavily a few times over things I didn't understand, muttered a blessing over the tea and biscuits that Michal had imperceptibly laid out for us, and turned to me with curiosity and anticipation.

Now I realized how small the apartment was. We were sitting in a hallway that was also the living room, eight square meters with room for a small table and a few chairs. Every accessible part of the walls was covered with bookshelves, and each shelf was overflowing with books, many in expensive leather bindings, brown and purple with gold lettering, some more worn than others. Here were commentaries on interpretations, and interpretations on commentaries, various editions and versions of the basic texts of Judaism, collections of prayers and blessings, recorded Hasidic stories and teachings and commentaries on them. In the narrow passages that led farther into the apartment, more books were stacked.

How many more books would have fit in Ramot Polin if the architect had designed rectangular buildings?

Shimon showed me three other small rooms and a kitchen. All nine children slept on mattresses in a single room, huddled together on the floor. One room was Shimon and Michal's. The kitchen had a dining area. In a small windowless room, actually a storage closet, Shimon had set up his study. Hundreds more books were stacked on the floor and on a desk. On a wall above the desk two yellowed pictures of bearded men in large headdresses were pinned. One was said to be a rabbinic ancestor of Shimon, the other one of the great holy men of Hasidic Judaism,

Rabbi Nachman of Bratslav. The shelves of the study were filled with carefully labeled audio cassettes: recordings of lectures, discussions, interpretations. On the table hummed a small tape recorder with a copy function, and with copying in progress.

Little by little, the inhabitants of Ramot Polin had tried to free themselves from their architectural straitjacket. An empty space between angled walls had been made into a balcony where the sukkah for the autumn harvest festival could be erected.

What does Shimon think? And why?

"We need a long time," he says.

I realize after a while that we need time for different things. I want to talk about him, he wants to talk about the others. He looks suspiciously at the class photo.

"Am I in it?" he asks sincerely.

I tell him with whom I've been in contact, and he gets visibly excited. For Shimon, I am not a time machine but a spaceship. Every name, every new memory brings a forbidden world to life. I note how close to the surface the associations are, and that not all of them are harmless. How do you erase your old life without denying yourself?

After a while, he fills in some gaps in his own biography. Yes, during his high-school years both parents were abroad and he stayed with relatives. I had been led to believe that he lived in abandonment and poverty—maybe it was the sandwiches, or the fact that Shimi never invited me to his home—but in fact his parents were on a diplomatic mission to Poland, and whatever poverty there was in Shimi's life was emotional.

A year later, I would learn that his parents' postwar relationship with Europe had been anything but diplomatic. And that Itzhak "Pascha" Reichmann-Avidov and his wife, Dorka, both of whom had survived the Holocaust in a Jewish partisan unit in the forests of eastern Poland and Ukraine, must have returned to Europe with a sinking feeling in the pit of their stomachs.

And that Shimon Avidov had grown up in the darkest of Israel's shadows.

From early on, the disability of hemophilia excluded Shimon from the most important of Israeli societies, the Israel Defense Forces, a fate which he refused to accept as long as possible. Our summer together in a voluntary training camp for Gadna commanders suddenly appeared in a different and more tragic light. When a few years later, he was drafted to the regular army, he tried to get through by using false medical certificates, only to be "betrayed" by his comrades on the eve of the first combat exercise with live ammunition. Everyone knew that a small scratch would be enough to neutralize Private Avidov. He was subsequently deemed unfit for military duty and discharged.

People who had been deemed unfit for military service would be tacitly excluded from the many circles in Israel to which military service was an entrance ticket. When Shimon eventually joined the hippie colony in Rosh Pina, it only confirmed his status as an Israeli outsider.

It was in Rosh Pina that Shimon met Michal, an immigrant from South Africa, and it was from there that they began the journey back into Israeli society. For a year, Shimon worked as a veterinarian at a clinic in Yahud, where Ester had indeed seen him "with a goat on a string." Shortly afterward he set up his own practice in the prosperous coastal villa community Nof Yam, and by the early 1980s he had built up an effective business and an appreciative clientele.

After two years, Shimon closed the clinic in Nof Yam and moved with Michal to a small rented room in Jerusalem. The decision to "return" to God had been maturing for some time, influenced by new missionary impulses within Orthodox Judaism. One of the most prominent missionaries, an Orthodox rabbi named Adin Steinsaltz, had translated the Babylonian Talmud into English, and also published a relatively accessible Hebrew version with explanatory texts and drawings(!). His goal was to stop the defection of Jews from Judaism, which he perceived to be the road to the final destruction of the Jews. His target group was young Jews who had never had any contact with Jewish religious life, and who could therefore be equated, in the halachic sense, with "children raised by non-Jews." His golden opportunity was the moral and ideological vacuum left by a stagnant secular Zionism.

What Steinsaltz wanted to achieve was not a little extra Yiddishkeit to garnish an essentially modern identity, a few Shabbat candles here and a visit to the synagogue there, but a complete break with modern life. A Jew who wanted to return to God, to become a *baal teshuvah*, had to undergo a personal conversion. "The latter-day *baal teshuvah* of our time enters a new world . . . To accept Judaism in its entirety, it is not merely to set aside a certain corner of one's life as a sanctuary, outside the everyday flow of affairs, but to alter deeply that flow itself." *Teshuva* was a turning point in life that involved thousands of small steps, but had to begin with one big and decisive leap: "[T]here comes a certain moment of categorical change, a moment unlike any that came before or any that are to follow. One can pace up and down the shore or wade about in the shallows for a long time, even a lifetime, contemplating swimming but until one takes the plunge, you are not swimming."[1]

I was told that the recruitment of *baale teshuvah* had been particularly successful in artistic and cultural circles. A number of well-known Israeli entertainers had suddenly disappeared from the scene and reappeared in anonymous gatherings of black coats and big beards. Relationships with old friends and colleagues had been severed, contracts and jobs terminated, apartments and villas sold. They had taken the plunge. Sometimes overnight.

Shimon and Michal's move from Nof Yam to Jerusalem was their plunge, the decisive leap into a world that would henceforth govern every minute, indeed every second of their lives. Two modern people had, after careful consideration, chosen an existence that was largely incompatible with the values and practices of modern society. They had assumed duties and responsibilities that seemed to violate the "reason" of modern people. They had committed themselves to a way of life that could only be realized in the company of like-minded people. They could no longer live outside the institutional and social confines of Orthodox

Judaism. In family life, they had to assume their highly duty-bound roles as husband and wife. In community life, they must have daily access to a minyan, the circle of ten adults required to hold services. They must have a Torah school for their young children, a Talmud school for their slightly older ones, facilities for keeping the Jewish dietary laws, ritual baths for women and men, an Orthodox burial society, a mohel, and hundreds of other formal and informal institutions without which Jewish Orthodox life would be impossible. "For all these reasons," he concluded, "it is vital that a *baal teshuvah* find a suitable social environment as soon as possible."

"The offer of the apartment in Ramot Polin came as a gift from the Holy One, blessed be He," says Shimon.

At regular intervals, the children come forth to look at the strange guest in his odd clothes.

What had Shimon been looking for? And what had he found? A world without cracks. A world giving meaning to every action and event. A world providing divine guidance in every sphere of human life. A world that the Jewish Enlightenment had believed it could educate and reform. A world that Zionism had believed it could leave behind. A world that had been almost eradicated in the Holocaust.

It was certainly not a world that Shimon had inherited from his parents. Like so many others of their generation, they had despised it and fought against it. But it was the demise of this very world that the young Jewish partisans Itzhak and Dorka Avidov had once vowed to cruelly avenge.

UNTO THE THIRD GENERATION

In the early morning of June 23, 1992, I return to Ramot Polin. Shimon has asked me to accompany him to his yeshiva, a Talmud school, an hour's drive from Jerusalem, in an area inhabited by Jews before the 1948 war but now in the occupied West Bank. This is the day when Israel will elect Yitzhak Rabin as its prime minister and open a new chapter in its history.

"You are punctual," Michal says and smiles.

After a few minutes, Shimon comes home from morning prayer. He still has tefillin wrapped around his head and arms. We eat breakfast together: freshly baked bread, a boiled egg, a piece of melon, and, especially for me, a cheese pierogi.

The car is a Japanese van furnished with long side benches, a common design in Israel. Less common are the thick plexiglass windows. They protect not against modern high-speed weapons but rocks and guns. Shimon takes a pistol out of a black plastic bag, pushes a magazine into the butt, and puts it on the seat next to him. I don't ask anything, but he answers anyway.

"The Arabs hate us. We have broken their pride. They will never forget. Maybe the best thing would be to move them, but I don't know how to do that. Maybe self-government would be good. We shall see. In the meantime, there is war."

We make a pickup round. An elderly rabbi (one of the great sages of Jerusalem, Shimon says, Rabbi Zalman Nechemia Goldberg) gets into the front seat, and a few students, all reconverts, line up on the benches across from one another. After a while, one of them picks up a book of Tehilim (Psalms), quietly humming its texts along the way. At one point, food is slipped under our legs: two watermelons, a bag of bread, a bag of fried chicken.

Bat Ayin must be the yeshiva with the best view in the world. From the prefabricated hut on top of a hill in southern Judea, you can see for miles in all directions. The landscape is like a biblical etching by Gustave Doré. Well-tended olive groves and small patches of plowed fields spread across the rocky, centuries-old terraces. Flocks of sheep graze in the valley. Through the soon-to-dry June vegetation, the stones glow white and the clay soil red. A few hills away are the newly built white houses with red tile roofs of Betar, another national-religious settlement in the West Bank. Across the valley to the southwest, the sun-baked stone houses of the Arab village of Saffa shine in the bright morning light, the sense of proximity surreal. This area, hebraized Gush Etzion, was home to the only Jewish settlements to have fallen into Jordanian hands during the 1948 war, which seems to have given extra energy to the feverish settlement activities going on.

Before my eyes, factory-made mobile barracks are attached directly to the ground, one next to the other. Pipes and wires still lay bare. Israeli flags are everywhere. On the barracks serving as a post office, someone has attached a sticker saying, "Messiah is coming." On a nearby hillside new land plots are being parceled out. A tractor is already plowing furrows in the red soil. The visible remains of terracing indicate that the land has been cultivated before.

The yeshiva is housed in a large room furnished with wooden benches and bookshelves. The floor rocks when you walk on it. About fifteen people are gathered around Rabbi Goldberg, who is sitting at a desk with a glass of tea and two loaded tape recorders in front of him. The students appear to be between twenty and forty-five years old. Most wear crocheted skullcaps but are otherwise "secularly" dressed. From the waistbands of their worn jeans or cotton slacks, prayer knots protrude ostentatiously. Shimon, in his black coat, is noticeably different.

The difference is, of course, more than aesthetic. The crocheted skullcap and casual attire are the hallmarks of the religious settlers. The black-robed ultra-Orthodox are less predictable in their stance on settlements. Some see the State of Israel as a forbidden intervention into the divine scheme of things; some have embraced the settlers' messianic cult of the land; most are indifferent to the politics of the state except when it comes to subsidizing their way of life.

During a break we go for a walk. Shimon has taken off his coat in the heat. His white shirt and white vest stand out against his dark beard and black pants. The sidelocks are flapping in the hot dry wind. My shoes have thin soles and the stones and thistles go right through them. We walk past a group of settlers inspecting their newly allotted land. The ownership still seems to be disputed. Someone admits to this legally being someone else's land, but this doesn't seem to be admitting anything of significance.

As we walk down a dry riverbed quail fly up.

"The Arabs are hunting them," says Shimon.

He picks up a stone and weighs it in his hand.

"While living with the beatniks in Rosh Pina I began rethinking my life. What would I raise my children to be? What would I have to give them? Hashish? What had my parents given me? Nothing.

"During my veterinary studies in Italy, I had come into contact with Nietzsche, not directly at first, but indirectly, through the Israeli writer Pinhas Sadeh. I eventually realized that those who said that Nietzsche led to Nazism were wrong. Nietzsche wanted something else. He was looking for a new man, a man who could master the chaos and disorder of the world, a man who could find a way out of the *toho ve'boho*.

"That's what I was looking for. A way out of the *toho ve'boho*. Man must have a purpose. People who do not have a purpose must invent one. If you found a pencil on Mars"—he takes the pen out of my breast pocket and holds it up—"would you say it was by chance? No, you would realize that someone had made it, created it, and you would try to find out its purpose.

"Creation did not come about by chance. God gave us the Torah to give us the truth about its purpose and meaning. The Torah is a tree that keeps branching out, higher and higher, deeper and deeper, without end.

"At the age of five, I saw things that no one else saw. After a while I forgot about it, but I still had a strong feeling that this world was not the real world."

Things fall into place. The reticent smile, the look of surprised indulgence. Shimi never crossed the threshold to the rest of us. Our passions and ambitions did not touch him. The rules of our world remained arbitrary to him. It was a world where he could eat a live lizard one day and command his thin blood to stop the next. Shimon was born with a free relationship to material reality, you might say, and in addition he was born to parents who, for their own reasons, had not had much regard for it. Suddenly it seems less surprising that he had withdrawn from our world, than that he had stayed in it for so long.

Farther down the valley, the vegetation is greener and the traces of human hands more visible. Laboriously built stone walls line the valley and a well-tended olive grove lies ahead. Beads of sweat cover Shimon's forehead. Except from his not very field-like appearance, it almost feels like the old days. The eager, insisting voice could well have belonged to the thin fifteen-year-old boy in boots and a khaki uniform with whom I once hiked through the Red Gorge in the Negev desert.

"What were the dimensions of Noah's ark? $300 + 50 + 30 = 380$. If you multiply the numerical value of the letters in Yahweh and Adonai, one by one, what is the result? 380! What is the numerical value of the letters in the word peace, *shalom*, added to the number of letters [four in Hebrew]? $376 + 4 = 380!!!!$"

I see nothing but contorted numerical relationships, but I can see that in Shimon's eyes these are his keys out of the *toho ve'boho*.

"Spiritually, the world has never been at a lower point than now," says Shimon after a moment of silence. "Do you think it can continue like this? Do you think 'nature' has a solution to this?"

I'm not sure what he means by "this," but his gesture extends far beyond the hills on the other side of the valley.

We continue downward. The dry air is torn apart by two sonic booms. I watch the sky in vain. Shimon realizes that he is still holding my pen. And that his question hangs in the air.

"It is time for the Messiah to come. It is time for the prophet Elijah to herald his coming, as written in the Torah. Religion will again spread throughout the world. Redemption will come from the people of Israel."

He must sense how my questions are buzzing with the flies in the rising heat. Does he mean that King David's kingdom will be restored? With the Torah as its law? With a king of David's lineage? With the Temple on the Temple Mount in Jerusalem where Islam's sacred mosques stand today? Does he recognize the secular laws of the State of Israel—or only the divine laws of the Kingdom of Israel?

"What has happened has happened. We have become a people of conquest. Now we must bring the Torah back to Israel."

We reach deep into the wadi, the barracks of Bat Ayin disappear behind us, the path leads to a stone-walled olive grove; in between the olive trees there are figs, walnuts, and an occasional vine. The soil is carefully plowed. We sit down in the shade of a tree and lean against the wall. Shimon warns of scorpions.

It is indeed possible that Jews ask more questions than others, but the question that no Jew in Bat Ayin seems to have asked on this day of land distribution, plowing, and Talmudic studies is: What should we do with the Palestinians?

I ask the question.

Shimon is silent for a long time and his answer is vague and evasive. On the one hand, he says that he wants to live in peace with the Arabs; on the other hand, he says the intifada should have been dealt with harshly from the beginning, "because the Arabs want to kill us." On the one hand, prophecy tells him that the Temple must not be rebuilt by force, that the Jews shall return to Eretz Israel to prepare for the coming of the Messiah, not to build a secular state. On the other hand, the situation is what it is. The people of Israel have become conquerors. And conquests have their particular logic.

"What is it?" I ask.

"He who gives mercy to the cruel is cruel to the merciful."

After a while he repeats that the situation has no solution "according to the laws of nature." That it requires a divine intervention, a miracle.

I notice that he has brought his gun.

On the way home, we stop in Mea Shearim, an ultra-Orthodox neighborhood in the center of Jerusalem. There is something that Shimon wants me to have. It's late afternoon and the cooling streets are teeming with heavily dressed men and women. We enter bookstore after bookstore, all roughly the same, their walls covered with religious texts in leather bindings and gold. Each time Shimon walks up to the counter, I see the black-robed booksellers shake their heads or wave dismissively. In the fourth bookshop we find what we seek. An incorruptible looking Hasid bends down and takes a book from a shelf under the counter. I pay.

As we part ways in the car park below number 55 at the Ramot Polin space station, he takes my hand with surprising eagerness and warmth. Could I perhaps arrange for him to meet "the others"?

I promise to do my best. I also tell him that I want to meet his parents.

"My father appreciates what I've done," he says after a while. "Now he understands that I have something to give to my children."

I watch the black figure disappear into the darkness between the strange buildings, and take out the heavy folio-sized volume that he wanted me to have. It is the first part of Steinsaltz's illustrated edition of the Talmud, the tractate of blessings, the Masechet Brachot.

Later in the evening, it is announced that Yitzhak Rabin has won the election, and that the plowing settlers in Bat Ayin have lost ground in the Israeli parliament.

What Itzhak Avidov, a.k.a. Pascha Reichmann, had had to give his two children, I learned in full three days later, in an article published by the Israeli newspaper *Haaretz* entitled "The Avengers Are Coming Out."[2] It confirmed previously published information that immediately after the war a group of Jewish partisans in eastern Poland had planned to poison the drinking water in a number of German cities. Six million Germans for six million Jews was the unspoken motto of the operation. Named Operation Din (*din* is the Hebrew word for "judgment," but also an acronym for *Dam Israel Notar*, the blood of Israel is to be avenged), it went as far as having members of the organization infiltrate the waterworks in Nuremberg and Hamburg, waiting for the poison to be delivered. The article also claimed that a lethal poison had in fact been acquired and was on its way.

For various reasons, some of them coincidental, Operation Din was not carried out and only parts of a Plan B, a much smaller and more targeted operation, were brought to action. On April 13, 1946, a delivery of bread intended for German SS prisoners in a camp outside Nuremberg was poisoned with arsenic. The perpetrators claimed afterward that 2,800 had become sick and 900 had died, but an article in *Süddeutsche Zeitung* on April 24 claimed that only 2,283 had been sickened and none had died.[3]

Vengeance is the child of all wars. But no other "war" was like the Holocaust, and no other revenge was like that which a few Jewish partisan remnants gathered in the Lublin area under the leadership of Abba Kovner from Vilnius, later a poet in Israel, later a witness in the trial of Eichmann in Jerusalem, had sworn to enforce. The second most senior leader of Operation Din, and the head of the organization in Europe, was Pasha Reichmann, alias Itzhak Avidov, the father of Shimon.

To this day, he believes that Operation Din should have been carried out.

The ragtag bands of surviving Jewish youngsters who roamed the smoldering ruins of the Holocaust, who had lost everyone and everything but who now faced silence and indifference, even hostility, must have been among the loneliest of people in postwar Europe. Many contemplated suicide, quite a few took the plunge. For some, the idea of total revenge, a final outcry that would reverberate around the world, became the only reason to live on.

Pasha and Dorka Reichmann-Avidov had survived the end of the war in a Jewish partisan unit in the mountains and forests around the town of Baranovichi in Belarus. The leader of the group, Eliezer Lidovski, later testified to their mood as they began to realize what kind of war they had survived:

> When I returned to Rovno [in Ukraine], I met hundreds of Jewish partisans, and I will never forget their mental state. There was such total hopelessness that I had not even seen in the ghetto or in the partisan camps. Without any will to live . . . Everyone began to ask: What is the meaning of it all? Why have we stayed alive? . . . I met with Pasha and some other comrades and said: We have to do something, if only to save the partisans from desolation.[4]

Shortly afterward, Pascha encountered the man who would show them the way:

> I met Abba Kovner the night he arrived in Lublin. He was leaning against the railing of a staircase and asked, "Well, what's going to happen?" I told him that I would not leave [Europe] without taking revenge on the German enemy. Abba embraced me and kissed me. Trembling and full of emotion, he said: "Pascha, this is the only thing I have had in my head all the time. To this I have devoted time, much time."[5]

Until April 1946 and the bread-poisoning operation at Stalag 13 on the outskirts of Nuremberg, Kovner's and

Reichmann's revenge organization was entirely focused on the main operation. Reichmann set up headquarters in Munich, while other members of the group took strategic positions throughout Germany. Kovner traveled to Palestine to seek organizational support and obtain a suitable poison.

What Kovner and his group would have used the poison for, had they had the chance, we will never know. In December 1945, on board a British warship going from Alexandria to Toulon, Kovner, disguised as a soldier of the British Jewish Brigade, was arrested by the British authorities and spent the following months in prison, first in Toulon, then in Cairo and Jerusalem. Decades later, people who had been on the ship claimed that he had brought the poison with him, packed in cans of tinned milk that he kept in a tarpaulin bag carried over his shoulder. When the ship was stopped outside the port of Toulon and Kovner was told to report to the bridge, he handed the bag to an uninitiated Jewish soldier. When Kovner did not return, he threw the bag through a valve into the sea, believing it to contain compromising explosives or weapons.[6]

The conspirators' version is that the big plan was still valid, and that it was the one for which the poison had been intended. The men who had infiltrated the waterworks in Hamburg and Nuremberg had located the places where the poison was to be added and marked the pipes to be excluded. There are also letters from Kovner in August 1945 urging the organization in Europe to concentrate on Plan B. Time had run out. German cities were beginning to fill up with Allied soldiers and their families, non-German refugees, and even Jews. It was no longer easy to "kill Germans." Kovner was probably also influenced by the lack of support in Palestine for a "total war of the Jews against the Germans." He could not even raise the issue with more than a few confidants.

Be that as it may, after the bread-poisoning action in Nuremberg, Operation Din effectively died. In the summer of 1946, Pasha and Dorka arrived in Palestine along with several others in the group of avengers. For decades their story remained hidden and forgotten, the conspirators themselves didn't want to tell it, perhaps to hide their failure, perhaps because few would understand, let alone accept, what they had set out to do.

This did not mean that they had forgotten, or that others had. The idea of revenge had been on the minds of many more survivors than the apocalyptic avengers of Operation Din. In fact, revenge was a strong impulse immediately after liberation. And once the desire for revenge had subsided or was repressed, the memory of the injustice and humiliation festered like a dark stain in people who looked perfectly normal and healthy on the outside, and who gave birth to seemingly perfectly healthy and normal children. Like the submerged part of an iceberg, they formed an invisible reservoir of unresolved anger and bitterness, of frozen hardness and fear, stored beneath the surface of the emerging new state.

Indeed, calls for revenge were at times widespread. A prominent political figure, Meir Yaari, the secretary-general of the left-wing Zionist kibbutz movement, raised the issue in a farewell speech to the Jewish Brigade traveling to

Europe in February 1945: "We cannot make a distinction between the German masses and their leaders. There is not only a Nazi top layer but also a huge middle layer about which we do not know how long it will take for the poison in their souls to dissipate. We must not let mercy and reconciliation lead us astray."[7]

As news of the death camps began to spread, high-pitched demands for revenge were expressed in normally cautious Palestinian Jewish organizations and newspapers. "May every hand in Israel be stretched out to avenge the victims," proclaimed the Hebrew Writers' Union. "The murderers must know that the day of vengeance will come, as it is written: 'An eye for an eye, a tooth for a tooth,'" read an opinion piece in *Haaretz*. In the Labor Zionist party organ *Davar*, a heated debate took place in the late fall of 1944 between those who demanded that the issue of revenge be placed at the top of the Zionist agenda and the editorial board, which warned against emotional outbursts that could endanger "our national interests." *Ha'olam*, the Jerusalem-based organ of the World Zionist Organization, published an article calling for the killing of a German prisoner of war for every Jew killed, which in turn prompted a response from the magazine's editor who argued that a distinction must be made between individual Germans and the German nation. Revenge against individual Germans was unforgivable, he wrote, "but I am prepared to impose on the German people as a whole an unlimited amount of suffering and torture to be endured for hundreds of years, until the sin has been burnt up and purified." In 1944, the Hebrew writer Nathan Alterman published a collection of poems that was ostensibly about God's plagues on Pharaoh's Egypt, but which could easily be rendered a more contemporary interpretation:

Righteous in its judgment is the sword,
but wherever it extends its arm
it leaves behind
like the taste of salt
the tears of the innocent.[8]

Many argued that the idea of revenge was incompatible with the ethics of Judaism, and that the German leaders responsible must be prosecuted and tried according to the law. Some were already saying what Hannah Arendt some ten years later would put in writing: that this was an evil so radical that it could neither be punished nor forgiven.[9] The pro-Soviet faction of the Zionist movement seemed happy to delegate the avenging role to Comrade Stalin. The avengers themselves seemed to have made the calculation that with an apocalyptic act of vengeance they would make continued Jewish existence in Europe all but impossible and provide the Jewish state with its ultimate raison d'être.

In the spring of 1945, Itzhak and Dorka Avidov had believed that the purpose of their lives was to avenge six million murdered Jews. Fifty years later, they still pondered what went wrong. Who betrayed us? What if we had succeeded? Second thoughts and regrets marked their lives like unhealed wounds.

An unredeemed past is what they had had to give to their children.

Retired insurance executive Itzhak (Pascha) and retired teacher Dvora (Dorka, a.k.a. Karol) Avidov lived in a townhouse filled with books and art on Six Day Street in Ramat Hasharon, a lush and prosperous middle-class community just north of Tel Aviv. They greeted me with warmth and curiosity. Itzhak was a vital man in his seventies, of medium height and proportionate build, with well-trimmed gray hair, and with a certain eagerness in his voice and gestures. I could easily imagine him as a young man with burning eyes, lean cheeks, and unruly black hair, much like Kovner in the photos from the Jerusalem courtroom in 1961. Dorka was a vivid and intense lady of about the same age who offered coffee and homemade cakes in the living room, but who very soon let me know that her role in this family story was not that of the housewife.

They asked me about my meetings with Shimon, about our shared past, about Sweden, about myself, but both were fully aware of why I had wanted to see them. After fifty years, they too were eager to tell, to explain, to justify. In the recent burst of publicity, Operation Din had been portrayed as a mindless, immoral, and unrealistic revenge fantasy of an isolated group of desperate but not very capable survivors. Key elements of the narrative had been called into question and the whole project had taken on a nimbus of insanity, and Itzhak and Dorka were no longer alone with their memories and doubts. A battle for history had begun, and no niceties were needed before we got to the heart of their story.

Itzhak was born into an Orthodox Jewish family in the small town of Zduńska Wola near Łódź in Poland. As a teenager in the turbulent years before the war he was drawn to communism and its promise to abolish antisemitism. In November 1939, he and Dorka fled from the Nazi-occupied part of Poland into the Soviet part. The first year they hid with a Ukrainian woman who had taken a liking to them, but in the summer of 1941 they went "straight to the forest" and joined a communist partisan unit. Here they were quickly converted to Zionists as they discovered that Russian and Ukrainian communists disliked Jews as much as other Russians and Ukrainians, and that communism was not the solution to the Jewish problem.

Instead, Jews had to form their own partisan units. They were less well equipped, more vulnerable, often harassed by others, but intensely aware of what was happening to the Jews around them. From the edges of the forests in Belarus, Ukraine, and eastern Poland, they witnessed villages burned down, mass executions carried out, mass graves dug, and transports to death camps rolling by.

"When we came out of the forest and returned to the cities, and saw the people living much as they had before, in their houses with their families, with only the Jews, our families, our world, our friends, our loved ones, missing, we all thought: We don't want to live in a world where this could have happened. How could we continue our lives, maybe travel to Palestine, without taking up the cause of the murdered?

"We met Abba Kovner's partisans in Rovno in April and May 1945, and we became obsessed with the idea of doing something so shocking and cruel that the world would never be able to doubt what had happened and why it had been done. We were not possessed by murderous instincts, we were certainly not Nazis, but we could think of nothing else, and we felt that our response had to be as unbelievable as the murder of the Jews had been, or no one would believe it. We didn't want to kill for the sake of killing, like the Germans, we just wanted to convey to the world that what the Germans had done was so incredibly insane, that the revenge had to be insane as well.

"We were tormented by so many questions. How could seemingly normal people do this? How could a cultured people who loved Chopin, Mozart, and Beethoven, millions of educated and well-read people, say to the Jews: You are not human, you are nothing, you are insects, flies, you have no place under the sun? Should the Jewish people not give a response to that? Should we not give a response to the two Germans who came to my sister in Zduńska Wola and took away her three-year-old child? Should we remain silent?

"But six million Germans? Children? Women?

"For us, coming out of the forests, there were no limits. Six million, sixty million, six hundred million, children, women, what did it matter? The Germans, that was all that mattered. We didn't think of surviving the action ourselves, the plan was that one of us, two at most, would be left to testify."

Dorka passed the cakes around for the fourth time. Itzhak pulled out a picture of his parents. He had found it after the war in the house of his childhood, where other people now lived. The two of them had been talking nonstop for an hour and a half, taking turns, interrupting each other, trying to see if I had understood. I had expected some kind of detachment from the past, maybe even a sigh of relief that Operation Din never happened, but in this friendly, educated, middle-class home in north Tel Aviv, two people were living with a nagging feeling of having failed their mission.

"We should never have left Europe before the mission was accomplished," said Itzhak. "I still mourn that we did not succeed. If we had, the Jewish people would be safer today."

I looked at him in amazement.

"Don't you see?" he pleaded. "The witnesses have not yet died, and there are already those who deny that the Holocaust happened. Would they have been able to do so if we had succeeded? If the memory of our catastrophe had been inseparable from the memory of our revenge?"

What could I say?

It was dusk when I said goodbye to the Avidovs in Ramat Hasharon. A cool breeze was blowing from the sea. It was the week after the historic handshake between Rabin and Arafat. Toward the end we talked politics. Itzhak and Dorka were in the peace camp. The Jews must not become a people of force, they said. The Arabs must be given full rights, Israel must give up land for peace. Both were upset by the abuse of Holocaust symbols for right-wing nationalist purposes; Rabin and Arafat in Nazi uniforms, the PLO compared to the SS, Israel confronting another Auschwitz.

Paradoxically, almost all the avengers, including Dorka and Itzhak, had belonged to the left-wing Zionist movement Ha'shomer Ha'tzair. The same young people who were willing to kill millions of anonymous Germans, good and bad, were also embracing the utopian vision of a world without conflict, violence, social classes, and, of course, without racism and antisemitism. Perhaps they needed a vision big enough to continue living for. Perhaps revenge and vision were linked in the same twisted way that a bloody revolution was linked to the classless society.

At the door, they asked me if I was going to see Shimon again.

"Yes," I said.

"You know, he has always been a seeker," said Dorka. "He could have started to believe in Jesus. There are Jews who do that."

I suspect she favored Rabbi Nachman of Bratslav after all.

My meetings with Shimon prompted a rapidly organized reunion of our class. For the longest time I suspected he wouldn't come, but when we gathered at Ester's house in suburban Yahud, he arrived more punctually than most; in secular Israel, no party starts before nine in the evening, no matter when it is due to begin. A little later, Alex and Chaja arrived from kibbutz Nir Oz on the border of Gaza, followed by Gili, Ronit, and Miriam from Tel Aviv and its suburbs. They could have come from even farther. Geographical distances are not obstacles in Israel. Human distances may be. Between Ramot Polin and Yahud there are four miles—and four light-years.

Meeting Shimon was not the culture clash that some had feared. He didn't mumble prayers in his beard, he didn't rant about the sanctity of the Torah, he wasn't absent or strange. He took the fruit from the table and drank the coffee. In fact, he was so unmistakably the same person as before, the same laugh, the same slightly surprised look, that the conversation soon flowed freely. Old photos were brought forth, stories were told and retold, shared experiences were remembered, ties were reestablished.

We left a few hours after midnight. I felt a strong sense of affinity with these people, whose story was so much my own, whose lives I had shared for a few crucial years, but whose future destiny had been shaped in a crossfire of historical upheavals. They had tried hard to live normal lives as modern, educated Europeans. They had built fine careers and tasteful homes, they had beautiful children and didn't look too bad themselves. Materially, they were better off than many Swedes in similar positions. They had tried to live as if everything were normal—when in fact nothing was. There was an element of anxiety and restlessness in their life stories. Surprisingly many had tried to emigrate or settle abroad, some had rediscovered their European identity, others were searching for new ideals in the void of ideals lost.

Back then, everything had seemed so clear and obvious. Now, we all saw the shadows behind us.

IV

THE LOST LAND

■

"There is nothing more sacred on earth than
human blood.
That is why our country is called the Holy Land."
"Is my hometown Haifa also sacred?"
"Every place in our country has been sanctified
by the blood of the slain . . .
and will continue to be sanctified, my son."

—EMILE HABIBI, *THE SECRET LIFE OF SAEED: THE PESSOPTIMIST*

THE LAND UNDER THE STONES

> I shall carve the name of every stolen plot of earth
> and all along the former borders of my village,
> which houses were blown to pieces, what kind of trees
> were torn up,
> what wildflowers were crushed,
> just in order to remember. And I shall carve every act of
> my fateful drama, every phase of the catastrophe,
> everything, large and small,
> in an olive tree in the backyard of my home.
>
> —TAWFIQ ZAYYAD

I remember Tetley raising its shutters early in the spring of 1967, which doesn't necessarily mean that it was unusually warm that year, just that it wasn't particularly cold. The owners of the little outdoor teahouse under the towering elms in Kungsträdgården in Stockholm proceeded from the assumption that if it wasn't too cold to sit outside without freezing your ass off, there was no place you'd rather do it than right there. So there I sat in the afternoons, drinking tea and watching the days get longer. In Vietnam the National Liberation Front (NLF), was about to give the USA a run for its money, in China the Cultural Revolution was gearing up to rescue communism from the blind alley of Soviet revisionism, in the West monopoly capitalism hung by the fragile thread of false consciousness, and in the bright Stockholm evenings the world seemed transparent and clear. By the end of May it must have become quite warm, as I remember the burgeoning elm trees casting their restless, murmuring shadows over the ever gloomier news reports from the Middle East.

At the time I was studying mathematics at the University of Stockholm, and some months earlier I had joined Clarté, a traditional leftist student organization that had turned Maoist and was now spearheading the movement against the war in Vietnam. You might say that my joining the group was pure coincidence, but in retrospect it was inevitable that I would eventually link up with the revolutionary left. Barely three years had passed since my involuntary "descent," and I missed the wide panoramas, the clearly articulated goals and ideological fellowship that Israeli society had to offer. For at least six months after my return to Sweden, I spoke Swedish with a Hebrew accent, and for even longer I regarded my descent as a temporary retreat. I was actively involved in the Zionist youth movement Ha'bonim (the builders), and the first two summers I made my way back to Israel by train and boat masquerading as a travel guide (I was seventeen at the time so may the travel agency and my fellow travelers forgive me), doing my little part to keep the Zionist dream alive.

The antiwar movement, with its elements of idealism, self-sacrifice, and ideological commitment, both challenged and strengthened my pro-Israeli convictions. It challenged them by broadening my perspective from Israel to the larger world. It strengthened them by propounding ideas and values seemingly reminiscent of those I had embraced in Israel. In fact, Israel was often described in the same terms as Cuba, as a country of collective farming, a socialist welfare system, and a people's army to its defense.

Until now, I'd had little reason to question my image of Israel. The established Swedish parties, not least the Social Democrats, still viewed the new state and its institutions with awe and admiration. European intellectuals and opinion makers looked at Israel as the happy ending to the Holocaust nightmare, a way to absolve their guilty conscience, a laboratory where the dreams of postwar reconstruction were about to be realized. To the extent that the Palestinian refugees were mentioned at all, they were generally seen as being directly or indirectly responsible for their own fate; in any case, the State of Israel was rarely held accountable. The Palestinians were an Arab problem, pure and simple. The very real and occasionally bloody conflict between the Zionist pioneers and the native inhabitants of the land quickly faded from memory. New realities and borders were soon taken for granted. Nobody could possibly picture the tiny, pencil-thin country as a threat to Arab security interests. Quite the contrary, it was the Arab countries who threatened the Jewish state and refused to acknowledge its existence or even mention it by name; nor did they think twice before engaging former German Nazis as military advisers.

There were those who tried to present a different and darker picture of Israel, using words like "conquest," "colonization," and "expulsion," but few in Europe took them seriously.

Neither did I.

Consequently, in the spring of 1967, I was deeply concerned for the survival of Israel. In May, the headlines went black. On May 14, the Egyptian president Gamal Abdel Nasser dispatched two army divisions to cross the Suez Canal into Sinai and take positions along the Israeli border. On May 17, Nasser demanded that the UN withdraw its monitoring forces from Sinai, Gaza, and Sharm el-Sheikh at the Straits of Tiran at the entrance to the Red Sea, which, to the surprise of many, the UN's secretary-general U Thant agreed to and implemented two days later. On May 22, Egypt blocked the Straits of Tiran from all traffic to the Israeli port of Eilat. Egyptian and Syrian rhetoric became increasingly belligerent. On May 30, Jordan joined the Egyptian-Syrian military pact. On June 4, Iraq followed. Regardless of your view of the roots of the conflict and the plight of the Palestinian refugees, few were untroubled by the prospect of Israel being militarily defeated and politically annihilated.

At Tetley, however, anxiety gradually gave way to a new certainty. A growing number of comrades had now learned that the world revolutionary avant-garde in Beijing was not on the side of Israel but on the side of the Arab states, and that in the struggle between imperialism and the peoples of the Third World, Israel was on the side of imperialism, and that Israel's rapid and astonishing victory was not to be celebrated but to be seen as defeat in the larger scheme of things.

For my part, I was determined to show that the cause of Israel was fully compatible with all the other and greater causes to which I was committed. Soon after the war I went to Israel to bolster my position. I arrived in late June, when the presence of Israeli troops along the Jordan River and the Suez Canal, and in the Golan Heights near Damascus, was still a new and unaccustomed fact of life. With the exception of Jerusalem, these conquests seemed anything but permanent. On June 19, a week after the end of the war, the Israeli government even adopted a proposal to return most of the occupied territories to the Arab countries in exchange for recognition and peace. Perhaps the Israelis knew in advance what the answer would be. In any case, the logic of peace was soon lost, and the logic of occupation was taking hold. New geographical and demographic realities emerged, especially in and around Jerusalem. Palestinian neighborhoods near the Western Wall were demolished, villages were erased, maps appeared without the 1949 "green" armistice borders. I pored over newspapers and magazines, engaged in discussions with all and sundry, toured the still-smoking and deserted Golan Heights, learned of the new refugee camps on the other side of the Jordan, noted the rapidly growing public opinion in favor of a Greater Israel, got to know Jewish Israelis who were critical of Zionism, and made my first Palestinian Arab contacts. New histories were put into my hands, old truths were questioned, and hitherto unknown perspectives became visible. I remember this first postwar summer in Israel as a time of relief, hope, confusion, and a nagging sense of deception.

This was the summer I discovered the land under the stones.

The occupation of new territories soon made clear that Israel was not just about territory. Before 1967, one could have been forgiven for thinking that if only there were secure and recognized borders, the conflict would come to an end and peace would break out. After 1967, it became increasingly evident that the geographical dimensions of the territory were secondary to its ideological significance. What mattered was the Jewishness of the territory, not its size. Those who opposed retaining the occupied territories generally did so out of concern for the Jewish character of Israel. Those who wanted to colonize them also wanted to make them Jewish.

Prior to the 1967 war, the ideological conquest of the land had been pursued within the armistice borders, partly through the continued but little-noticed Judaization of Arab lands, mainly in parts of the Galilee where Arabs were still in the majority, and partly through the irrigation and cultivation of the northwestern Negev desert between Beersheba and Gaza. After the war, Israel was in control of territories that had at least as much emotional, historical, and religious value as even the coastal and Galilee areas. If the Jews could claim a historical right to Judaize the former Arab cities of Haifa, Tiberias, or Jaffa, they could reasonably claim an even greater right to Hebron and Jerusalem. And if they could not claim the right to Judea and Samaria (as the territory of the West Bank soon was called), on what grounds did they have a right to the Galilee?

Those who feared the agonizing consequences of the question did not ask it. Those who pushed for further Judaization of the land asked it with increasing fervor. "The land is ours if we occupy it and build on it," read one of the many proclamations reflecting the changing public mood after the victory. A war fought in defense of what most of the world had come to accept as a legitimate territory led to a territorial conquest that most of the world considered to be illegitimate, not to say illegal.

Before the 1967 war, Zionism was able to successfully justify its state-building project by reference to the Holocaust, European betrayal, the international community's responsibility for the Jews, Israel's smallness, the intransigence of the Arabs, and the world's admiration for the vitality of Israeli society. The carefully cultivated Zionist myth that the Jews had come to live in peace with the Arabs, that the Zionist project had not harmed the Arabs of Palestine but had benefited them, that it was the Arabs who had caused the refugee problem, was still credible in much of the outside world. For a time, Israeli claims to the newly occupied territories were bolstered by arguments for more secure and defensible borders, and were characterized, at least on the part of the Labor Party, by caution and ambiguity. But the genie was out of the bottle. Previously suppressed arguments for colonization and Judaization were now brought out into the open. The 1967 war, ostensibly a war between states, revealed with disturbing clarity the inherent conflict between an ideology based on the colonization and Judaization of the "Land of Israel" and the people who happened to live there.

Jewish Israelis who recognized the historical conflict, and perhaps always had, hoped to draw a clear line between the new and the old territories. Without a sharp distinction between Jewish rights to pre-1967 Israel and Jewish rights to Judea and Samaria, the ideological edifice of Labor Zionism would collapse. If the religious settlers who tried to colonize Hebron were given the status of Zionist pioneers, the status of the Zionist pioneers would be diminished, and the struggle for a Jewish state would be compromised. They tried as much as possible to defend the old Zionism against the new, but in vain. When their own history was not turned against them, they were beaten over the head with newly created facts on the ground. In the years after 1967, the Labor Zionist ideology was destroyed by its own irresolvable contradictions. What remained was a battlefield of naked conflicts of interest between Jews and non-Jews, of blatant military occupation, of ethnic and messianic terrorism, of cynicism and self-deception, and, in a few cases, of rethinking and resistance.

For me it was all a profoundly unnerving experience. I had already realized that my adolescent perception of Israel was limited and naive, that there were things there I had never even dreamed of looking for, much less taking to heart. Even before the 1967 journey, I had come to understand, at least on a theoretical level, the dimensions of the refugee problem, and I slowly began to shake my well-held belief that the Zionists had settled an empty land, or at least a land where they did not encroach on anyone. I was ready to find spots on the sun, to nuance my image of Israel, to meet criticism halfway, in order to save at least something of my own past.

But nothing could prepare me for the feeling of emptiness and bitterness that spread as the ideological veils were torn away and one pioneer myth after another was cut to shreds. Close, close beneath the land I had once rooted myself in and loved, lay a land filled with violence, injustice, and hatred. And in between, a growing layer of lies, falsified history, and plowed-up house grounds. I felt deceived, betrayed, and robbed of my memories. Nothing in Israel was the same anymore. My carefree, sunny, buzzing Tel Aviv had become a strange and inhospitable city. People I had just been close to became unreachable. The political hypocrisy made me sick. The historical ignorance and indifference became unbearable. I stepped out of the circle of tacit codes and signals, and became an outsider with unacceptable, dangerous thoughts in my head. I could no longer travel across the country without seeing what was missing rather than what was there. Once, I had hiked across the Galilee without noticing the scattered remains of stone foundations that sometimes lined my path. Now I saw the stones everywhere. I became obsessed with tracing the names of the villages buried beneath the groves and fields of the kibbutzim and moshavim of Israel. These once enticing collectivist societies, whose distinctive entrance signs bearing the symbol of Keren Hayesod, the Jewish land fund, had once signaled future and community, were becoming ideological bastions of a system built on conquest and expulsion. In all the many ways I had once identified with Zionism, I now identified with its historical critics.

The reassessment was certainly a radical one, and it was the most painful and most profound of my political experiences. What I was to discover during my frantic fact-finding tours in the summers of 1967 through 1970 would permanently immunize me against every form of nationalist rhetoric, every demand for blind allegiance. In retrospect, I realize that it was the Palestinian issue that kept me within the radical left during these years, not the other way around. On a matter that was crucial to my identity, the left had been correct and I had been wrong. Most of my new Israeli friends were on the radical left, a phenomenon due more to the peculiar political landscape in Israel (the only party where you were legally permitted to be an anti-Zionist was the Communist Party) than a consequence of the anti-Zionist position itself. There was no logical reason to why you had to be a communist to be enraged by the expulsion of people from their homes, the ethnic monopolization of the land, the overt and covert discrimination of a minority population. In that sense the critique of Zionism was based on basic liberal and democratic principles. Nevertheless, stepping out of the ideological community of Zionism came at a high personal cost and demanded a considerable strength of conviction.

In my Swedish Jewish environment, I was met with incomprehension and outright hostility. Whatever facts I brought forth to bolster my case were either angrily denied or ignored. Soon I was considered a traitor, a Jewish self-hater who had turned against his own people. I found myself not only deceived of my Israeli past but maligned about my motives as well. I felt like the Israeli Jewish woman Irit in David Grossman's book *Sleeping on a Wire*, who, when she marries Rasan, a Muslim Arab, finds herself living in a strange and frightening land:

> I suppose I was very naïve when I lived in Tel Aviv. [. . .] Israel was something holy for me. I was very patriotic. Then suddenly it all became questionable. I met Rasan and I witnessed things I couldn't believe were happening here. I began to be frightened. I discovered all kinds of things I hadn't known about the Jewish people, my people. The world changed before my eyes. I was afraid for my life and that of my partner. I thought, One day they'll come and bang on the door and take us away, and no one will lift a finger.[1]

Once the gates to the land under the stones had opened, nothing could be the same. My hardwired emotional links with the land were slowly breaking down. The landscape whose smells, colors, and light had evoked memories of hikes, friends, and wide vistas now evoked the feeling of something forever lost. And if I was experiencing a loss, how much more so did those whose land lay beneath the stones? At times, I could hear their voices:

We are from Ruwais . . .
We are from al-Hadatha . . .
We are from ad-Damun . . .
We are from Mazraa . . .

And we are from Shaab . . .
We are from Miy'ar . . .
And we are from War'at as-Sarris . . .
We are from as-Seeb . . .
We are from el-Bassa . . .
We are from el-Kabri . . .
We are from Iqrit . . .
We are from Kufr Bir'im . . .
And we are from Dair el-Qasi . . .
We are from Saasaa . . .
We are from el-Ghabisiy . . .
And we are from Suhmata . . .
We are from as-Safsaf . . .
And we are from Kufr Inan . . .[2]

What had I discovered? Human nature and the relentless march of history, said those who knew but had said nothing before. History was replete with peoples who had displaced other peoples, and of borders being redrawn and redrawn again.

What I had discovered, however, was something other than the relentless march of history. It was the deliberate rewriting of history. Maybe those who were now saying what they hadn't said before were right: Israel had only done what so many other nations and states had done before it. It had done to the Palestinians what the Russians did to the Volga Germans, or the Poles to the East Prussians, or the Turks to the Greeks, or the Americans to the Indigenous peoples, but that was not what I had been told. I had been brought up believing that Israel was a blessing not only for the Jews but also for the Arabs, that we had taken nothing from anyone, conquered nothing that was not ours, cultivated nothing that was not waiting to be cultivated.

What I discovered was that I had been living a lie.

The most scrupulously constructed lie concerned the period just before and after Israeli independence in 1948, since that was when the conflict between the theory of peaceful coexistence and the reality of Jewish colonization came to a head. The founding of the Jewish state confronted Zionism with its moment of truth, a chance to make good on its declared ideals of democracy and minority rights in terms of military objectives, geographical borders, and national laws. In the space of a few years, Zionism was faced with one historically decisive choice after another—and consistently chose the path to ethnic domination and ethnic cleansing. Between the words of the Israeli Declaration of Independence of May 14, 1948, promising "complete equality of social and political rights to all its inhabitants irrespective of religion, race, or sex" and the deliberate expulsion and declassification of the Arab inhabitants of Palestine, a gap emerged that could only be bridged by a massive falsification of history.

Until 1948, the Zionist movement had not been pressed to demonstrate in practice what was meant by a Jewish state. Indeed, the very notion of a Jewish state had been largely taboo in public discourse until 1937, when the British Peel Commission presented its proposal for a partition of Palestine into a Jewish part and an Arab part, with Arabs initially in the majority in both. Drawing what appeared to be the ultimate conclusion of its own reasoning, the commission proposed that a quarter of a million Arabs be transferred out of the Jewish part and a thousand Jews be transferred out the Arab part. The 1944 opposition platform of the British Labor Party went even further and recommended the evacuation of Palestine's entire Arab population to the surrounding countries. The idea of removing the Arabs from the prospective Jewish state was, of course, openly expressed by the revisionist movement but periodically also by Labor Zionism, one of whose leaders, Berl Katznelson, envisaged large-scale population transfers in the wake of the Second World War, including an exchange of Jews for Arabs in the countries of the Middle East. David Ben-Gurion was openly supportive of the idea, most notably in a speech to the 1937 session of the World Zionist Congress in Zurich, but he later backed down for tactical reasons. Nevertheless, the Zionists who voiced any moral scruples in this regard were few and far between.

More than anything, the idea of transfer emphasized the zero-sum nature of the conflict. One man's meat was another man's poison. Land awarded to Jewish settlers was land taken from Palestinian Arabs. Jewish majority meant Arab minority. Jewish state meant a state where non-Jews had a subordinate position. When the goal of a Jewish state was first openly proclaimed by Ben-Gurion, at a specially convened Zionist conference at the Biltmore Hotel in New York on May 11, 1942, in the darkening shadows of the Holocaust, the Arab Palestinians were referred to only as "our Arab neighbors," not as prospective citizens of the future

Jewish state. The extent to which Zionists had shut their eyes to the heart of the conflict was all too evident from the shocked reaction of those who had most fervently believed that they were engaged in a project aimed at furthering the interests of Arabs as well as Jews: "Ben-Gurion's proposal completely disregards the fact that a million Arabs live here together with us—as if they did not exist at all," wrote Meir Yaari, the leader of the Ha'shomer Ha'tzair.[3]

At the time of the adoption of the UN Partition Plan in November 1947, the conflict was still defined in terms of which people were to control what territory. In a complicated maze of demarcation lines, with special enclaves and zones to separate the two communities as much as possible, the Jewish state was allocated more than half the area of the Palestine mandate, although Jewish institutions at the time owned only about 7 percent of the land. In the prospective Arab state, Arabs owned three-quarters of the land; in the prospective Jewish state, the Arabs owned one-third of the land and were still in the majority. Arabs also owned most of the land (80 percent) in the proposed internationalized zone around Jerusalem. In the Jewish part, just under 10 percent of the land was in Jewish hands.[4]

Just how little territory the Zionist agencies had managed to acquire during forty years of colonization was made painfully clear by the fact that even after the territorial gains in the 1948 war and the 1949 armistice agreement, they still owned only a little over 8 percent of Palestine. A small percentage of the added territory had been controlled by the British Mandate government but consisted mostly of rough terrain, roads, and woodlands. The rest of the land, especially the arable parts, was in Arab private or institutional ownership.

By 1961, thirteen years later, more than 92 percent of the lands of the State of Israel had been transferred into Jewish hands by ways of physical pressure and legal artifice. The widespread reports that the Arabs had fled voluntarily, leaving behind empty houses and fields to be taken over by newly arrived Jewish immigrants, was a convenient but essentially false description of what had taken place. While it was true that a great many Arabs had fled, just as people always do in times of war, the tens of thousands who attempted to return after the war were confronted by closed-off villages, blown-up houses, and expropriated land. What's more, the distinction between flight and expulsion was at times nonexistent. It was in the interests of the Zionist project to make as much of Palestine's land as possible available for Jewish settlement.

The first military operations to gain control of Arab-owned lands were conducted in the spring of 1948, before the termination of the British Mandate and the Israeli Declaration of Independence. A long-prepared military operation, Tokhnit Dalet (Plan D), drawn up by Yigael Yadin (né Sukenik), the wartime commander of Haganah, was put into action in order "to gain control of the territory of the Hebrew state and defend its borders."[5] It consisted of eight war operations designed to connect the enclave of Jerusalem with the Jewish-controlled territory and to expand its borders. In the face of often fierce Arab resistance, Jewish forces succeeded in capturing several areas that had been allocated to the Arabs in the UN plan or included in the

UN-supervised international zone around Jerusalem. Cities like Tiberias, Haifa, Jaffa (with the status of a special Arab enclave), Safed, and Akko (located in the Arab part) were completely or partially emptied of their Arab inhabitants. In cases of armed resistance, the plan proscribed that the enemy force would be destroyed and the population expelled beyond the borders of the state.[6] It was also during this period, on the night of April 9–10, 1948, that the massacre of Deir Yassin, an Arab village outside Jerusalem, took place and 250 inhabitants—men, women, and children—were murdered in a demonstratively brutal manner. The act, carried out by members of the armed Jewish nationalist organizations Irgun (Etzel) and Lehi (the Stern Gang), spread intended and predictable terror among the Arab inhabitants of Palestine.[7]

Until March 1948, not a single Arab village had been vacated or evacuated, but in the two months that followed, the Jewish forces, taking deliberate advantage of the gradual withdrawal of the British, succeeded in conquering and partially emptying Arab-populated areas both inside and outside the zones allocated to them by the United Nations. Operation Yiftach, launched on April 28, was directed at the Arabs of the eastern Galilee. Operation Khametz, launched on April 27, took control of Arab villages around Jaffa in preparation for its final conquest. Operation Matateh, launched on May 3, captured and destroyed the Arab villages connecting Tiberias to the eastern Galilee. Operation Ben-Ami, launched on May 14, captured Acre and cleared parts of the western Galilee of Arabs.[8] The military officer in charge of the coordinated actions, then

Palmach Commander Yigal Allon, was later to summarize the purpose and the results:

> Thanks to these local offensives, the continuity of Jewish territory was secured, as well as the penetration of our forces into Arab territory.
>
> The widespread Arab flight made it easier for our forces to control large areas of land, while at the same time put pressure on the enemy, forcing him to devote all his energies to receiving and organizing refugees. It is easy to imagine the sense of defeat that these refugees brought with them to the Arab territories. If the Arab states had not decided to invade, there would have been no obstacle for Hagana's forces to reach the natural borders of Western Israel in the same offensive, as the local enemy forces were by now completely paralyzed.[9]

The Arab attack on Israel on May 15 had the express purpose of thwarting the partition of Palestine and the creation of a Jewish state, but resulted in a further expansion of Jewish-controlled territory. As late as September 1948, during a cease-fire in the war, Ben-Gurion toyed with the idea of conquering the whole of the former mandate and emptying it of its Arab population. When asking his military commander Allon how many Arabs could be expected to flee on their own, Allon had replied: "As many as you decide." According to Ben-Gurion's plan of attack, a large Israeli force would overtake the fortress of the Arab Legion at Latrun and in a single thrust reach the western shore of Jordan, from where it would join units that had encircled

THE LAND UNDER THE STONES

Jerusalem from the south. "I assumed," he later noted, "that most of the Arabs of Jerusalem, Bethlehem, and Hebron would flee, as had the Arabs of Lod, Jaffa, Haifa, Tiberias, and Safed, and we would have control of the full expanse of the country north and south of Jericho." The day before the operation was to be launched, UN mediator Folke Bernadotte was assassinated in Jerusalem by members of the Stern Gang, and the plan was thwarted.[10]

Nevertheless, Zionist military actions during this period could still be presented as crucial to the survival of the state. Although there had certainly been Jewish transgressions to reckon with, the end still seemed to justify the means, not least in the immediate years after the near-eradication of Europe's Jews. That, at any rate, was how I learned to see Israel's War of Independence, and that is what I had convinced myself of for a long time.

What I would hopefully never have convinced myself of was the rationale for the newly founded state to establish laws and institutions with the sole function to seize land and property from fully present Arab owners and hand it over to Jewish colonizers. The Judaization of the land might have been an explicable modus operandi for a national-colonial movement in quest of territory, but hardly so for a professed democratic state committed to the equal treatment of all its citizens.

When, in the late 1960s, I came across the Israeli Arab lawyer Sabri Jiryis's paragraph- and statistic-filled book about the situation of the Arabs in Israel, originally published in

Hebrew (and subsequently translated by me into Swedish), it was with a growing sense of disbelief and amazement. Surely this could not be true. Could there really exist laws that made it possible to declare fully present Arab landowners as "present absentees" (*nochachim nifkadim*) in order to confiscate their land?[11] Could there be permanent emergency laws authorizing arrests, curfews, the sealing off of Arab villages and fields, the expulsion of Arab inhabitants, and the destruction of their property without a trial? Could it be that an entire population group was de facto excepted from basic aspects of the rule of law?

It didn't take long to verify most of Jiryis's claims, it was all there to be seen for anyone who cared to look. Jiryis himself was under administrative house arrest in his home in Haifa when I met him in January 1970. The administrative directive issued on April 25, 1969, by David Elazar, the commander of the Northern Military District, in accordance with the emergency laws, ordered Jiryis

- not to live outside the municipal boundaries of the city of Haifa
- not to change residence within the city of Haifa without police authorization
- not to cross the boundaries of the city of Haifa without police authorization
- to report daily to a police station (at 15:45)
- to stay at home from sunset to dawn

A month later, on February 20, 1970, Jiryis was put in administrative detention with the same disregard for jurisprudence. Shortly thereafter, he was allowed to go into exile in Lebanon. I suspect that this was the intended outcome. Administrative orders under the emergency laws did not require judicial approval, could not be appealed, and could be extended indefinitely,

When exploring the land under the stones, I would encounter the emergency laws everywhere. There was hardly an Israeli Arab family that had not been touched by them in some way. Meanwhile, in Jewish Israel one could live a whole life without knowing that the laws existed, even though they formally applied to Jews as well. And those who did know mostly did not care, or justified the laws as necessary for the security of the Jewish state.

It was a different story when the Defense (Emergency) Regulations were introduced by the British in 1945. Then it was the armed Jewish militias who were the main target and leading Palestinian Jewish lawyers at the time denounced them as an expression of "legalized terror." Ya'akov Shimshon Shapira, later Israel's attorney general and minister of justice, declared that

> the system established in Palestine by the defense laws is unprecedented in any civilized country. Even in Nazi Germany there was nothing like it . . . There is really only one type of regime similar to the one we have now—the regime of an occupied country . . . It is our duty to explain to the world that the defense laws imposed by the British government in Palestine undermine the foundations of justice in this country.[12]

The emergency defense laws of the British Mandate were taken over by the State of Israel in 1948 and have essentially been in force ever since. Over the years they have formed the basis of a legislation aimed at expanding and consolidating Jewish control of the land within the borders of the State of Israel, instituting a de facto discrimination against the Arab population. The most effective of the emergency powers in this regard is Article 125, which authorizes the Israeli military to close an area and restrict the movement of its residents. In the 1950s, it was routinely used to exclude Arabs from areas to be used for Jewish settlements. In the Zionist definition of national security, an Arab village was a security risk while a Jewish settlement was a security asset. Article 125 was supplemented in 1953 by the Israeli Land Acquisition Law, the main purpose of which was to retroactively legalize the de facto usurpation of Arab lands and to establish rules for financial compensation. Among other things, the law made it possible to validate the transfer of land "which was not in the hands of its owners on April 1, 1952." The fact that the land was "not in the hands of its owners" because they had been physically shut out from it by means of Article 125, didn't matter to the law. The law also applied to Arab land which, between May 14, 1948, and April 1, 1952, had been taken "for the purposes of essential development, settlement or security."[13]

The list of Arab villages wiped off the map in this way during the first years of the State of Israel's existence is long, but the legal arbitrariness of the process is perhaps most clearly symbolized by the two Maronite (Christian) villages of Ikrit and Biram in northwestern Galilee near the border with Lebanon. Neither village had taken part in any fighting and neither had shown any hostility to the Jewish forces, but both were forcibly evacuated by Israeli soldiers on November 5 and 15, 1948, respectively. The Ikrit people allowed themselves to be transported by truck to Rama, an Arab village farther south, with the explicit promise that they would be able to return within two weeks, that they would only have to take the bare necessities with them, that during their absence the houses and fields would be guarded by Israeli soldiers. Asked to leave the village for a few days "until the area had been cleared of hostile elements," the people of Biram did so without suspicion since they knew several of the soldiers evacuating them—they had housed them in their village weeks before. So they handed over the keys to their houses and went to their olive groves to sleep under the open sky. From a small hill nearby they could keep an eye on village. It was November and it was raining hard, and they saw people moving among the houses down below.

When, after two weeks, they began to wonder what was going on and sent a delegation of elderly men to the village to get the army's help to return, the houses were broken up and emptied, and the remains of furniture and furnishings were scattered in the streets. They were told that the land was not theirs and they were forced to leave at gunpoint.

When, after a year and a half, it became clear to the villagers of Ikrit that they wouldn't be allowed to return, they brought the minister of defense and the military commander before the Israeli Supreme Court. On July 31, 1951, the court ruled in support of the villagers' claim to their homes and property. The state had argued that since the villagers were no longer living in their villages, which were now closed military zones under Article 125 of the

Emergency Law, they could not be considered permanent residents anymore. The villagers pointed out the obvious, that they were not in their villages because the army had ordered them to leave. "We hold," the Supreme Court wrote, "that the defendant [the state] can no longer deny that the plaintiffs are permanent residents."

When the people of Ikrit happily approached the military commander to have the sentence enforced, he referred them to the minister of defense, who referred them to the military commander. On September 10, 1951, as the execution of the sentence seemed imminent, the military commander issued a new decree based on an emergency law from 1949 stating that Ikrit had to be evacuated for security reasons and that all its inhabitants had to be expelled (served with "exit orders"). The villagers again approached the Supreme Court, which was scheduled to hear their case on February 6, 1952. But on December 24, 1951, Christmas Eve (yes, that too), Israeli army units entered the village and blew its houses into bits and pieces.

The residents of Biram suffered a possibly even more bitter fate. In September 1953, almost five years after they had been lured away from their village, they too were vindicated by the Supreme Court, only to witness from a nearby hillside how, on September 16, 1953, in a gigantic show of force, Israeli infantry and aircraft blew up, shelled, and airbombed the empty village, leaving no house standing. The lands of Ikrit and Biram were immediately taken over by neighboring and newly established Jewish agricultural colonies. Scattered stones, a reopened cemetery, and a restored church are all that remain of Ikrit.[14]

THE LAND UNDER THE STONES

Many years later, in January 1970, I would find myself walking in the ghostly remains of a similar operation. On June 11 and 18, 1967, after a formal cease-fire had taken effect, three Arab villages in the Latrun area between Tel Aviv and Jerusalem—Yalo, Emmaus, and Beit Nuba—were razed to the ground. Two and a half years later, the yellow-white stones of the demolished houses were still clearly visible underneath rapidly growing eucalyptus plants and twisted iron rods. A nature reserve, Canada Park, was in the making, and within a few years all traces of the three villages would be wiped out.

We found some of the former villagers living in the Kalandia refugee camp outside Ramallah. Ibrahim, a forty-five-year-old man with a face marked by another twenty years, had managed to save his photo album and showed us pictures of solid stone houses, colorful orchards, and smiling people. That was Yalo. He also showed us a photo of a white-haired man in traditional Arab dress: "This is my father. He was killed when they destroyed the village. He was old and could not move without help."

Amos Kenan, a well-known Israeli journalist, author, and previous member of the Stern Gang, took part in the operation and wrote down what he had experienced:

> The platoon leader told us that there were orders to blow up three villages in our area: Beit Nuba, Emmaus and Yalo. We were ordered to search the houses in the village and capture armed men. Unarmed men were to collect

their belongings and told to go to the nearby village of Beit Sura.

Beit Nuba was built of fine carved stone; some houses were simply magnificent. Each house was surrounded by an orchard, olive trees, apricots, vines, cypresses. Everything was well looked after. Among the trees were well-tended vegetable gardens.

In one of the houses we found a wounded Egyptian commanding officer and some very old people. At noon the first bulldozer arrived and demolished the first house on the edge of the village.

Within ten minutes, the house and everything inside the house had been turned into a gravel pile; the olive trees, the cypresses were uprooted . . . After three houses were destroyed, the first group of refugees arrived from Ramallah. We didn't shoot, but we took up positions and soldiers who knew Arabic met to give the warning. There were people so old they could barely walk, mothers with children in their arms, mumbling old ladies, small children. The children were crying and asking for water. Everyone was carrying white flags.

We told them to go to Beit Sura. They told us that they had been chased away everywhere, that they had not been allowed to enter a single village, that they had walked on the roads for four days, without food, without water. Some had died on the way. They asked to come back to their village and said that otherwise we might as well kill them. Some of our soldiers started crying.

More and more groups of refugees arrived, eventually numbering in the hundreds. They could not understand why they had been told to come back (they had been urged to return by Israeli radio broadcasts) when they were forbidden to enter the village. We couldn't stand their prayers. Someone asked why we destroyed their houses instead of taking them over ourselves.

We drove them away. They continued walking southwards. Like lost cattle. The weak died. In the evening we realized that we had been deceived, also in Beit Sura bulldozers had started to destroy the village and refugees had been forbidden to enter it.

We were beside ourselves in our group. At night we were ordered to put guards on the tracked tractors, but the group was so furious that no soldier would accept the duty. The next morning we were removed from the area.

None of us understood how Jews could behave like this. None of us understood why these poor farmers were not allowed to take their stove, their blankets, some food.

The chickens and pigeons were buried in the ruins. The fields were destroyed before our eyes. The children who disappeared crying down the road will be guerrillas in nineteen years, until the next war.

That is how we lost our victory.[15]

Numerous Arab villages would be wiped out in the newly occupied territories after 1967, and for some time security concerns were used to mask ideological goals. It was a security interest to settle the Latrun area in order to safeguard the passage between Tel Aviv and Jerusalem, as it was a security interest to settle the Syrian Golan Heights, where hundreds of abandoned Arab villages were destroyed. The Golan, annexed early on by Israel, became the object of a classic Labor Zionist colonization, with secular Jewish collective farms established on the ruins of Arab villages, often with only a slight hebraization of the Arabic names. The village of Khispin became Kibbutz Kasrin, Ain Ziuowan became Ein Ziwan, the tourist resort of Neve Ativ was established on what was once the village of Jobata, etc. Traveling the area in those first years of upheaval I saw abandoned toys lying outside still-standing houses in the not yet demolished ghost villages pocking the harsh but fertile highlands.

In the West Bank, by contrast, the security motives for Jewish settlements were soon hard to distinguish from the religious-national goal to establish Jewish control of the Land of Israel. Those within the Israeli government who wished to pursue the security argument (Allon and Dayan) quickly succumbed to the ideological pressures. The national-religious Jewish settlements in Hebron and Kiryat Arba, in the middle of a major Arab population center, and with no security relevance whatsoever, were established with the approval of the Labor government, as did one after another of new national-religious settlements established on seized Arab land, in open deviation from the "security" locations devised by the government (the Allon Plan).[16]

Rapidly, the distinction between the reasons for settlement disappeared. Under the definition of security that had evolved in Israel before 1967, the establishment of Jewish settlements was by definition a security measure since it strengthened the Jewish character of the State of Israel and thereby its ability to exist as a Jewish state. The Israeli law professor David Kretzmer has put it this way: "The notion of 'state security' in Israel . . . is intimately bound to the definition of the state as a *Jewish* state . . . Security of the state is synonymous with the security of the Jewish collective, and that is often seen as being dependent on promoting 'Jewish national goals.' Acts that strengthen the Jewish collective are also actions that promote security."[17]

With security so defined and applied, the physical and legal displacement of the Arab population, both inside and outside the 1967 borders, was neither accidental nor incidental.

Arguably, the most important legal tool for bringing Arab-owned lands under Jewish control was a 1950 law allowing for the seizure of land and property of people categorized as "absentees." The law created a special authority for the administering of "absentee property," with discretionary power to reject and evict "wrongful" owners and to resell the property to owners more suited to the "development of the economy and the state." In the category of "wrongful owners" were individual Arab property owners or representatives of collectively owned Arab property who had left Palestine or gone to areas within Palestine "held at the time by forces seeking to prevent the establishment of the State of Israel or fighting against it after its establishment." The law took no account of whether the thus "absent" owner happened to be present when the property was declared "absent property," as it was sufficient that he had been absent "for some time . . . after 29 November 1947."

About half of the remaining Arab population in Israel thus came to be known as "present absentees." Formally, the authority had the right to return "absentee property" to owners who turned out to be present, but as a practice it did not return land claimed by Jewish settlements.[18]

With the use of this law some 70 percent of the territory of the State of Israel came to be defined as "absentee property" and was largely transferred to Jewish ownership. Considering that the state-owned land taken over by Israel from the British Mandate government constituted about 2 percent of the country's territory, that only 10 percent was owned by Jewish interests, and that consequently about 88 percent was tied to Arab ownership (a lot of desert, to be sure), one realizes the extent of the "absentee problem." The direct arable land thus made available for Jewish colonization was two and a half times greater than the hitherto accumulated Jewish land holdings in the country, according to the estimates of the UN Mediation Commission in Palestine. Of 370 Jewish settlements established between 1948 and 1953, 350 were on "absentee property." In 1954, more than a third of Israel's Jewish population lived on "absentee property." Almost a third of the country's new immigrants were housed in emptied Arab neighborhoods and towns. Agricultural products from "abandoned" Arab lands, not least olives for export, played an important role in the economy of the State of Israel during its early years.[19]

Along with the Defense (Emergency) Regulations, the Land (Acquisition for Public Purposes) Ordinance, and the Land Acquisition Law of 1953, the Absentee Property Law could be applied so that more than 92 percent of the land in Israel came to be owned or managed by institutions that were not only defined as Jewish but were also directly or indirectly prohibited from leasing or selling land to non-Jewish interests. Not only would Israel's "present absentees" never be able to regain their land; they would never be able to buy or lease any other.

Once I began to see the land under the stones, I also began to see Israeli society's deeply embedded pillars of oblivion and denial. It was less the discovery of unknown historical injustices that troubled me, than the new state's unwillingness to even see or acknowledge them. An injustice can be examined and to some extent compensated for, but denials and lies penetrate the soul of a society and corrupt it. People whose history you do not recognize, indeed whom you even refuse to acknowledge as "present," you cannot respect. And people you cannot respect, you will begin to despise. In the Israel of the early 1960s, the Palestinian Arabs were anonymized and rendered invisible, their hatred of Israel made incomprehensible, and their standing as citizens formally and practically denigrated. They were seen as an unwanted burden, not as a potential asset.

Very soon, Israelis came to see it as natural that a ministerial post in Israel could not be entrusted to an Arab, that the prime minister's adviser on Arab affairs was routinely recruited from the Israeli security service, that parties which gave voice to national aspirations of the Palestinian Arabs were dissolved. I got used to the argument that political power in Israel must be based on Jewish votes only.

For those who were not used to it, the experience could be shocking. In November 1995, in the days following the assassination of Yitzhak Rabin, a Swedish colleague and I had a conversation with a well-dressed Israeli woman at Kennedy Airport in New York. She was on her way home to Tel Aviv and we naturally expressed our distress at what happened.

"But of course, Rabin did not have a majority for his peace policy," she said.

"Why?" my colleague asked in amazement. "Did he not have the government and the parliament behind him?"

"Yes, but he did not have a Jewish majority," she explained. "He had to rely on Arab votes."

I was familiar with her reasoning, my colleague was not. She was not used to a society where de facto citizenship and human rights was determined by ethnicity and religion. She, like so many others, was not aware of the formal and informal discrimination of the Arab minority. Nor had she reflected on the fundamental conflict between a state based on the equal rights of all its citizens and a state giving preference to citizens of Jewish ethnicity. The Law of Return of 1950 stipulated that a Swedish citizen born to a Jewish mother had a stronger right to Israeli citizenship than a Christian or Muslim Arab born in the country. This overt legal distinction based on blood lineage could perhaps be defended as a temporarily justified response to the Holocaust, giving preference of entry and citizenship to people who on the same criteria had been targeted for extermination by the Nazi regime. The Law of Return was in that sense a consequence of the Nazi Nuremberg Laws of 1935.

But for how long? How long could Israel be balancing a constitutional democracy's demand for equal rights before the law "irrespective of religion, race, or sex," with the demand for special rights for people with a Jewish blood lineage? How long before the demands of a Jewish state came into conflict with the demands of democracy?

ON THE BARRICADES

Whoever is not with me is against me.

—MATTHEW 12:30

Leaving Israel, I always give Ben-Gurion Airport an extra hour in addition to the check-in hours stipulated by Israeli security regulations. I know what to expect, I don't see it as pointless routine, but I am annoyed by the routine nature of the process. My name triggers an alarm on the computer screen at the entry control, the young, usually female officer gives me a blank stare, presses a button, and asks me to wait. After a while, sometimes half an hour, a plainclothes security officer takes me to a small room behind the scenes where a fully predictable interrogation begins. Where have I been? Whom have I met? Why have I come? I don't know what they already know, but they are usually satisfied with my answers. I also don't know what they keep in the file they have on me, but I assume it is filled with almost thirty years (at the time of this edition, more than fifty years) of information about meetings with Israeli Palestinians and left-wing radical Israelis, with secret intelligence reports on the Palestinian solidarity movement in Sweden; meetings, conferences, tape recordings, surreptitious photographs, yellowed newspaper clippings. Perhaps they could cleanse the file a bit, but why would they do that? Rather a superfluous piece of information than a piece missing, must be the archival principle of every security service.

I assume they still keep records of my visit to the Jordanian capital, Amman, in September 1970. They should. I traveled as a delegate of the Swedish Palestinian solidarity movement (and a rookie journalist) to the Second World Congress of the General Union of Palestinian Students, during a period of increased Palestinian armed actions against Israel and a growing conflict between the Palestinian organizations and the Arab world. I managed to escape two weeks later, in a taxi to Beirut via Damascus, from King Hussein's devastating attack on the Palestinian bases in Jordan. Over my head (the artillery salvos against the Palestinian headquarters in the city center grazed the roof of my hotel), and before my eyes, a movement was being crushed, which only a few days earlier had proudly demonstrated its military and civic virtues. We were taken on tours of hospitals, schools, sewing sessions, and spectacular military training displays. Various Palestinian letter combinations competed for our attention. The air was buzzing with strategies and theories.

On the last day of the conference, September 6, one of the Palestinian organizations, the Popular Front for the Liberation of Palestine (PFLP), hijacked three passenger planes from Pan Am, Swissair, and TWA. The Pan Am jumbo jet, because of its size, was ordered to land in Cairo, where the passengers were evacuated and the plane was blown up, while the other two, a DC 8 and a Boeing 707, were forced down with passengers and all at the "Airport of the Revolution," a desert field near the town of Zerka north of Amman, where they were joined three days later by a British BOAC plane. We were invited to witness the surrealist spectacle. In the distance in the sweltering heat, the fuselages of the planes with their ill-fated cargo glistened like giant alien insects, and even farther away the ominous dust of mobilizing Jordanian tanks. After declaring war on "Zionism and imperialism," and calling for the overthrow of all "reactionary" Arab regimes (including the Jordanian), the young chain-smoking PFLP leaders in their khaki shirts and dark glasses eventually released their hostages in exchange for convicted Palestinian terrorists in British, German, and Swiss prisons. By then blowing up the planes they handed King Hussein all the pretexts he needed to blow up the Palestinian movements.[1]

The increasing terror against Jewish and Israeli targets was a sign of Palestinian weakness. Very soon after the 1967 war, the hopes for a Palestinian uprising in the occupied territories were gone. Israel had consolidated its military control, the Palestinian inhabitants were adapting to the new rulers, the possibilities for a Palestinian guerrilla movement to gain a foothold in the confined terrain of the West Bank were nonexistent, armed commando raids had produced many martyrs but no results. The strategy of conducting the armed struggle from across the border had spurred conflicts of interest between the Palestinian organizations and their Arab hosts.

Moreover, Palestinian commando raids against Israel regularly led to massive military reprisals against villages, towns, and vital installations in the host countries, creating growing tensions between Palestinians and neighboring communities. This was particularly evident in southern Lebanon, where the Palestinians had no traditional foothold, and where they antagonized the local Christian and Shia populations as the Israeli military reprisals across the border escalated. The decision of the Palestinian organizations to establish bases in Lebanon, thus drawing the country into confrontation with Israel, was almost certainly the first step toward the disintegration of Lebanon. In January 1970, clashes between Palestinian guerrillas and the local population were reported in southern Lebanon, and in Jordan, recurrent skirmishes with the Jordanian army foreshadowed what was to come.

Yasser Arafat's organization, Al-Fatah, and thus the majority of the PLO, hoped to balance their own interests with the interests of the host countries and the need for support from the Arab population within Israel. There were even those who argued for a policy that directly or indirectly recognized the interests and claims of Israeli Jews in Palestine. Among the Palestinian leaders I met in Amman that black September in 1970 was a plainclothes, bespectacled, slightly bald man named Nabil Shaath. Shaath was most likely the author of a series of articles in Al-Fatah's English-language organ, which for the first time seemed to accept Israeli Jews as part of a new "democratic, progressive, and anti-imperialist" Palestine. The articles explicitly polemicized against paragraph 6 of the PLO Charter (adopted in July 1968, and revised only in April 1996), which stipulated that only Jews living in Palestine before the "Zionist invasion" would be considered Palestinians—that is, allowed to remain in the country. The articles also warned against adopting anti-Jewish stereotypes and prejudices. Otherwise, they ignored most political realities, overestimating the strength of the Palestinians, underestimating the strength of the Israelis, disregarding the logic of hatred, fear, and revenge. They portrayed a Palestine where every intractable conflict would have a revolutionary solution, where Jews, Christians, and Muslims would embrace in the struggle for "a progressive, open and tolerant country for all of us," and where, consequently, "all of us" could invest "our" hopes and dreams.[2]

I was, of course, deeply captivated, not least by the recognition of the Jewish dimension of the conflict, which was central to me. A new and more realistic attitude on the part of the Palestinians toward the actually existing Israeli society could perhaps halt Israel's development of increasingly harsh and extreme positions and actions. In the light of other revolutionary expectations at the time, this one seemed no more utopian than any other. While the PLO's charter remained unchanged, and the Palestinian leadership probably said one thing to the outside world and another among themselves, I am convinced that Shaath had come to realize that the future of the Palestinians lay in a settlement with Israel, not in desperate hopes of military victory or world revolution. Twenty-three years later, not unexpectedly, he would play a central role in the negotiations leading up to the Oslo Accords.

The problem of Nabil Shaath and the Palestinian movement was of course that Israel had no interest whatsoever in negotiating with them, except to confirm their defeat. For

Golda Meir, Israel's prime minister at the time, there was no such thing as a Palestinian people.[3]

How to resist from a position of weakness? This was the seemingly unsolvable equation facing the Palestinian resistance. Until September 1970, the impression of political and military strength had been created by successful and skillfully marketed activities in the Jordanian refugee camps, by maintaining a high international profile, and by more or less accurately reported armed raids into Israeli territory. "Commandos shake the status quo and the US-sponsored peace scam," was a headline in the English-language newspaper *Fatah* that was distributed to the delegates in Amman.[4]

After the September massacre in Jordan and the subsequent expulsion of the Palestinian resistance movement from Jordanian territory, it became clear that armed struggle was a losing strategy. It certainly sharpened tensions, hardened Israeli repression, and kept the conflict simmering, but if sharpening tensions was the only achievable goal, there were other, more effective means of achieving it. As early as the summer of 1968, groups within the PLO had begun advocating for and carrying out international terrorist operations against Israeli and "Zionist" targets throughout the world. They represented the ever-latent current among Palestinians hoping for a new order to come out of chaos. Moreover, the struggle for chaos was easier than the struggle for a new order.

In these years, the order that would be born from chaos was dressed up in secular terms. The methods of terror would provoke a final confrontation between the "progressive" socialist forces of the world, led by China and the

Soviet Union, and the "reactionary" forces led by US imperialism and Zionism. In a revolutionary Armageddon, Israel would disintegrate and a new socialist, classless, secular (but simultaneously Arab) Palestine would rise.

The fact that the PFLP was suspended from the PLO Central Committee after the September 1970 hijackings had no practical significance. In fact, the defeat in Jordan seemed to intensify and popularize the Palestinian strategy of terror, with Palestinian groups increasingly joining the international band of bomb-throwing vigilantes who left ruin and death in West Germany, Japan, Italy, and Ireland in those years. In May 1972, three members of the Japanese Red Army used automatic weapons and hand grenades to mow down nearly a hundred people at Lod Airport outside Tel Aviv, killing twenty-six. In September 1972, eleven Israeli athletes were captured and killed by a Fatah-affiliated organization called Black September.

In September 1970, I witnessed at first hand the weaknesses of the Palestinian movement, among them a disturbing lack of realism when it came to their view of Israel and the Israelis. They still told themselves that Israel could be made to disappear through the right combination of political radicalism and revolutionary upheaval. They ignored the fact that newly created facts were facts as well. At most, they were ready to recognize Israeli Jews as human beings, but not as a people.

I myself, like the small Jewish anti-Zionist movement in Israel, had a different experience and a different view.

If fifty years earlier there had not been an Israeli Jewish people, there certainly was one now. This people had to be reckoned with in any Palestinian strategy, otherwise the strategy would fail. With the rise of terror, and the definition of virtually all Israelis and Jews as legitimate targets, any such strategy was abandoned. For this and other obvious reasons, I and many with me opposed terror as a method, which was not self-evident in parts of the Palestinian solidarity movement in Sweden and subsequently led to its split. One faction regarded the hijackings as "the poor man's bombs" and declared its support for PFLP, the most terror-prone of the Palestinian organizations. As in all such contexts, the split was total and irreconcilable.

The Swedish and Israeli security services of course paid no attention to such distinctions. Anyone within the sphere of Palestinian solidarity was a suspected terrorist and the subject of police scrutiny. In the summer of 1972, Omar Sufan, a Fatah sympathizer in Stockholm, had his hands ripped off by a letter bomb, and shortly afterward a popular Swedish weekly trumpeted that a group of Swedes, including myself, were "at the top of the letter-bomb list." From an official Israeli perspective, I was a security risk of the first degree and deserved a well-stocked intelligence file and an interrogation at the airport.

Already then, I knew that I had a special role to play. I was the Jew who supported the Palestinians, I was the alibi for anti-Zionism not being antisemitism. I was not the only alibi, of course, and not everyone saw me that way, and the role was absurd after all. What trauma required all Jews to speak with one tongue when it came to Israel?

But the trauma existed and the role was a fact: The presence of a single Jewish Auschwitz survivor in a Palestinian refugee camp (it happened) could do more for the Palestinian cause than a whole brigade of non-Jewish volunteers. The most potent criticism of Zionism in those years was launched by Jewish intellectuals like Noam Chomsky, Maxime Rodinson, and Nathan Weinstock. With no comparison, I was a young man still, I came to be part of the same category of "inner" critics, or, as it was often called, Jewish self-haters. In the latter capacity, I became the target of much anger and bitterness, sometimes even hatred and threats. The space for Jewish dissent on the issue of Zionism was nonexistent.

My visible presence in the Palestinian solidarity movement may have taken the edge off the most reflexive accusations for antisemitism and the most misleading attempts to equate Zionism with Judaism, but within a few years Palestinian activists would be sucked into the fiery vortex of the struggle between Israel's security services and Palestinian resistance groups, and be accused not only of antisemitism but of espionage and terrorism as well.

At the same time, the line between antisemitism and anti-Zionism became increasingly difficult to uphold. Partly because many Jewish communities and organizations identified themselves with the State of Israel and its policies, partly because historically entrenched antisemitic stereotypes could all-too easily be mobilized for anti-Zionist/anti-Israeli propaganda.

In the first years after the war of 1967, I wanted to believe that its spectacular outcome would bring a new momentum to the relationship between the Jews and Arabs of Palestine, that their intertwined destiny would become more apparent, the need for mutual reconciliation more pressing, and that the logic of colonization and Judaization could thus be countered.

What initially strengthened my belief was, paradoxically, the denials with which I was confronted as I brought forth what I saw as indisputable facts in the matter. My first and most shocking experience was the reaction to the Swedish translation of Jiryis's book. A reviewer called the book "a terrible example of falsification" and Jiryis himself "a bitterly lonely" Arab in Israel. His ample quotations from existing legal texts were said to be "distortions or outright lies," with Jiryis representing "the small minority of large Arab landowners who had had their land expropriated in Israel's first decade, when the overriding need was to settle the hundreds of thousands of refugees and other immigrants who, often destitute, poured into the country."

Based on a similar view of things, the same reviewer demanded that my contribution to an anthology on the "conflict in the Middle East," in which I detailed the Israeli emergency laws and their effects on the Arab population, should be excluded since it contained "false information." In my response, with facsimiles of house arrests, housing restrictions, and travel bans, I was sure to have proven that the emergency laws were a living reality for Israel's Arab population. Upon which the reviewer stated that emergency laws were "a perfectly normal thing: is there any state on earth that does not have it and does not apply it to those suspected, or more than suspected, of conspiring for its downfall?"

As the occupation tightened, a more critical view of Israel gained credence and support. The Israeli government, with Golda Meir and Moshe Dayan as its emblematic leaders, had become convinced that the occupied territories could be kept indefinitely and the Palestinians be suppressed forever, that status quo was a victory, and that initiatives to negotiate a lasting solution to the conflict were anti-Israeli conspiracies.[5] Meir not only denied the existence of the Palestinians but also divided the non-Jewish world into two groups, "those who have murdered us, and those who have taken pity on us. It is better to be alive and maligned than dead and pitied."[6]

Dayan, the hallowed war hero, who had come to personify the faith in Israel's invincibility, also came to personify the paternalism and contempt that characterized many Israelis' view of the Arabs. In the immediate aftermath of the war, he advocated political restraint and caution, but he soon became an opponent to any idea of peace for territory. Six months after the war, he attacked people within the Labor Party for hesitating to call the newly conquered territories "liberated."

In September 1973, in a manifesto for the upcoming Israeli elections, the governing Labor Party stated: "At the Suez Canal there is calm. Our positions in the Sinai Desert, in Gaza, in Judea and Samaria and on the Golan are secure.

The bridges are open and Jerusalem is united. New settlements are being established and our policy is strong."

On October 12, the holiest day of the Jewish year, Yom Kippur, the election campaign was interrupted by Egypt's attack across the Suez Canal, six thousand Israeli soldiers were killed in a war on the verge of panic, and six years of military-political illusions were shattered.

The years between 1967 and 1973 have been called the era of the Israeli empire. These were the years when military-minded technocrats like Rabin, Peres, and Dayan took over from the ideological puritans of Labor Zionism. Earlier social and cultural taboos rapidly lost their force. Members of the political and military elite began enriching themselves by acquiring expensive houses, landed estates, and illegal bank accounts abroad. These were the years when the hubris of military superiority prevailed on the logic of political self-preservation. Millions upon millions of dollars were invested in new colonization projects in the West Bank, in the establishment of cities and ports in North Sinai, and in a bloody war of attrition along the Suez Canal. These were the years when political and religious extremism was allowed to fill the void opened by the ideological collapse of Labor Zionism, and the inherent contradiction between the principles of democracy and the imperative of Judaization became apparent.

Above all, these were the years when the potential of turning military victory into political strength was squandered, when the prospects for peace and reconciliation were weakened rather than strengthened. These were the years that further sharpened the conflict with the Palestinians, and created the political conditions for Menachem Begin's nationalist takeover in May 1977.

Being on the barricades of the Israeli-Palestinian conflict in these years was a desolate journey from hope to despair. Between increasingly polarized positions, the space for political action vanished. Begin made explicit what previously had been shrouded in anguish and equivocation. He was elected on a platform asserting the "eternal and inalienable" right of the Jewish people to the Land of Israel, clarifying: "Between the sea and the Jordan, there will be Jewish sovereignty alone."[7] This was also what his government immediately set about to realize, hectare by hectare. Anwar Sadat's peace initiative on November 9, 1977, his breathtaking visit to Jerusalem ten days later, and Israel's separate peace with Egypt on March 26, 1979, changed nothing in this regard. The peace agreement's already modest demands for Palestinian autonomy remained empty words. Instead, relentless steps were taken to undo the geographical and political conditions for any meaningful concept of Palestinian autonomy. After a few more years I decided to exit from the Israeli-Palestinian battlefield altogether. I no longer saw any way out, only a never-ending spiral of violence and extremism. The Israeli chapter of my life had to be closed.

Which proved easier said than done.

During the Easter holiday of 1980 I traveled to Israel for the first time in ten years. My status as an Israeli "inhabitant" (*toshav ha'aretz*) had been canceled (or so I believed), and thereby the threat of being recruited to the Israeli army upon arrival. However, it didn't take long to notice the hardening political climate, and not much longer before a sense of commitment was awakened and broken contacts were reestablished.

I will never forget the scenic though depressing journey in a small Israeli-registered Autobianchi, generously loaned to me by my unwitting and ever-forgiving cousin, filled to the brink with a one-year-old child, a pregnant wife, the anti-Zionist activist Uri Davis, and his elderly mother, on a narrow, breathtaking tarmac loop from the southern Jordan Valley through the hills of the West Bank toward the main Ramallah–Nablus road, passing a small village called Kafr Malik, where the journey came to a halt. In the midst of the village, a herd of goats blocked the road, and the small car was squeezed from all sides by a foul-smelling, bleating mass of animals. Behind them we saw the shepherd's black-and-white keffiyeh rising. Then his face. Then his eyes, dark and hard. He raised his staff and shouted in a hoarse, angry voice. The herd was about to devour us. More and more villagers gathered around the car. More and more eyes stared at us.

Then Uri rolled down the window and said something in Arabic. The clouds cleared, the faces softened, the goats retreated, and the road opened. No one in the car said anything for a long time.

That evening we stayed with a professor of English in Birzeit, the rebellious university town outside of Ramallah. As darkness fell, he served us the olive oil of the house and showed us why the villagers of Kafr Malik had come to hate. From the surrounding hills rapidly disappearing into the night, a string of blue-white headlights illuminated the military patrol roads and the barbed-wire rolls encircling the religious settlements of Beit El, Ofra, Rimonim, and Kochav Ha'shachar.

We had seen the evil seed of the occupation ripen, and a new provocative, uncompromising, religiously driven Zionism showing its pale, inhuman face.

BLOOD AND SOIL

The land of Israel has an element of life in it, of spirit.
To give up a single part is like giving up a living organ.

—HANAN PORAT, FOUNDER OF GUSH EMUNIM

Jerusalem, September 21, 1993. The evening is mild and pleasant. In the facade-lit parliament building on the hill of Givat Ram, the Oslo Accords between Israel and the PLO are being debated, and the park area on the outside is filling up with thousands of people. In small and large groups, hour after hour, they ascend on the steep, winding access roads. The teenage girls wear white blouses, dark skirts, sandals or low-heeled shoes, and small rucksacks. They sing as they clap their hands. On high-raised poles, the blue-and-white Star of David soars toward the sky.

If I don't look too closely, I am transported back thirty years in time. The Spartan dress, the collective marching and singing, the shining eyes of certainty could be a scene taken from a Zionist youth gathering in the early 1960s; dedicated pioneers en route to plant another tree, establish another kibbutz, harvest another crop, defend another border, celebrate another national memory, explore yet another place of Jewish significance in the Land of Israel.

A closer look at the young men breaks the illusion. They too are dressed simply, in white cotton shirts, dark trousers, and sandals. But they do something that no Zionist pioneer did in 1962, they pray. Some with their hands to their temples, others with their hands clutching a prayer book. They are all wearing crocheted skullcaps, some with a large prayer shawl or an Israeli flag wrapped around their shoulders, some have donned their tefillin, and prayer tassels protrude from beneath their shirts.

Also breaking the illusion are the young mothers with their headscarves, long sleeves, and swarming children. The praying men and the chaste mothers are gathering not to celebrate yet another Zionist achievement but to protest a looming Zionist betrayal.

Betrayal of what? The cute little kids in the park are wearing T-shirts with a montage of Prime Minister Yitzhak Rabin in a black-and-white Palestinian keffiyeh and the word *ha'shakran* (liar) in red. An elderly man in a blue cap carries a placard proclaiming: "Liars and traitors negotiate with terrorists!" A group of youngsters has gathered around a banner demanding: "The Land of Israel for the Jews." Another banner proclaims: "Rabin killed the Jewish state." At ad hoc stands you can buy books and pamphlets reflecting a diversity of beliefs—within a narrow spectrum of ideas that in any other context would be considered unreal. Here are those who believe that the goal of Zionism is to rebuild King Solomon's Temple and restore King David's kingdom. Here are those who believe that Zionism's goal is to complete the messianic redemption of the world through the ingathering of the Jews to the land that God promised

Abraham, and the establishment of the Torah as its law.[1] Here are Rabbi Schneerson's black-robed missionary patrols proclaiming the latest edict of their Messiah: "We must not cede any part of the Land of Israel!" Here are groups regarding the agreement with the PLO as a national suicide and the prelude to another Shoah.

I descend from the hill in the footsteps of a group of youngsters clapping their hands and singing the Zionist pioneer song, "Eretz zavat chalav u'dvash"—a land flowing with milk and honey.

Thirty years earlier, I could have been one of them.

With the emergence of a religiously driven movement for Jewish territorial supremacy, Zionism was supplemented with an element impervious to worldly political and military calculations. The fulfillment of God's plan had its own rules and morals. Jewish land was more sacred than Palestinian lives. The laws of the Torah were more valid than the laws of the State of Israel. The armed trailblazers for the messianic redemption gave themselves the right to steal, destroy, displace, and kill. In the trenches of the Messianic Kingdom, mass murderers could be hailed as martyrs and the assassination of a prime minister be seen as an act of God.

This monster in the making was initially regarded with sympathy and even affection in large parts of official Israel, as it spoke a language that many recognized and wished for things that many deep down longed for. During the 1970s and '80s, the religious settlers were showered with grants, subsidies, and positions as they became a key force in the settlement enterprise. They were seen as wild, unruly, but nevertheless vibrant new shoots on the Zionist tree.

On closer inspection, the new shoots had deep roots as well. The idea that the return of the Jews to the Land of Israel would bring about the coming of the Messiah had been promulgated by two Eastern European rabbis in the mid-nineteenth century, in opposition to the prevailing rabbinic edict forbidding the hastening of the coming of the Messiah. For another hundred and twenty-five years, Jewish Messianism and secular Zionism coexisted side by side, carefully separated by a wall of mutual distrust and contempt. When the wall finally came down, in the national-messianic frenzy stirred by the "miraculous" return to the whole Land of Israel, it was soon understood why Jewish sages and rabbis had fought so hard to control it. The infusion of Judaism's millennial messianic yearning into the Zionist state-building project unleashed explosive forces in both secular and religious Zionism. In the state-sponsored colonization of the "Land of Israel," they could mutually confirm and radicalize each other. The religious Zionists saw the secular Zionists as unwitting instruments of God; the secular Zionists saw the religious Zionists as ideological pioneers. When the umbrella organization of the settler movement, Gush Emunim (Bloc of the Faithful), was formed in March 1974, in the national depression after the October War of 1973, it succeeded in mobilizing widespread public support. In its manifesto, Gush Emunim portrayed itself as the standard-bearer of historical Zionism: "Our aim is to bring about a large movement of reawakening among the Jewish people for the fulfillment of the Zionist vision in its full scope [. . .] The sources of this vision are the Jewish traditions and roots, and its ultimate objective is the full redemption of the Jewish people and the entire world."[2]

Eventually, hundreds of thousands of Israelis would come to share the beliefs and ideas of Messianic Zionism, not because they were having a religious awakening or were personally prepared to settle in "Judea" and "Samaria," but because the movement appealed to already existing Zionist values and sentiments, adding an element of zeal to the still-living Zionist goal of settling the whole Land of Israel.

There were ominous signs early on. The Land of Israel Movement (Ha'tnuah le'maan Eretz Israel ha'schlema), founded in September 1967, gained broad public support by openly stirring messianic sentiments and demands.[3] The conquest of "Samaria" and "Judea" was portrayed as an event of biblical dimensions: "The victory of IDF [Israel Defense Forces] in the Six-Day War has situated the people and the State of Israel in a new and momentous period. The whole of Eretz Israel is now in the hands of the Jewish people, and just as we are not allowed to give up the State of Israel, so we are ordered to keep what we received there from its hands: the Land of Israel."[4]

The manifesto was signed by an impressive array of political and cultural personalities in Israel, religious and secular, and according to the historian Ehud Sprinzak, "probably the most distinguished group of names ever to have joined a public cause in Israel."[5] It included, of course, the full gamut of revisionist veterans from Begin's right-wing nationalist party, but also prestigious names associated with Labor Zionism, from well-known war heroes and kibbutz pioneers to key intellectual figures such as the national poet Nathan Alterman and the Nobel laureate author S. Y. Agnon. The labor governments of Eshkol and Meir pretended there was no contradiction between a policy for occupation and settlement and a policy for recognition and reconciliation.

Subsequently, there was no open conflict between the demands of the settler movement and successive Labor governments. It was a Labor government who initiated the annexation of East Jerusalem and the expropriation of large tracts of Arab land for Jewish settlement; who drew up plans for the colonization of the Jordan Valley and "strategic" parts of the West Bank and the Golan Heights (the Allon Plan). It was also a Labor government that helped to establish the first and most extreme of the religious settlements in the newly occupied territories.

On April 4, 1968, thirty-two Jewish families moved into the Park Hotel in the center of Hebron, in the midst of seventy thousand Arabs and in defiance of official government policy. The new guests proclaimed that they had only come to celebrate the Jewish Passover in the City of the Patriarchs, but they stayed on for good. It soon emerged that the "visit" had been given a green light by the deputy prime minister, Yigal Allon.

The leader of the Hebron settlers was Moshe Levinger, a bony, slightly stooped man in his thirties and a student of Rabbi Zvi Yehuda Kook, who in his Jerusalem Talmud school, Merkaz Ha'rav, had long taught that the Jewish settling of the Land of Israel was a divine decree, and who, in a sermon in May 1967, on Israel's Independence Day, had predicted the Jewish "return" to Hebron, Shechem (Nablus), and Jericho.[6] Accordingly, as soon as the Israeli army reached the Western Wall a month later, Rabbi Kook was brought there by two paratroopers, where he promptly proclaimed before "all Israel and the whole world that by divine decree we have returned to our home, to our holy city, never to leave it again." For Levinger, Rabbi Kook was God's prophet and the June War was God's plan.

Less than a year later, when Levinger let it be known that he was going to fulfill God's plan in Hebron, Allon equipped him with three Uzi submachine guns for the "visit." Allon also lobbied the Israeli government to let Levinger's group stay in Hebron under military protection, and thereafter repeatedly gave in to Levinger's increasingly aggressive and challenging behavior. Allon himself revealed his role to a respected Israeli journalist the day before his death in 1977. By then, Allon had seen Rabbi Levinger initiate one violent provocation after another, and seemed to have regretted playing with the messianic fire.

Before the war of 1967, Rabbi Kook's Messianic Zionism had few followers. His interpretation of the State of Israel as an instrument of God, and the Jewish return to the Land of Israel as a means of preparing for the coming of the Messiah, made him an outsider to both Orthodox Judaism and secular

Zionism. Nevertheless, he represented, albeit in a more activist form, a rabbinical interpretation of Zionism that had been formulated by his father, Avraham Yitzhak Hacohen Kook, the first Ashkenazi Chief Rabbi of Jewish Palestine.

Kook the Elder was born in Lithuania in 1865 and came to Palestine in 1904 to be the rabbi of the Jewish community in Jaffa. He was already convinced that political Zionism was the finger of God and the settlement of the Jews in Palestine the beginning of the redemption (*atchalta d'geula*). With references to sources in the Kabbalah, the Jewish mystical tradition, he proclaimed that a divinely inspired course of events could very well be promoted by ungodly agents, and that the pioneers of Zionism were unwittingly walking in the footsteps of the Messiah, *be'ikvata d'meshicha*. The "secular cloak" of Zionism would eventually be transformed into the "crown of holy splendor."[7] The task of Orthodox Jews was not to oppose the Zionist pioneers but to facilitate their enterprise and infuse it with a messianic spirit.

Rabbi Kook thus showed great ingenuity in reconciling the strict injunctions of Jewish orthodoxy with the practical problems of colonization. The Torah stipulated that every seventh year must be a sabbatical year (*shanat schemita*), during which Jews must let the land rest and not sow or harvest, which, if applied literally, would have caused the collapse of the Jewish agricultural enterprise. In view of the approaching sabbatical year of 1909, Rabbi Kook issued a ruling that would allow Jews to farm the land during a sabbatical year if they temporarily sold it to non-Jews. The ruling sparked fierce Orthodox opposition, but Kook defended it as an emergency ruling for the survival of the unwitting heralders of the Messiah.

With rulings like this, Rabbi Kook initiated a radical reinterpretation of the position of Orthodox Judaism regarding the coming of the Messiah. The prevailing interpretation was unambiguous: Human hand must not hasten the End. The return to Zion and the Messianic Redemption could only happen by divine intervention, not by human action. Against this, Rabbi Kook argued that there would come a time when God's plan required human action, and that the time was now. The Zionist return to the Land of Israel was a step in a divinely ordained process whose paths must remain mysterious and inscrutable. Secular, God-denying, socialist pioneers had their assigned role in it, as did Jew-hunting mobs in Europe, as did the First World War. In 1915 he wrote: "It is our firm conviction that universal devastation and the Jewish distress will usher in the redemption promised by the omniscient Architect of History."[8]

And a year later: "The Jewish national self-realization in a world rocked by war constitutes a critical stage in the eventual establishment of the universal Kingdom of Heaven. Israel's restoration mirrors the Divine brilliance that irradiates all the facets of life [. . .] We are facing a spectacle of unparalleled grandeur. Evidently, society is undergoing a profound transformation, wherein Israel's historical reassertion is an integral element."[9] The Balfour Declaration of 1917 was "divinely inspired" and Hitler's rise to power in 1933 one of the "international developments affecting the Jewish people which . . . combine to further the goal of Israel's ingathering into our Holy Land."[10]

Had Rabbi Kook lived, he would undoubtedly have added both the Holocaust and the founding of the State of Israel to his divine chain of redemption. At his death in 1935, however, he left behind enough statements and predictions for his messianic interpretation of Zionism to live on. "We must concentrate on land acquisition with the same fervor as the pious worship of God," wrote Rabbi Kook. The injunction to settle the land could even offset the injunction to preserve life (*pikuach nefesh*) in case the former were to clash with the latter. Kook's teachings urged pious Jews to swallow their anger at violations of Jewish law in the realization of the Zionist enterprise, from the raising of pigs to the desecration of the Sabbath, providing it with unflinching "halachic" arguments for colonizing and settling the whole Land of Israel.[11]

Kook's ideas remained an almost invisible building block in the Zionist edifice, an untapped source of ideological energy, a pioneering spirit not yet awakened. In a dilapidated and neglected Talmud school in West Jerusalem, his less charismatic son, Rabbi Zvi Yehuda Kook, was still praying for the day when the pioneers of Zionism would become the warriors of God.

Thirty years later the day arrived. With the seemingly miraculous return to the whole Land of Israel, Messianic Zionism made the leap from periphery to center. A Zionism that had once promised to normalize the relationship between the Jews and the world was now conquered from within by a movement that sought the opposite. It was openly hostile to Christianity and Islam (the confrontation between the people of Israel and the "gentiles" was part of the apocalyptic scenario). It sought to have Israel leave the "hostile" organizations and institutions of the non-Jewish world (such as the United Nations). It set itself above secular laws and regulations, it humiliated and provoked the Palestinian Arabs and openly challenged "universal" morality.

Kook the Elder's idea that the Zionist settling of the land could take precedence over previously prevailing halachic injunctions was driven to its extreme by Kook the Younger, who proclaimed that it might be right "to kill in order not to sin" (*jehareg uv'al ja'avor*). In the run-up to the messianic age, giving an inch of Eretz Israel to non-Jews was as great a sin as worshipping foreign idols. It was with this ruling in mind that Rabbi Levinger threatened to commit suicide when Israel returned the Jewish settlements in Sinai to Egypt in 1982. And got out of his car in the center of Hebron in September 1988 to shoot dead the shoe-shop owner Khayed Salah.[12] This also gave rabbinical sanction for settlers to terrorize, injure, and murder Palestinians, usually with impunity. When, in July 1983, Levinger's son-in-law and members of the armed Jewish underground movement, Ha'machteret ha'yehudit, mowed down thirty-six Palestinian students in the courtyard of the Islamic secondary school in Hebron, killing three of them, Rabbi Levinger declared that "whoever did this has sanctified God's name in public."[13] When, in February 1994, Baruch Goldstein killed twenty-nine worshippers in the Ibrahimi mosque in Hebron before being killed himself, he was declared a martyr and hero by leading settler rabbis and a memorial was erected in his honor in Kiryat Arba. A religious pamphlet published a few months later was entitled *Baruch [blessed] Be This Man*.[14] Rabin's murderer, Yigal Amir, only did what he had been commanded by his rabbis to do.

The messianic interpretation of Zionism also came with the command to rebuild King Solomon's temple in Jerusalem on its former site, which is where now stands the third holiest mosque in Islam, Al-Aqsa. The Chief Rabbi of the Israeli military, Shlomo Goren, had the Israeli flag raised on the golden Dome of the Rock, and on August 16, 1967, Tisha B'Av, the Jewish memorial day to the destruction of the Temple, Rabbi Goren defied the military and halachic ban for Jews to set foot on the Temple Mount and proclaimed in full uniform that he would build a synagogue in the open area between the Dome of the Rock and the Al-Aqsa mosque. He left behind a book-shaped Torah (*chumash*) and a prayer stand—and set up an office on the site. Panic ensued in the Islamic world—and in the Israeli government, which quickly closed the office and removed the Torah book, assuring that neither Rabbi Goren nor anyone else would ever be allowed to build anything on the Temple Mount.[15]

Since then, the site of the two mosques has been a target for the most extreme elements of Messianic Zionism. In 1969, a non-Jewish Australian tourist set fire to the Al-Aqsa mosque "to hasten the return of Christ," recalling the connection between extreme Jewish and extreme Christian messianic beliefs.[16] In 1980, Rabbi Meir Kahane and his brother-in-arms Baruch Ben-Yosef (Andy Green) were arrested for conspiring to blow up the Dome of the Rock and detained for six months, in a rare "Jewish" application of the 1945 Emergency Laws. In April 1982, Alan Goodman, an American Jew, walked into the compound with an automatic rifle and opened fire on the guard outside the Dome of the Rock, resulting in two dead and nine wounded, including some Israeli police officers. In April 1984, it was revealed that the Jewish underground movement that had been behind the attack on Palestinian students in Hebron and the car bombings of three Palestinian mayors also had far-reaching plans to blow up the Dome of the Rock. The mastermind was Yehuda Etzion, a leading figure in Gush Emunim, who believed that a proper bomb in the right place would hasten the messianic times. He had become increasingly critical of the settler movement's collusion with the Israeli state and hoped that the destruction of the mosques would create the appropriate apocalyptic conditions for the restoration of King David's biblical kingdom. Etzion gave voice to a contempt for the laws and institutions of the State of Israel that were cultivated in the Talmud schools of the settler movement, and which ten years later would radiate from the smirking face of Yigal Amir, the assassin of Yitzhak Rabin.[17]

This line of thought, seemingly disconnected from reality, gained a following within the religious settler movement in the 1980s. Between 1983 and 1986, *Nekuda*, the movement's official organ, published dozens of articles calling for the "Judaization" of the Temple Mount. In 1986, twelve thousand ultranationalist Jews from Merkaz Ha'rav, Kook the Younger's Talmud school in West Jerusalem, marched to Mount Olive in East Jerusalem to watch a sound and light show entitled "The Temple Mount is the Heart of the People."[18] As early as December 1978, disciples of Zvi Yehuda Kook had settled in the Muslim part of Old Jerusalem with the express purpose of preparing for the rebuilding of the Temple. Their Talmud school, Ateret Cohanim (the priestly crown), became the center of successive provocative attempts to Judaize the area around the Temple Mount. One house after another was purchased by fake front companies and turned into well-guarded Jewish fortresses in the midst of densely populated Muslim quarters. Ateret Cohanim began to study the long-obsolete sacrificial rites and laws that would be practiced again when the Temple was rebuilt. They also initiated genealogical research to determine which Jews were of Levitical, priestly lineage and thus permitted to serve in the Temple. They began constructing and reconstructing fabrics, costumes, dyes, musical instruments, and sacrificial vessels. A worldwide search for strains of red cattle took place in order to fulfill the injunction for priests to purify themselves in the ashes of a red heifer (Leviticus 19:1–10).[19]

Ateret Cohanim was not a crazy and isolated sect in 1980s Israel. It received political support from the nationalist right, financial support from a nationalist government, and moral support from former defense minister Ariel Sharon, who in December 1988, through Ateret Cohanim, bought himself a large house in the Muslim section of Old Jerusalem, decorated it with an Israeli flag and a seven-armed candlestick, surrounded it with military guards, and declared his support for continued Jewish settlement in the Muslim quarters.[20]

The Judaization of Arab Jerusalem also gained significant political and financial support from right-wing Jewish circles in the United States. Leading Israeli and American politicians hosted fundraisers for the Jerusalem Reclamation Project, an American support organization for Ateret Cohanim. At its first fundraising dinner in Los Angeles in 1987, then Israeli UN ambassador Benjamin Netanyahu spoke; in 1989, Sharon and the New York City mayor Ed Koch spoke. At these events tens of millions of dollars were donated to Ateret Cohanim for the purpose of buying Arab property.

On Easter 1990, two days before Good Friday, Ateret Cohanim's American friends got cold feet when hundreds of armed Jewish settlers occupied and evacuated St. John's Hospice, a building in the Christian quarter of Old Jerusalem. The seventy-room property near the Church of the Holy Sepulcher was run by the Greek Orthodox Church and used as a hostel for Arab families and European pilgrims. The settlers renamed the house Neot David (Meadows of David), raised an Israeli flag, and invited Sharon to visit. On the same day, they began throwing furniture and religious decorations onto the street outside, including crucifixes and images of saints. A Byzantine cross embedded in the pavement was covered with a piece of plywood painted with a blue Star of David. The takeover of St. John's Hospice provoked protests and condemnation worldwide, the Greek Orthodox Church sought to have the purchase through yet another front company overturned in court, and the timeless conflict between Christians and Jews flared up in a reversed balance of strength.

Despite the protests and the negative publicity, Ateret Cohanim continued its extensive purchases of properties in both the Muslim and Christian parts of the Old City. The support of the Israeli Likud government continued until the coming to power of the Labor Party in the summer of 1992. Only a few months earlier, in March 1992, Ateret Cohanim and the Ministry of Housing had announced plans for a large apartment complex near Herod's Gate in the Muslim quarter. The incoming Labor government dampened the messianic homebuyer activity, but did not stop it.

The line between religious and secular fanaticism was not always easy to see. One of the most articulate Temple-building movements, Ne'emanei Har Habayit (The Faithful of the Temple Mount), was led by a shy, well-read man with a slight limp in his sixties who, in a gentle voice and with a wry smile, told anyone who would listen that the two mosques on the Temple Mount should be moved to Mecca to make way for a new Temple building. I met Gershon Salomon in December 1989, in his large three-story house in East Jerusalem, in a Jewish neighborhood built after the June 1967 war. He walked me through rooms overloaded with bookshelves and national religious symbols: flags, cups, candlesticks, mosaics, old maps, and one wall covered with a giant aerial photograph of Jerusalem and the Temple area.

Salomon was not overtly religious. His parents had fought in the Irgun, Begin's armed underground movement. He himself had made a career in Herut, Begin's right-wing nationalist party, as a municipal politician in Jerusalem. When Begin took power in 1977, Salomon believed that the time for a new Temple had arrived. When Begin signed the 1978 Camp David agreement, returning Sinai to Egypt, he organized an opposition faction that would evolve into the ultranationalist party Tehiya (Rebirth). Tehiya was the political manifestation of a fusion between Jewish Messianism and Jewish nationalism. The Talmud-studying disciples of Rabbi Kook and the gun-toting settler-activists of Rabbi Levinger were rubbing shoulders with the ideological and political heirs of the Stern Gang. Steely-eyed settler fanatics like Daniella Weiss were joining forces with calculating military strategists like Yuval Ne'eman. Ne'eman was Israel's Dr. Strangelove, a prominent nuclear physicist and the mastermind of Israel's nuclear weapons program, also the minister of energy and science under Menachem Begin and Yitzhak Shamir, providing philosophical and intellectual arguments for war, settlements, occupation, and expansion.[21]

Salomon radiated a similar disquieting combination of intelligence and fanaticism. His words were well chosen and fell in the right order, cause and effect were connected, he seemed to understand the meaning of what he was saying, but something in his perception of reality was twisted and skewed. For example, I could not understand how he could be lame after a war injury from the 1950s and at the same time have participated in the military liberation of the Temple Mount in 1967. Mythomaniac, perhaps, but every autumn at Sukkot (Feast of Tabernacles) he managed to convince both his supporters and his enemies of his intention to enter the closed mosque area to found the Third Temple.

Barely a year after our meeting—on October 8, 1990, the morning of the Sukkot holiday—Salomon's "peaceful" march to the Temple Mount provoked the worst incident so far in the history of the Temple movement. Thousands of Muslims flocked to the defense of the mosques, while tens of thousands of Jews celebrated Sukkot on the Western Wall plaza below. Salomon's group was stopped at the entrance to the mosque grounds and retreated after a moment of flag-waving, but rumors were spreading, people gathered, and the situation got tense. A tear gas grenade went off, stones began flying, live shots were fired. Forty minutes later, nineteen Palestinians lay dead on the Temple ground.

A year later, Salomon, with his gentle voice and wry smile, announced that this time he would hire a helicopter to lay the foundation of the Third Temple. He didn't get permission for a helicopter, but he did get a thousand Israeli soldiers to protect his flag-waving march through the Muslim quarters surrounding the Temple Mount.

Salomon only has to succeed once, and he is not the only one who keeps trying.

Was this Judaism? Well, clearly Judaism could also be this. Judaism had no church, no central authority, no binding interpretation. Like Sabbateanism, Zionist neo-Messianism could make references to biblical and Talmudic sources. Every Jew was free to interpret and apply the scriptures and commentaries according to his ability and influence, and to issue a religious, halachic ruling wherever appropriate. Such a ruling had authority as far as it was respected by other Jews, no more and no less. Many of the leaders of the religious settlers were considered halachic authorities. The endorsement by Israel's chief military rabbi Goren of Rabbi Kook's rulings regarding the conquest of land was no freak aberration. Dov Lior, the rabbi of Kiryat Arba, who in February 1994 had martyred Baruch Goldstein, the perpetrator of the Hebron massacre, was a respected Talmudic scholar considered for a seat on the Supreme Rabbinical Court, the Israeli authority in charge of reviewing religious rulings and regulations. He was turned down by Israel's attorney general only after it was revealed that he had given his consent to medical experiments on non-Jewish prisoners.[22]

A less established but nonetheless influential rabbi among the religious settlers was Yisrael Ariel, who had not only blessed the mass murderer Goldstein but had also ruled that those Palestinians who would choose to stay and live in the Land of Israel (which, according to Ariel, should include all of Lebanon and much of Syria and Iraq) would be considered "alien residents," with no right to have a state position or to have jobs that might put them in a superior position to Jews. At most, they would be allowed to make a living as shepherds and petty traders. "The land of Israel is intended only for those who have Jewish blood. The Jews have no right to cede a single part of it to a non-Jew or even to a Jewish convert."[23] In the same spirit, in 1980, Rabbi Israel Hess published an article in the Bar-Ilan University student newspaper entitled "The Genocidal Commandment in the Torah," in which he argued that the Arabs were the modern-day equivalent of the Amalekites of the Bible, and that it was a divine command to wipe them out.[24] Few others went as far publicly, but the notion of the Arabs as Amalek gained traction in religious settler circles.[25]

From a core of extremist halachic interpretations and rulings, an extreme manifestation of Judaism took shape. In hundreds of state-sponsored Talmud schools, and in special schools for combined Talmud studies and military service (*yeshivot hesder*), young men and women were educated in the halachic arguments for occupation, mosque demolition, and ethnic cleansing. They were taught that anyone who delays the redemption by ceding holy ground to Israel's enemies is a traitor and deserves to die. Amir was only doing the bidding of his rabbis when on November 4, 1995, in the name of God, he assassinated the prime minister of Israel.

In one respect, the similarity between Messianic settler Zionism and Messianic Sabbateanism was striking; acute expectations of a pending redemption were made to justify extreme actions and interpretations of the law. In another respect, the dissimilarity between them was as striking; Sabbateanism was a movement among mainly poor and powerless people, harming no others but themselves. Messianic settler Zionism, by contrast, was born armed to the teeth with the military and economic power of a secular state.

There is, of course, another Judaism, and yet another one. Judaism, like Christianity, can be universalist, socially radical, tolerant, strict, orthodox, conservative, and liberal. Judaism has been the source of central currents of moral thought in our civilization; the care for the weak, the love of the stranger, the right of the outcast. The many Jews in Israel and around the world who have watched the violent manifestations of religious settler Zionism with increasing horror and dismay have sometimes dismissed it as an extremist deviation from mainstream Judaism.

Unfortunately, they are wrong. Messianism is not an aberration in Judaism (nor, for that matter, in Christianity). The belief in the coming of the Messiah, and the belief that this coming is associated with the return of the Jews to the Land of Israel, is a central vision and an authentic impulse. It was an impulse that led to the devastating Jewish revolts against the Roman Empire in the century following the destruction of the Second Temple, that brought about Christianity, that gave rise to recurrent messianic outbreaks in the Jewish world, and that, explicitly or implicitly, became a powerful source of inspiration in the nascent Zionist movement.

This was also the impulse that gave birth to a militant, armed, land-worshipping, messianic extremism gaining power and influence in the State of Israel.

The most severe critic of neo-Messianic Zionism was Professor Yeshayahu Leibowitz, one of Israel's most interesting Jewish thinkers. Immediately after the 1967 war, he warned that any merger between Zionism and Messianism would be fatal to both Israel and Judaism. It would bring about a blasphemous deification of the nation, a fetishistic cult of the soil, and eventually new varieties of Sabbateanism, nihilism, and religious apostasy. The powerful apocalyptic forces within Judaism that the Jewish sage Maimonides had hoped to contain and neutralize, Rabbi Kook & Co. had swung open the doors to.

Leibowitz's writings and statements took on an increasingly prophetic character, as messianic arguments for colonization and occupation replaced secular and security policy arguments. In an article written in 1988, forty years into the State of Israel, Leibowitz returned to 1967 as a fateful historical turning point:

> On the seventh day [of the Six-Day War] we had to decide—and we were free to decide—whether that war was one of defense or of conquest. Our decision turned it into a war of conquest, with all that this implied. Not only was the character of the state altered; the very foundation of its existence assumed a new aspect. [. . .] Israel ceased to be the state of the Jewish people and became an apparatus of coercive rule of Jews over another people. What many call "the undivided Land of Israel" is not, and can never be, the state of the Jewish people, but only a Jewish regime of force [. . .] When nation, country and state are presented as absolute values, anything goes.[26]

Leibowitz feared that the merging of messianic and political goals would eventually lead to a fascist social order, a fear that was deeply rooted in his own strictly Jewish Orthodox outlook and morality. He could argue against the messianic claims of religious Zionism in its own terms:

> After all that has been said about the "religious" and pseudo-religious and even halakhic reasons for maintaining Jewish rule over the territories and their Arab inhabitants, and for the annexation of the territories to

the state of Israel, I have nothing to add to what already
appeared in the Scriptures, the same Scriptures to which
the national religious fools appeal for support for their
lust for conquest. Two thousand six hundred years ago,
the prophet Ezekiel foresaw Gush Emunim and the arguments of its leaders and rabbis.[27]

The Land of Israel was a conditional bequest, not a property contract, Leibowitz argued. The only legitimate task of the State of Israel was to create conditions for Jews to live as Jews, not to put itself in the place of Judaism and Jewish values. The values of Judaism could only be realized by morally striving people, not by the machinery of a state—a state that wanted to attribute inherent, divine motives and values to itself and its actions was a fascist state.

As soon as Menachem Begin was given the task of forming a new government in May 1977, he requested an audience with the then eighty-six-year-old Zvi Yehuda Kook, to kiss his hand and receive his blessing. Shortly thereafter, Begin traveled to the front line of religious settler Zionism, an Israeli army camp near the Arab village of Qadum. The camp contained twenty Jewish families that the Rabin government had evacuated three years earlier from Elon Moreh, an illegally occupied hill just south of the city of Nablus. With a Torah scroll under his arm, Begin promised to return Elon Moreh to its settlers, exclaiming "there will be many more Elon Morehs."[28]

And thus, a decade of unrestrained land usurpation began.[29] The hitherto few Jewish settlements on occupied land multiplied, and the number of settlers increased dramatically. The continued Judaization of Samaria and Judea became official policy, the organizations of the Jewish settlers were embraced by the Israeli state and rendered official status, political power, and financial resources. East Jerusalem was annexed, expanded, and Judaized. Jewish land ownership in the West Bank accelerated, first through the expropriation of "absentee" property and expropriations for "security" reasons, then through expropriations for "public purposes" (roads and water for new settlements), systematic legal assaults on Palestinian claims to landownership,[30] the classification of large tracts of land as "state property" and thereby amenable to expropriation without appeal, and finally through land and property purchases by masked interests. In 1981 alone, more land was transferred to the State of Israel than in the preceding twelve years of military occupation.[31]

And this was only the beginning. As soon as the ink had dried on the peace agreement between Israel and Egypt in September 1978, the Begin government embarked on a comprehensive program to block the promise of Palestinian autonomy enshrined in the document. Under the direction of Matityahu Drobles, the head of the settlement department of the World Zionist Organization and a veteran of Begin's Likud Party, a strategy for the Judaization of the West Bank and Gaza was concocted. The Drobles Plan stipulated that Jewish settlements would be established throughout the Land of Israel, "not only around the settlements of the minority population [that is, the indigenous Arabs], but also in between them [. . .] in accordance with the settlement program adopted in the Galilee and other parts of the country, with the objective of reducing to the minimum the possibility for the development of another Arab state in these regions."[32] In this way, sixty-five to seventy new Jewish settlements would be established over a five-year period, and the Jewish population in "Samaria, Judea, and Gaza" would multiply in size.

This plan, viewing the occupied territories as an inseparable part of the Land of Israel, had not been drawn up by some odd messianic rabbi in an obscure outpost settlement but by the Israeli government. Secular politicians now spoke the language of messianism, and religious settlers spoke the language of secular power. These were the years when a fusion of military ruthlessness and religious fanaticism constituted the political base for a succession of hardcore nationalist governments. It allowed for messianic goals to justify increasingly brutal and repressive means, for pointless wars to be launched, for Palestinian life to be diminished and deprived of hope, for possible avenues of reconciliation to be closed.

The result was a growing list of unpunished settler acts against Palestinians, and a growing list of arbitrarily and harshly punished Palestinians. In 1984, an official Israeli legal commission accused the military occupation authorities of deliberately turning a blind eye to settler abuses, of deliberately ignoring Palestinian allegations of violence and property destruction, and of entering into a "conspiracy of silence" with the settlers and the local militias.[33] The following year it was revealed that the underground Jewish terrorist organization Ha'machteret had been responsible for 384 acts of violence and 23 murders in four years. Some of the public was horrified, others hailed the perpetrators as heroes. The twenty members were convicted of murder, accessory to murder, and membership in a terrorist organization and sentenced to heavy prison terms, but all were released early, the last in 1990.

Documents and newspaper articles from these years testify to a growing legal and democratic decay. The moral rot of the occupation gradually penetrated everyday Israeli life. No one could hide or turn their back anymore. Everyone was affected in one way or another; as conscripted soldiers, as their parents and relatives, as citizens of a small country with small circles. In the name of the state, or with the state's tacit consent, a policy was implemented that made for increasing division and introspection within Jewish Israeli society. The effect on the Palestinian population was depression, desperation, and, finally, rebellion.

When the intifada broke out in December 1987, the Begin and Shamir governments had spent more than a billion dollars on new settlements, many times more than on equivalent housing projects inside Israel itself, thus tempting a new and growing category of Israelis to cross the former geographical and moral boundary. In towns like Ariel, Givat Ze'ev, Ginot Shomron, Karnei Shomron, Nofim, and Ma'ale Adumim, well-educated young couples could buy a four-bedroom house with a garden and a view of the pastoral hills of Judea and Samaria, in communities with well-equipped schools, subsidized electricity and water supplies, good social services, and an unspoiled environment, for the same price as a cramped apartment in central Tel Aviv. The new settlers were able to commute the relatively short distances to their high-paying jobs in Tel Aviv or Jerusalem on newly built "Jewish" roads with newly established "Jewish" bus lines, and thus came to associate the settlement policy with a private standard of living that would have been unthinkable under other circumstances.

While many may have convinced themselves that their choice of housing was purely pragmatic, no one could reasonably fail to note the overtly political intentions behind the generous financial subsidies. They could not completely avoid confrontations with an increasingly frustrated local Palestinian population, nor could they completely detach themselves from the fact that their comfortable existence was ultimately built on expropriated Palestinian land and secured by a military occupation force. In the long run, it was certainly difficult for many not to be politically influenced by daily contact with a project that was so fundamentally permeated by the attitudes and values of religious messianism and extreme Jewish nationalism. Voter support for territorialist parties soon reached above the Israeli average, and the recruitment base for extremist ideas and actions widened.[34]

One of the most aggressive settler militias emerged in Ariel, the largest and most secular of the new settlements in the West Bank, a half-hour motorway ride from Tel Aviv's northern suburbs. In the late 1980s, ten thousand people lived here in what seemed like any other Israeli residential suburb, with well-planned playgrounds and lush gardens. Nevertheless, during the intifada it became the home to devastating citizen raids into the neighboring Arab village of Biddya, on whose land parts of Ariel had been built. Once in a while, as when a Jewish man from the neighboring settlement of Alfei Menashe was found burned to death in his car in February 1989 (due to a leaking gasoline hose, as it turned out), up to three hundred armed men from Ariel would enter Biddya, overturning cars and smashing windows, dragging people into the streets and beating them, in some cases to death. The routine also included burning the villagers' olive trees, standing as deep-rooted evidence of the land being cultivated and thus difficult to expropriate, and which the militant Ariel residents therefore decided to destroy. In June 1989, the Likud activist Ron Nachman, at the time the mayor of Ariel, suggested that Arab migrant workers in Ariel be required to wear special color signs so that they could be quickly identified. When someone reminded him of the yellow Star of David in the Nazi empire, he withdrew the proposal. In the 1992 election that brought Rabin and the Labor Party to power, 80 percent of Ariel residents voted for the Likud Party of Shamir and Sharon or for one of the parties further to the right.

Yet at its founding in 1978, Ariel had been dominated by people close to the Israeli Labor Party, which a few years earlier had planned Ariel as a link between Tel Aviv and the "strategic" agricultural settlements in the Jordan Valley, and whose trade union–owned institutions, construction companies, and banks had played a central role in the establishment of Ariel. As the motives for occupation shifted, so did alliances and loyalties. The settlement offensive had transformed beyond recognition not only the occupied territories but the political and cultural climate in Israel as well.

It has been said that uprisings come not from lack of hope but from hope betrayed. The Palestinian uprising of December 1987 was no exception. Without the hope awakened by an emerging Jewish Israeli opposition to the policy of occupation and settlements, the intifada might not have lasted for as long as it did (until the Madrid peace conference of 1991). Not that the Shamir government's suppression of the intifada was conducted with kid gloves, on the contrary, but with each beating of children and women, each smashed face, each live ammunition fired at stone-throwing youngsters, each settler attack on Palestinian villages, a shudder went through parts of the country. Israelis returning from mandatory reserve duty in the occupied territory brought with them new stories of fear, humiliation, and shame.

One of the more shocking testimonies came from Jacques Pinto, the journalist and section commander in the Israeli army who in 1989 published a diary of his service in the occupied territories during the first year of the intifada. In August 1988, his company had relieved a military guard in Ramallah, north of Jerusalem, with instructions to act with "aggressiveness and firmness," since the Arabs understood "only one language, that of violence." Pinto quickly realized that the mission was militarily impossible, politically ineffective, and morally indefensible. He noted: "The more effective our reprisals and collective punishments, the more the population closes ranks around the perpetrators." The diary recounted military operations to remove Palestinian flags from roofs and minarets, collective punishments of ailing old people and crying women, indiscriminate shots in the dark against Molotov cocktails and stones, the shooting of a masked insurgent in the Al-Amari refugee camp: "Behind the face mask was a thirteen-year-old girl. A week later she died in a Jerusalem hospital; her name was Nahal Touchi and she became the two hundred and fifty-second victim of the intifada." Pinto soon came to see his task as an officer as "defending at all costs what still remains of lucidity and humanity in our country." He became increasingly convinced that Israelis and Palestinians "in a kind of blind madness" were driving each other to mutual destruction. "If we do not quickly find a common solution, we will destroy each other."[35]

How deeply this sense of fatal destiny had penetrated established Israeli society was perhaps most clearly demonstrated by Chava Alberstein, my cousin by marriage and one of Israel's most popular singers over the years. I first met Chava in the summer of 1967, when she was still a young, pimply-faced talent with an acoustic guitar, a pure voice, and her entire recorded output on a CBS 45 rpm disc. During the following summer visits, I got to chill out in her tiny apartment in Tel Aviv, carefully navigating between music and politics. Over the years she became a major star, a national symbol, drawing sell-out crowds wherever she performed. When the State of Israel celebrated its fortieth anniversary in 1988, she was one of the citizens given the honor of lighting the memorial torches at the Western Wall. It would take a lot to have a song by Chava censored by the Israeli state radio.

In December 1989, two years after the outbreak of the intifada, it happened. The Likud-dominated radio board decided to ban Chava's version of the traditional Jewish Passover nursery rhyme "Chad Gadia." This ancient Aramaic text tells the story of the kid that Father fetched, the cat that scratched the kid that Father fetched, the dog that bit the cat that scratched the kid that Father fetched, the stick that beat the dog that bit the cat that scratched the kid that Father fetched, the fire that burned the stick that beat the dog . . . etc. The chain of events ends with the angel of death killing the butcher, who slaughtered the bull, who drank the water, that put out the fire, that burned the stick, that beat the dog, who bit the cat, who scratched the kid that Father fetched. But in Chava's version, the chain of events turns on the Israelis themselves. "Why," she asked, "am I singing 'Chad Gadia' now? Father hasn't come, and Passover is still far away." And in an answer to the Jewish child's traditional question at Passover dinner, "what makes this night different from all other nights," the lyrics continued:

This night, this year, it is me who has changed.
Once I was a lamb, a kitten gentle,
Today I am a tiger, a raging wolf.
Once I was a pigeon,
Once I was a deer,
Now I no longer know who I am.[36]

An Israeli morning radio host ignored the ban and got the chairman of the radio board on the phone with "Chad Gadia" playing in the background. The chairman threw a tantrum on the air, while Chava Alberstein sang her song to the last verse.[37]

This was the rift from which not only a Palestinian uprising could emerge but also a growing Jewish resistance to the messianic and right-wing nationalist direction in which Israel was heading. The rift was further widened by the declared intention of the Shamir government to use settlements, confiscations, and military force to push the occupied territories toward a de facto annexation. In the 1988 Israeli elections, new parties emerged with one far-reaching proposal after another on how to "take care" of the Arabs. Raful Eitan, the hero of Sabra and Shatila, was elected to parliament on the promise of making Palestinian life in the occupied territories even more unbearable. With roadblocks, curfews, and deportations, Palestinian life would be shattered and the uprising stifled within days: "If they set up a roadblock, I will send ten tanks. If they throw stones, I'll close the road from Nablus to Ramallah and let the Arab who wants to buy rice in Jenin take the road via Jericho."[38]

Another brute, Rehavam Ze'evi, for some reason nicknamed Gandi, and with several corruption scandals on his CV, launched Moledet (The Fatherland), a new party with the sole agenda of emptying Israel and the occupied territories of Arabs. The party took as its symbol the Hebrew letter *tet*, as in "t" for transfer, and launched the slogan "We here, they there, and peace be upon Israel."[39] Ze'evi argued that a "peaceful" transfer in 1988 was no more immoral than the forced transfer in 1948. Four years earlier, Rabbi

Kahane's proposal for a forced transfer of the Palestinian Arabs had been met with disgust and condemnation. Now, Ze'evi's proposal to "create a negative magnet that would encourage the Arabs to leave," was awarded two mandates in the Israeli parliament. What Moledet meant by "a negative magnet" became clear as Ze'evi accused previous Israeli governments of allowing Palestinian universities and secondary schools to operate, of failing to strangle the Arab economy, of failing to stop the influx of Arab labor into Israel, of continuing to give Palestinian Arabs an alternative to emigration.[40]

The transfer idea was also entertained, albeit less explicitly, in the settler movement's own party, Tehiya, which ran on a platform of indefinite military martial law in the occupied territories: All Palestinian associations, institutions, newspapers, universities, and schools with the slightest connection with the intifada would be closed; all remnants of civilian law would be abolished and replaced by military martial law; any outbreak of Palestinian violence would be met with a crackdown and yet another Jewish settlement. In an election pamphlet, Tehiya advocated that 650,000 Palestinian refugees in the West Bank and Gaza be "exchanged" for Jews in the neighboring Arab countries, with full transfer as the desired outcome. In the 1988 elections Tehiya won three seats in parliament, and in 1990 took a seat in Shamir's government, the most extreme in Israel's history so far. Even within the Likud Party, it became legitimate to advocate transfer and the rule of terror in the occupied territories.

While the ruling parties in Israel pushed for expansion, confrontation, and messianic redemption, the opposition was radicalized toward peace and reconciliation with the Palestinians. For the first time, groups within the Israeli elite spoke out in favor of direct contact with the PLO, and some moved from words to action. The recently taboo two-state solution was suddenly the talk of the town, not least after Arafat's recognition of Israel in 1989 and the subsequent recognition of the PLO by the United States. The combination of desperation and hope that had given rise to a Palestinian revolt now seemed to crystallize into a historic peace option, still infinitely distant but politically energizing and inspiring.

In the Israeli elections of June 1992, the alternative had not yet been formulated and expressed. There was only the growing sense that two different and fundamentally incompatible views of society had emerged, and that Israel was at a crossroads. Some warned that the internal conflict could degenerate into civil war. Democratic debate and compromise required that all parties respect the values and principles of democracy. However, the parties of the nationalist and messianic settler movements had made it increasingly clear that their Israel was based on higher principles than democracy, and that they had no intention of respecting political decisions that would block the path to resettlement and redemption.

The 1992 elections did not resolve the conflict, but at a critical junction tipped the balance of power in a new direction. The most extreme right-wing parties, Tehiya and Moledet, were wiped out, and the idea of land for peace gained political power. The Rabin government's first action was to freeze settlement projects in the West Bank and Gaza and to slow the flow of state funds to the institutions of the settler movement. An alternative vision for Israel, based on a comprehensive Middle East peace settlement, was publicly articulated. The historic step a year later, the Oslo Accords with the PLO, and the breathtaking handshake between Rabin and Arafat in front of the White House, stemmed from the growing realization that the "facts on the ground" established by the previous governments had to be countered by other facts.

It also meant that the conflict intensified. The democratic ambiguity stemming from the contradiction between the Zionist aim of creating a majoritarian ethno-Jewish state and the universalist ideals proclaimed at the founding of Israel had now resulted in an open conflict, marked by growing anti-democratic and anti-Arab attitudes among young Israelis. In a survey from the mid-1980s, one-third of secondary-school students identified with positions taken by the racist party of Rabbi Kahane. Anti-democratic views were three times more common among religious students. Seven in ten students in religious vocational schools said they "hated" Arabs.

In January 1994, just a month before Goldstein's massacre in the Hebron mosque, Professor Baruch Kimmerling, one of Israel's leading sociologists and historians, argued that the situation in Israel was comparable to the situation in the United States before the American Civil War. There was no room for compromise between the idea of an ethnocentric, xenophobic, and theocratic Israel based on messianic expectations, and the idea of an Israel based on peace, reconciliation, and democracy. "The fundamental choice we face,"

Kimmerling wrote, "is whether one collective identity should be allowed to dictate the rules of the game for another."[41]

The idea of assassinating the prime minister of Israel was born among messianic settlers radicalized by the Oslo Accords and the specter of a land-for-peace agreement with the PLO. Rabbinical calls for disobedience and rebellion followed immediately, and in the fall of 1995, a number of settler rabbis declared Rabin a traitor, a *moser*, a person who "delivers" Jews to non-Jews, and that anyone who delivers the Land of Israel to its non-Jewish inhabitants "forfeits his life."

Two days after the murder, Yigal Amir faithfully and defiantly echoed the edict of his rabbinical authorities in a packed Tel Aviv courtroom: The Jew who gives Jewish land to the enemy is to be killed. The command to save Jewish lives is more important than the command not to kill. "Therefore it is right to kill a prime minister who shakes hands with the worst murderers of the Jews and releases terrorists who will kill Jews in a few days. Such a person is not a prime minister in my eyes."[42] Amir's Talmud teacher at Bar-Ilan University, Rabbi Moshe Raziel, was asked if he had shed any tears for the murdered Rabin. "No, not a single one," he replied.[43]

A few months later, Shlomo Aviner, one of the leading settler rabbis, gave his view of the situation:

> There are two conflicting views of the Land of Israel. One sees the land, the territory, as a means. The land should

enable the nation to physically exist and develop its cultural and spiritual life. This school of Zionism, which once made every effort to expand our homeland, now demands that we reduce it for the sake of peace: better a small house of peace than a large house of conflict. The second view sees an organic bond between the land and the people: without land no people, without people no land. It sees Zionism as a movement not for relocation, but for rebirth. The bond between the land and the people is, to borrow a metaphor from Isaiah, like the bond between the bride and groom. A groom would never dream of sharing his wife with anyone else, even if his life was at stake.[44]

Two days after the handshake in Washington, DC, a few hours before the onset of Rosh Hashanah, the Jewish New Year, I sit on the emptying beach beneath my hotel in Tel Aviv, reading David Grossman's book on the Palestinians in Israel, *Sleeping on a Wire*, as two men come up me.

"That little Pole hasn't understood anything," says the older of them, pointing to my book. A wreath of gray hair decorates his tanned bald head, and a sailor tattoo covers his right shoulder. The two men discuss me between themselves in Hebrew until I ask them, in Hebrew, to stop. The man with the tattoo kneels by my towel to discuss, while the other comes and goes with ever new suggestions on what I should read instead of "that one."

No doubt Ya'akov Kaplan is a remarkable man, erudite and polyglot, pronounces names of Swedish cities like Gothenburg and Kiruna with a hardly noticeable accent, says he was born in Estonia but remains demonstratively mysterious about his past.

Soon I notice his fondness for words like "carnage" and "slaughter" and "war." "The handshake in Washington is just the beginning," he says. "Soon Jews will be shooting at Jews. You know that Rabin was already shooting at Jews in 1948?"

"You mean Altalena," I say.

He seems surprised that I know anything at all.

"What is your option?" I continue.

"There will probably be a war anyway, but a son of a whore like that doesn't understand it." He points to Grossman's book again. "No, I'm sorry, not son of a whore, then I must apologize to the whores up there." He points to Yarkon Street, along which the seaside hotels are lined up.

"Your option," I insist.

"Transfer," he whispers with an indifference charged to the point of explosion. "Move them out. Everyone does it. Sweden too."

"And America," adds the literary adviser just passing by. "And Germany."

"That idiot Begin never got it, cursed be his memory, *zichrono le'klalla*."

"We will not do it with threats and impropriety, but with civility and firmness, with the Bible in one hand and Machiavelli in the other. We will learn from the Finns, the Romanians, the Estonians."

"If I'm a refugee, I don't care about the purple line or the green line or any other line, I care about me. Which is what this schmuck, idiot, doesn't understand." He points again to Grossman.

"Peres, *ha'nevela*, that bastard!" adds the literary adviser.

"When I visited the synagogue in Stockholm I bought a postcard for five crowns and asked, 'Why does it cost five crowns and not fifty öre,' and they answered that the surplus went to Keren Kajemet in Israel. So I said that they should not send their money here, to traitors and embezzlers like Peres and Begin, but help their own poor instead. If they send money for a cannon, they will at most get a gun."

I rise from the sand and wade into the emerald-green water. Kaplan follows me.

"Soon they will be here," he says.

"Soon this will be the Hong Kong of the Middle East," I say defiantly, looking out on never-sleeping, ever-growing Tel Aviv.

He gives me a pitiful look.

I ask him what he will do with his Arab-empty country.

"They won't be able to escape," he says, as if he didn't hear my question. "Rabin, Peres, Beilin!"

"Escape?"

"These *dreckim*, assholes, they shall not be able to escape when the Arabs come. Even if I have to slaughter them myself."

I am freezing in the warm water.

"No one will save them, at least not Tsvah Haganah Le'Ishmael, Ishmael's Defense Forces" (a pun on Tsvah Haganah Le'Israel, Israel's Defense Forces).

He gives orders in a military voice: "A. B. Yehoshua, Amos Oz, David Grossman, *al ha'kir*, against the wall!" Kaplan sprays imaginary bullets from an imaginary machine gun, then laughs and swims a few strokes.

I walk back onto the almost empty beach. Never-closing Tel Aviv is closing for the holiday.

On the lifeguard cabin someone has hung a white sign with text in red: "No lifeguard on duty."

The sea appears calmer than ever.

V
THE LAND REVISITED

2006: A FUNERAL

On the night of October 26, 2006, my aunt Bluma dies, and thirty-six hours later I find myself on a flight to Tel Aviv. Jewish funerals are speedy affairs and I have only a margin of eighteen hours. The news of Aunt Bluma's death was unexpected and the decision to attend her funeral was spontaneous; but as I settle into my seat, thoughts and memories come forth. The thoughts of stories silenced and links severed. The memories of glittering eyes, contagious laughs, the unruly mix of Polish, Yiddish, and Hebrew, the indomitable joie de vivre against a backdrop of unmentionable experiences.

Bluma was born in 1915 in the village of Chełm in eastern Poland, noted in Polish folklore for its fools (as is the Swedish city in which I was born, Södertälje). She was eleven years older than her youngest sister and the only remaining member of the Staw family with a living memory of the place where my mother was born. Many years ago, on a tape for which they no longer make recorders, I asked her for memories of Chełm. As she reminisced about the local *Wunderrabbi* and his miraculous cures and blessings (in case of difficult childbirth, tie a prayer book to the bed), I couldn't be sure whether she was just telling tales. Although I didn't understand everything she said, I did understand that whatever she managed to tell me will be as much as I will probably know of the world from which my mother came.

My mother, Hala (Chaia), was only five when my grandfather Jankiel (Jacob) and grandmother Rachela (Rachel), with five daughters and one son, left Chełm to seek their future in the teeming industrial city of Łódź. And only thirteen when the Germans occupied Łódź and imprisoned its Jews in a ghetto. And only seventeen when, in September 1944, the surviving members of the family were transported from the ghetto of Łódź to the selection ramp in Auschwitz, where most of the stories were silenced for good. Grandfather Jankiel and grandmother Rachela went straight to the gas chambers, as did my aunt Dorka with her one-year-old son, Ovadja, my eldest cousin. The four younger and childless sisters were deemed capable of work and, after spending two days under the never-ending smoke from the never-stopping crematories, they were transported to Stutthof concentration camp on the Baltic coast east of Gdansk. In Stutthof my aunt Bronka died. In Słupsk outside Gdansk, a month after liberation, my aunt Sima died. "Somewhere" in southeastern Poland, having escaped Łódź before the ghetto, my uncle Shlomo died.

After liberation the two surviving members of the Staw family, my aunt Bluma, who was now thirty, and my mother, Hala, who still was only nineteen, headed back to Łódź in search of something or someone to continue living

2006: A FUNERAL

for. Neither found what they were looking for. Instead, Hala found my father-to-be in a transit camp for Jewish Red Cross refugees in the village of Furudal in central-northern Sweden. In August 1946, she managed to travel from Poland to Sweden. It was not an easy feat, and she succeeded because she traveled with a false story under a false name, which is why I don't get too upset about asylum seekers who are compelled to do the same.

Aunt Bluma stayed for a few more years, started a small business in wholesale textiles, married Leon, and gave birth to two sons, my cousins Jacob and Isaac. But anti-Jewish sentiments remained rampant, and the few surviving Jews returning home soon realized that they had no home left. The pogrom in Kielce on July 4, 1946, confirmed that a thousand years of Jewish history in Poland had come to an end.[1] Within a few years, a large part of Poland's remaining Jews had left the country. In 1949, Poland opened the door for Jews to emigrate to Israel and the last representative of my family on Polish territory closed it behind her without ever looking back. My mother never returned to Poland; my aunt Bluma did once, when she was almost ninety and no longer afraid of anything in this world.

I change planes in Vienna. For a few years now there have been no regular direct flights between Israel and Sweden, or any other Scandinavian country. Tourism has dropped and the business climate has cooled. Israel inspires ever less curiosity and ever more consternation and aversion. The forty years of occupation have come to be regarded by many as scandalous, the founding of ever new settlements as provocative, the building of a security wall on largely Palestinian lands as unlawful, and the wielding of military force as disproportionate. Some people are weeding out Israeli oranges and avocados from their food baskets and nonstop flights to Tel Aviv from their itineraries.

The greater part of the passengers on the flight from Vienna are Israelis. The trolley with preordered kosher meals is as stocked as the trolley with standard chicken. A Christian group from Norway occupies a few rows at the back of the plane. Christian groups seem insensitive to the cycles of war and violence in the area, or rather inversely sensitive: the more troubled the region, the more reason to travel there. I get the feeling that the group on the plane is traveling to demonstrate solidarity with their Christian Palestinian brethren in Ramallah or Bethlehem. I fear that other Christian groups are traveling in order to demonstrate solidarity with the repossession of the Holy Land by the Jews, thereby, they believe, hastening the battle of Armageddon and the second coming of Christ.

The new terminal building at Ben-Gurion Airport is spacious and bright; one walks enormous distances through gently sloping and generously glass-walled arcades. Newcomers receive an impression of openness and normality, at least until they arrive at the passport and security controls, although these are not much worse than anywhere else. Nowadays, everybody everywhere is a potential terrorist. In that respect, Israel has become the world—and the world has become Israel.

It's only on the way out of the airport zone that Israel unmistakably becomes Israel again. Or rather, it's on the way out that I realize how much the airport zone symbolizes the country Israel has become. It's a large zone, the size of a small city. You must travel awhile along broad boulevards lined with lush palm trees and confusing road signs before you reach its boundary, which is as heavily fenced and controlled as the border between states. Inside the fence there are not only runways, airport terminals, shopping arcades, hangars, hotels, car parks, administration buildings, and everything else you would expect to find within the boundaries of an airport, but also farmed fields and orchards and other things that you would rather expect to find outside.

A well-stocked mini-Israel, I reflect. A small fortress within a large.

A last refuge in a final siege.

This is not the first time I keep thinking of Masada when entering Israel. Not only because I was raised in the belief that the State of Israel was the closing of a parenthesis opened two thousand years ago by the fall of Masada. But also because for a long time I have been troubled by the link between a mass suicide in a besieged mountain fortress in the Judean desert in AD 73 and the self-perception of Israel. By the image of an eternal fortress under eternal siege. By the yearly swearing-in ceremony of military units on the ruins of Masada, taking the oath that Masada must never fall again. By the national motto *ein brera*: no choice. No choice between fortress and failure. Between survival and suicide.[2]

In the 2005 documentary *Avenge But One of My Two Eyes* (*Nekam achat mishtei einai*), Israeli filmmaker Avi Mograbi reveals the continuing existence of an ominous suicide cult at the ideological and mythological heart of the

Jewish state. In one scene we are shown groups of Jewish youngsters gathered at the top of Masada, huddling in the strong wind, covering from the blinding sun, dizzy from the breathtaking view, being told the story about how and why nine hundred Jews choose to commit collective suicide rather than to fall into the hands of the Romans. And why it was the right thing for them to do.

"What are you hearing?" the teacher in a knitted skullcap asks his students as they close their eyes against the wind. He keeps asking until they hear what they are supposed to hear (which takes a few rounds): the sound of heroism and self-sacrifice. What they are supposed to conceive is that the people of Masada did the only thing conceivable.

"Do you see the remains of a wall down there?" another teacher asks another group of students on another occasion, pointing down from the precipice. "It was built by the Romans in order to seal off the besieged Jews. It was once two meters high and surrounded the whole fortress. And do you see the piles of stones at intervals of about two hundred meters? These were the watchtowers."

The students look and nod. Had they been able to look farther, all the way to Bethlehem or Jerusalem, they would have seen another wall, considerably longer, considerably higher, and considerably harder to penetrate—not built two thousand years ago by the Romans to fence in Jews, but today by the Jewish state to fence out Palestinians. In certain stretches, the wall is not a wall but an electronically monitored metal fence surrounded by broad security zones, deep trenches, barbed wire, and military patrols. Nevertheless, the word "wall" is justified: even where the wall is "only" a fence, its aim is to wall off the Palestinians in a territory that less and less resembles a state and more and more a prison.

Throughout the film runs a phone conversation between the Israeli director, in full view, and an invisible Palestinian friend somewhere on the other side of the wall, at times under curfew. "I am preparing to be dead," says the friend. "When people here no longer have anything to live for, they will want to die."

At a locked gate in a fenced part of the wall people are waiting to cross, but no one is opening. The camera observes them through the wire. The hours pass, the sun moves, Israeli patrol cars move back and forth, people gesture, plead, give up. "This is the end," says a man in his forties. "We have nothing to live for."

Invisible soldiers behind dark holes in massive watchtowers or in heavily armored vehicles bellow warnings and commands to a never-ending stream of people who day and night are humiliated by the whims of armed force. In yet another scene in the film, a sick woman is brought to an ambulance waiting beside an armored vehicle and a tank.

"She's bleeding," explains a man carrying the woman's belongings in a green plastic bag. "I don't care. Get out!" rasps a metallic loudspeaker voice from the darkness behind the barred window in the armored vehicle.

The man is pleading.

"Just get out!" screeches the voice in broken Arabic. "Get out!"

The ambulance has its red emergency lights flashing.

"Only to Beit Furik," pleads the ambulance driver.

"Go back! Get out!" The armored vehicle turns around and advances threateningly. The ambulance reluctantly drives off. Left at the checkpoint are the woman and her relatives, an elderly man in a red-and-white keffiyeh, a young woman in a gray headscarf carrying a small child, a teenage girl, and a small boy.

"May God humiliate them as they have humiliated us," says the young woman to the camera. The young girl cries incessantly. The armored vehicle and the tank stay motionless in the background.

"Don't be afraid, my little one," says the young woman. "God sees us. God will help us. God will liberate us from them." Then she cries too.

"Try to imagine how they felt," says a guide to one of the groups on top of Masada. "Try to understand why they did what they did."

"Romans, we won't give up," a group of school children shouts into the abyss. "Romans, we won't give up." The echo bounces back from the surrounding mountains.

"Come and stay with us for two days and try to understand how we live," says the Palestinian voice on the other side of the wall. "Try to understand why we no longer fear death. Why it doesn't matter to me whether I live or die."

How to make a hero of a suicide killer? The biblical tradition knows. Let me die with the Philistines, Samson begs God when deprived of his strength and with his eyes gouged out he is brought before the masses to be humiliated. Strengthen me one last time, he then pleads to God, so that I may avenge one of my two eyes.

The story of how Samson regains his strength and brings down the pillars of the temple on himself and three thousand Philistines has been conveyed to generations of Israeli school children as a tale of heroism. In the national mythology, Samson is inscribed as *Shimshon Ha'gibor*, Samson the Hero.

"Who among you can imagine what Samson feels when he stands there?" asks a female teacher in Avi Mograbi's film. "He feels that it's better to commit suicide," answers a child, "because then he can decide for himself when to die, and then he can also kill Philistines."

In a following scene, a group of Palestinian men has been arrested at a checkpoint and ordered to stand side by side with their heads turned away. One of the men turns his head back and is ordered to stand on a small stone. "Look what they are doing to us," says the man to the camera while balancing on the stone.

Another man turns his head back and is ordered to stand on another stone.

Ten men in a row, two men balancing on stones. A cold wind takes hold of their jackets and sweaters. No one is moving. No one is allowed to cross the checkpoint.

The only things crossing freely are the poisonous seeds of humiliation.

My first memories of Aunt Bluma are from the late summer of 1956. Gamal Abdel Nasser had nationalized the Suez Canal and the tensions along the 1949 armistice lines were higher than usual; a new war between Israel and Egypt seemed probable and Bluma thought it a was an opportune time to take the children and visit her sister in Sweden. How three adults and four kids managed to share two small rooms on Hertig Carls väg in Södertälje Södra I can't remember. It is only with hindsight that I understood why they really came. This was before the era of charter flights and the decision to embark on such a long and demanding journey must have been a tough one.

During nine weeks of summer, two red-headed rascals from the cultural cacophony of inner-city Tel Aviv tried to make themselves at home in the Swedish *folkhemmet* (people's home), but with little success. They spoke a foreign language, didn't understand our games, "borrowed" our unlocked bikes, shouted my name outside the home of my polio-stricken friend Berra, where I used to hide among his books and magazines. Yet, toward the end, Jacob, the elder of the two, had picked up some Swedish and we slowly got to know each other.

Later in the fall I remember my father's worried head bending over the radio set in the corner of our living room, listening to crackling reports about the pending war that had finally broken out and which had resulted in Israel temporarily standing on the shores of the Suez Canal. By then Aunt Bluma and the cousins had gone back. I suppose that they couldn't have stayed on forever, and that Israel was home after all.

As we made our *aliyah* to Israel in 1962, Aunt Bluma's apartment on Shenkin Street became a second home to me. An unlimited number of mattresses and beds could magically be produced from sturdy wooden cabinets, and an unexpected number of people could, with no notice whatsoever, be accommodated in the two small bare-walled rooms on the second floor, overlooking a bakery that produced a lingering aroma of fresh bread and chocolate.

2006: A FUNERAL

On early summer mornings, before the heat had filtered through the heavy wooden blinds, Aunt Bluma put on the kitchen table a bowl of sour cream, fresh bread from the bakery, and a plate of finely minced vegetables, before hurrying away in her flowery dresses and broad-heeled shoes to a small textile business somewhere in the maze of narrow streets beyond the teeming Carmel Market. When she returned home it was mostly dark and the flowery dresses were damp with sweat, but before long a three-course dinner was miraculously produced, and the usual four chairs had been placed around the balcony table and the quartet of cardplayers had been seated, and the bids and the laughs and the stories and the smoke from incessantly burning cigarettes began mixing with the sounds and scents from a night of open windows and wounds.

Lightheartedness can be a form of self-delusion, and the lightheartedness I so distinctly associate with the people laughing away their evenings on Aunt Bluma's balcony was certainly not uncomplicated. They had all been to hell, and had all been forced to seek something to continue living for, and had all learned from hard experience that Israel was not a paradise. It was, to say the least, a complex-ridden people whose phobias and anticipations permeated the new state. And, to say the least, a complex-ridden political and military reality that they willy-nilly became part of. During the humid nights on Shenkin Street, you could imagine yourself being in any country on the Mediterranean. That is, if you shied away from what Israel was: an armed fortress, established on contested lands, by a highly traumatized people.

And for a time it seemed to work. Rapid advance is a way of keeping the past at bay. People who otherwise would have been consumed by a nightmarish past were now consumed by dreams of a new future. The borders of Israel were certainly narrow and unsafe, "Auschwitz borders" as the Israeli foreign minister Abba Eban called them in 1967. But the horizons were still wide and promising, and Israel still a country of the righteous and the justified. Righteous in their return to history and justified in doing what history demanded.

I remember them as fine years, those years when the hot-humid darkness outside the yellow cone of light above the cardplayers on Aunt Bluma's balcony was saturated with the scent of bread and the murmur of hope.

The Jewish burial ceremony is straightforward and beautiful. On a wheeled stretcher under the open roof of an outdoor chapel, Aunt Bluma is resting in a sack of broidered black velvet. The outlines of her diminutive body show through the cloth. A young rabbi in a black hat and coat steps up to a small podium behind the stretcher to say kaddish, the prayer for the dead. I was to understand that the family had gone to great efforts to get this particular rabbi for the funeral, but I am a bit surprised when I see him, since I would not have thought that an ultra-Orthodox rabbi would be the spiritual support of first choice for my aunt Bluma's mostly secularized, and in some cases openly anti-religious, family.

Then the young rabbi says something that makes an impression on me as well. He says it in the traditional mode of prayer, half singing, half lamenting, and at first his intonation obscures his words. Then I hear him intoning a parable about Abraham the patriarch and Bluma my aunt. "As Abraham once left his country and his family and his father's house to begin a new life in the land that God had promised to him and his children," chants Rabbi Dan Lau, "so did Bluma Genislaw, blessed be her memory, leave her country and her family and her father's house to begin a new life in the State of Israel."

Yes, Bluma had indeed left everything behind, and she had never looked back.

The stretcher with the body is rolled out under the bare sky and into an endless maze of narrow walkways through densely packed grave quarters. Most graves are traditionally modest, horizontal slabs of white stone, but all along the route of the funeral procession, enormous palaces in black or red marble have recently been raised, with golden inscriptions and portraits of the deceased etched into the stone. The inscriptions in Russian or Georgian testify to a newly arrived grave culture. Their size and their brazenness and the glaring contrast they form to the even sea of white stones surrounding them testify to a rapidly changing society.

We gather around an open grave that is neatly squeezed in between two white stones. Here Leon and his sister Carola are already resting, only one spot remains. The stretcher is lifted off the wheeled carrier and brought to the grave and slowly tilted forward so that the white-draped body can slide out of the black velvet sack and down into the red-white sand. With one shovel each, we all help to seal the last resting place of Aunt Bluma. Her grave, like Leon's and Carola's, will be marked by a flat white stone.

I stay for another two days. In the early mornings I walk with my cousins to the small Sephardic synagogue in Isaac's neighborhood to read kaddish for Bluma. Jacob has arrived with his wife and two children from Durban in South Africa, where he has lived and worked for many years. Jacob is the most observant among us. According to Jewish tradition, he has torn his shirt on the left side of the chest, close to the heart, and has made Isaac do the same. After prayer we go back to the shiva, the traditional "seating" in the house of the dead. Bluma lived her last years in a small apartment next to Isaac's, so it is in the home of Sara and Isaac that we put the extra chairs, set the table with the refreshments, and welcome all who wish to pay their respects to the dead, to comfort her family, and to share their memories. The Jewish tradition stipulates seven days of shiva. It is a fine tradition that offers many opportunities for comfort and reflection, and I would gladly have sat it through to the end.

The last afternoon I visit close friends, again in Ramat Hasharon, the posh suburb north of Tel Aviv. They have long been critical of Israeli policy and have long hoped for a change, but have become increasingly pessimistic and defeatist. We walk onto the roof terrace where we get a glimpse of the glittering Mediterranean in the west and the softly rising hills of the West Bank in the east. And invisibly along the foot of the hills, the wall.

"So we are locked in again," they say with an enigmatic smile on their faces.

Six months later I read a newspaper interview with Avraham Burg, the former speaker of the Israeli parliament, also the former chairman of the Jewish Agency, also the former runner-up to the leadership of the Israeli Labor Party in 2001. Burg's father, Yosef Burg, was a leading representative of early religious Zionism and a minister in several Israeli governments during the 1950s.

To make it short: Avraham Burg is not just anybody in Israeli society.

The interview is about Burg's new book in Hebrew, entitled (in translation) *Defeating Hitler*,[3] where Burg writes that Israel has become "a Zionist ghetto, an imperialistic, brutish place that believes only in itself."

The interviewer is clearly upset: "What you are saying is that the problem is not just the occupation. In your eyes, Israel as a whole is some sort of horrible mutation."

Burg: "The occupation is only a part of it. Israel is a frightened society. To look for the source of the obsession with force and to uproot it, you have to deal with the fears. And the meta-fear, the primal fear, is the six million Jews who perished in the Holocaust."

Interviewer: "So we are psychic cripples, you claim. We are gripped by dread and fear and make use of force because Hitler caused us deep psychological damage."

Burg: "Yes. The true Israeli rift today is between those who have faith and those who are afraid. The Israeli right's great victory in the struggle for the Israeli political soul lies in the way it has imbued it with absolute paranoia. I accept that there are difficulties. But are they absolute? Is every enemy Auschwitz? Is Hamas a scourge?"[4]

The next morning I take a taxi to the airport. With each visit, the traffic on the highway between Tel Aviv and Jerusalem is thickening and becoming more erratic. The surrounding landscape is shifting as well. New urban settlements incessantly encroach on agricultural lands, cranes and bulldozers in frantic action everywhere, and you can literally see the Israeli economy grow. The economic gaps are growing too, but in this respect Israel is no different from most other countries in the merry-go-round of profits in the expanding order of global turbo-capitalism. What nevertheless makes Israel different from all other countries is the fact that all this is taking place alongside, and in conjunction with, occupation, colonization, and demolition. Only a few kilometers away, sometimes at a stone's throw, the same people that are working hard to build a society, are working hard to destroy a society.

And working hard to build a wall separating construction from destruction.

It is indeed striking how one activity can be conducted practically within eyesight of the other with such indifference. How easily madness can be dressed up as normality. During the short summer of Oslo it became slightly more difficult. For a brief moment the standards of normality changed. For a while it was normal to think that endless occupation was a dead end and reconciliation with the Palestinians an open path. During the long winter that followed, the old normality reasserted itself; reconciliation is now the impossibility, and endless war and occupation the only possibility.

And herein lies the madness: Endless occupation is not a possibility, and military superiority is not a durable strategy, and a policy for locking the Palestinians out will increasingly lock the Jews in.

Self-destruction is a peculiar human capacity. The human species has the ability to build societies and to destroy them—and it might be the same humans that will do both. During a few years in the 1990s, many of us perceived a capacity to go from destruction to construction in Israel-Palestine, a unique window of opportunity created by unique circumstances.

At the time of this writing the window has closed.

My aunt Bluma is dead and buried, and with her one of the last living links to a generation that made its way to Israel with the hope of escaping the ghetto and overcoming Auschwitz. Little could she foresee that she would die within the walls of a new ghetto—in fear of another Auschwitz.

We get into the line of cars making its way through the security entrance to the airport. A routine glance by the guard and we are whisked through. Other cars are taken aside for a more thorough inspection. Security checks might take time, which one must take into consideration when flying out of Israel.

What I have not taken into consideration is the procedure at the passport control. It has little to do with security but all to do with my relation to Israel.

"May I see your Israeli ID card?" asks the young female passport officer after a lengthy gaze into the computer screen.

I answer that I do not have an Israeli ID card, that I am a Swedish citizen and always have been.

"You are an Israeli inhabitant," she says as if talking to a mischievous child.

"I lived here for two years, forty-five years ago," I answer.

"You still live here," she says laconically and slowly inscribes onto my Swedish passport, across the Israeli exit stamp, the word "inhabitant" in Hebrew and a number from the computer screen.

She might as well have said: "You will never be free of Israel."

I fear that she might be right.

2024: TANTURA

My revisit to Israel was planned before October 7, 2023, as was the Swedish republication of this book. There were already good reasons for both. On December 29, 2022, Israel had put in place a government with the intention of ending the last vestiges of democracy in the country, which in turn had given rise to the largest protests in Israel's history, which was reason enough to ponder anew where Israel was heading.

I write "the last vestiges," since I believe this book has shown that Israel was not a full democracy in the past either. In a democracy, all citizens are treated equally regardless of ethnicity, religion, and origin. Not so in Israel. Right from its founding in 1948, there was a gap between the Declaration of Independence and its promise of equal treatment for all citizens "regardless of religion, race, or sex," and the transformation of the remaining Palestinian Arab population into second-class citizens—or "strangers in their own land" to quote the title of a book by Fida Jiryis, the daughter of Sabri Jiryis, the Palestinian Arab lawyer and activist whom I had met in Haifa in 1970 and whom I hoped to meet again after fifty-four years.

The Israeli government that took office on December 29, 2022, included for the first time a party that in a previous incarnation had been labeled racist and banned from parliamentary elections, and in subsequent incarnations in the 1990s had been labeled terrorist, but which had received 10 percent of the vote in the 2022 parliamentary elections and a key position in Israel's new government. It was a party whose leader, Itamar Ben-Gvir, previously convicted of incitement to terrorism, now became the minister of national security, with the openly declared goal of expelling as many Palestinians as possible from Judea and Samaria and establishing Jewish rule over the entire Land of Israel—from the river to the sea.

It was a government that soon made clear that it wanted to remove the last legal barrier to such policies: the power of the Israeli Supreme Court to review "unreasonable" laws. This would give a free hand to the ruling majority to take control of the education system, the judiciary, the media, and the freedom of expression, as well as a free hand to annex the "whole Land of Israel."

The proposal for "judicial reform" was presented on January 4, 2023, and triggered widespread protests across Israel, on some occasions involving hundreds of thousands of participants. Leading representatives of virtually every sector in Israel demanded that the reform be stopped, former prime ministers and commanders in chief called for civil disobedience, senior reserve officers threatened to go on strike, and for a time it looked like Israel was heading for civil war, or at least for a historic watershed in determining what state Israel should be.

There had long been profoundly conflicting views on the matter, which was made clear, if it had not been before, by the assassination of Prime Minister Yitzhak Rabin in November 1995. The Oslo Accords two years earlier had provoked violent reactions from those within Israel who regarded any deal with the Palestinians as a betrayal and who were prepared to murder and massacre to prevent it.

The road to peace and reconciliation was certainly a difficult one, paved with blood and killing, easy to derail with murder and terror. Baruch Goldstein's massacre in Hebron was followed by a series of suicide attacks by the Islamist Hamas (an organization established with Israeli support to divide the Palestinians) on buses and civilian targets across Israel, and eventually by a full-scale Palestinian uprising, the second intifada, which effectively destroyed the already weakened Jewish-Israeli peace movement. The most devastating blow came somewhat surprisingly from the "left," as Ehud Barak, the prime minister of a short-lived Labor government, ominously declared that Israel had no partner for peace. In doing so, he cemented the notion that the only way to "negotiate" with the Palestinians was to suppress them. Israeli intellectuals who had embraced the idea of peace and reconciliation were transformed into pugnacious hawks. With shocking ease, most Jewish Israelis became convinced that the blame for the conflict rested squarely on the Palestinians.

For another decade or so, this view of reality seemed to hold. Israel was able to consolidate its suppression of another people without any noticeable effect on the daily lives of Israelis or Israel's position in the world. On the contrary, the world seemed to be gradually making Israel's reality its own. The Palestinian cause was moved further and further down the international agenda, while Israel's offers of military cooperation and high-tech weapons systems earned it a host of new "friends," including countries and regimes that only recently had made the Palestinian cause their own. At the end of 2020, under the auspices of Donald Trump, the so-called Abraham Accords were signed between Israel, the United Arab Emirates, Bahrain, Sudan, and Morocco, in which not a single word was said about the Palestinian cause. It seemed only a matter of time before Saudi Arabia would also join, establishing a new political and military-strategic reality where the Palestinians no longer mattered.

Paradoxically, the Palestinians would also play no role in the Israeli mass protests against the judicial reform in the spring and summer of 2023. While the streets and squares of Israel were filled with Israelis who demonstrated in defense of the rule of law and democracy in a sea of blue-and-white flags, the cause of the Palestinians was absent and Palestinian flags were not welcome.

The Israeli disconnect from reality could not be more manifest. On the one hand, a raging domestic conflict over what kind of state Israel should be, and on the other, a conspicuous inability (or unwillingness) to recognize the link between the erosion of rule of law in the State of Israel and the lawless rule over the Palestinians in the occupied territories. For most Israelis, the Palestinians were still anonymous figures in a nation-building narrative of good versus evil, of Israeli righteousness versus Palestinian intransigence. And although the veracity of the narrative had long since been picked apart by historians, it still had a role to play in making the protesters on the streets of Tel Aviv unwilling to link their cause to the oppression of the Palestinians.

In most other respects the narrative had lost much of its unifying power. Between the protesters demanding the rule of law and the messianic settlers demanding to take the law into their own hands, there was little room for compromise. Little room too with the rapidly growing ultra-Orthodox part of the population, which wants Israel to be a theocracy based on the laws and edicts of the Torah.

Questions that had been raised in the early days of the Zionist movement were being raised again.

What kind of state was a Jewish state to be?

What was meant by Jewish?

In short, there were good reasons for a revisit.

"Together we will prevail," it says in large blue-and-white letters on the train from Ben-Gurion Airport to Tel Aviv, and on the stations along the way, and on countless billboards and buildings. Israeli flags hang from balconies and windows and flutter from cars and trucks.

At temporary stands and memorials all over the city, also the pictures of the 251 Israeli men, women, and children kidnapped by Hamas on October 7, 2023. "Bring him (her) home now," it says under each of them.

At the stand on the sidewalk across from HaKirya, the Israeli military headquarters. I ask if there is a photo of Alex, and after a while we find him at the bottom left. "Alex

Dancyg (75)" it says, and below the photo in handwriting, "Nir Oz." I recognize him immediately, even though it's been thirty years since we met. We had planned to meet again, but it wasn't meant to be.

October 7 changed everything. Only the day before, Israel was about to consign the Palestinian cause to the dustbin of history and make the world accept its continued existence as an occupying power, instituting an apartheid-like system based on ethnic suppression, dislocation, and separation, but the day after, this no longer seemed possible. With its brutal attack, Hamas had burst the Israeli bubble of security and confidence, and with its brutal response, Israel had made the Palestinian cause the cause of the world. However outrageous the attack of Hamas, and however uncompromising its hatred of the "Zionist state," it had managed to seriously damage the credibility of Israel's foundational doctrine, that by military superiority it could and must suppress the Palestinians forever.

This doctrine should reasonably have been disproven long ago. Ever since the 1982 invasion of Lebanon, Israel's wars had been a succession of political and strategic defeats. The war in Lebanon in the summer of 2006 did not wipe out Hezbollah as intended, but strengthened it. The war in Gaza six months later did not destroy Hamas as intended, but strengthened it. Similarly, each new war to destroy Hamas (2008, 2012, 2014), or "mowing the lawn" as it came to be characterized, did not destroy Hamas but strengthened it. Even the war that was still raging when I landed in Tel Aviv, and which was supposed to wipe out Hamas "once and for all," will wipe out nothing but perhaps hundreds of thousands of lives and weaken Israel strategically and politically instead of strengthening it.

It was not long, however, before I discovered that the doctrine of military superiority was not only alive and well in Israel but that it reigned supreme. It had also become more self-assured, with declared goals like "total victory" and "total annihilation," and with unabashed attempts to deny or explain away the genocidal ferocity with which the war was conducted. On Israeli television you would search in vain for images of destroyed cities and camps, bombed hospitals and universities, massacres of men, women, and children. Instead, and repeatedly, there were images of Hamas's atrocities on October 7, as if to justify whatever atrocities Israel was committing in Gaza. There was also broad support for the aims and methods of the war in the public opinion polls. It was true that Jewish Israel was in a state of shock and anger, but it was also true that it was in denial. If the Palestinian cause had been invisible in the protests before October 7, it was even more so in the protests after. There were still people and organizations that dared to give voice to the Palestinian cause as well, but in Jewish Israel they remained a small minority, increasingly shunned and encircled.

The last time I met Alex Dancyg, my classmate from Secondary School Number Nine in Tel Aviv, Nir Oz was a lush, irrigated oasis in the agricultural belt of kibbutzim that borders Gaza, from Yad Mordechai in the north to Kerem Shalom on the Egyptian border in the south. I had intended to pick up our conversation where we left off thirty years ago, but Nir Oz was now destroyed and half of its four hundred inhabitants had been killed or kidnapped, with Alex among them, and there would be no more visits to Alex in Nir Oz.

During my visit in June 1992, we had been watching election campaign ads on television. In one of them, Daniella Weiss, the Valkyrie of the national-religious settlers, with her covered head and steel-blue eyes, speaks of blood and soil, while the heavily armed settler rabbi Moshe Levinger walks through occupied Hebron to the sound effects of gunshots.

"If they win, I will move," said Alex.

On my way home in the falling darkness of night, I listened to the settler radio station Arutz Sheva broadcasting a mixture of heroic Jewish tales, nationalist propaganda, and explanations of God's will in Hebron, Jerusalem, and other parts of the coming Kingdom of the Messiah. As I tuned in, a woman was speaking about a member of the right-wing nationalist terrorist organization Lehi, the Stern Gang, who later became David Ben-Gurion's personal bodyguard. The moral of the story was that Ben-Gurion would rather entrust his life to a right-wing nationalist "enemy" (that is, a true patriot) than to a "friend" in his own ranks (meaning, a potential traitor).

At a turn on the narrow road along the Gaza border, I am stopped by a policeman.

"You did not use your blinkers."

He is an older man with a slight European accent. How many wars has he experienced? Does he suspect me of something else? A few days earlier, a Mr. Kalman

Weinstock had fired a gun at a Mr. Amad a-Din on the road between Jerusalem and Bethlehem, on the sole grounds that Mr. Amad a-Din's West Bank–marked truck had been driving erratically.

"This is Israel," the policeman says for good measure before allowing me to drive on.

I returned to Nir Oz just over a year later, in September 1993, after the signing of the Oslo Accords. As a gift, I had brought a T-shirt made by a happy Palestinian restaurant owner in Jericho, covered with peace doves and olive branches and the word "peace" in three languages.

The next day Alex took me along to buy spare parts for an irrigation machine on a peanut field lining the Gaza border. On the other side, the city of Khan Yunis was clearly visible. Alex saluted the border, he even longed for it. He longed for an end to the ambivalence and the uncertainty. He longed for distinct borders and clear agreements. He longed for a divorce from the Palestinians. He did not like the Palestinians. He also made it clear that he liked the religious settlers even less, the hundreds of families, "madmen," who had taken root in Gaza.

"But from them I cannot divorce," he added.

"And not from the Palestinians either," I added in the first edition of this book. "Borders and gates can no longer protect the world of Alexander Dancyg."

Little could I then imagine how literally this would come true.

October 7, 2023, will go down in history as the day the Palestinian cause reentered Israeli history. The pogrom-like attack, the deadliest of its kind in Jewish memory, brought to life all the demons of Jewish history, as Israel's inability to guarantee the security of its inhabitants profoundly shook the argument with which the Jewish state had justified its existence: the need of a state where Jews would forever be safe from persecution and annihilation. Which had also been an argument for the suppression of the Palestinians; occupation and suppression was what Jewish safety demanded.

Israel's genocidal response also brought to life all the demons of Palestinian history. The disasters, the Nakbas of 1948 and 1967 were now joined by the Nakba of 2023, the deadliest of them all, erasing any historical distinction between Jaffa, Hebron, and Gaza. Between one Nakba and another.

Palestinian disasters that were about to be buried were coming to life again.

I decide to revisit Tantura.

In the early 1960s I lived in a Tel Aviv that dipped its feet in the sea, but in a sea that no sensible person would dip their feet in. At least, no more than their feet. The sandy beach was dirty and covered in lumps of tar, the water was murky and contaminated, and along the beach walk that today is lined with chic cafés and luxury hotels were small, sparsely lit establishments where, according to rumor, the countless cats roaming the kitchens and garbage cans were sometimes cooked and served.

Consequently, those who could, bathed elsewhere. We could, because my uncle had a 1955 black VW Beetle inherited from his brother, my father, and on memorable Saturday mornings, before the sun was up and while the beaches were still empty, we packed the Beetle to the limit and headed north along the coast. The most beautiful and least populated beach lay farthest away and was reserved for the long, hot weekends when the pressure on Israel's beaches was at its highest. I still remember the jolt of joy and anticipation when my uncle, with the drama of a circus ringmaster, announced the name of the destination.

The name was Tantura.

On January 21, 2000, the Israeli evening newspaper *Maariv* published an article about a hitherto unknown massacre of Arab villagers during the war known in Israel as the War of Independence. The article was based on a master's thesis submitted to the Department of Middle Eastern History at the University of Haifa by a senior graduate student named Teddy Katz, and which had passed with flying colors. Based on interviews with a total of 135 people, the paper described in more or less consistent detail what happened when Israeli soldiers of the 33rd Battalion of the Alexandroni Brigade captured the Arab village of al-Tantura on May 22 and 23, 1948.

What happened, apart from the village being occupied after a firefight, was that some two hundred villagers were killed outside combat. About a hundred were shot in revenge for an Israeli soldier killed after the surrender. The other hundred or so victims, men aged between thirteen and thirty, were picked out from the villagers assembled on the beach and taken to a wall near the cemetery where they were executed by a gunshot to the back of the head.

That al-Tantura had been emptied of its inhabitants and wiped off the map during and after the 1948 war was an undisputable fact. That a large number of its inhabitants were killed outside combat should also have been. It was not only Katz's interviews that provided evidence for what had happened, although the evidence was strong enough. In the archives of the Israeli army there was also a written report from the commander of al-Tantura warning of epidemics resulting from unburied bodies. Another report spoke of "irregular events" and "overreactions," and yet another informed that the "mass grave" had been checked and that everything was "in order," *ha'kol be'seder*.

Nevertheless, a bubble of denial soon covered the al-Tantura massacre. Under intense social pressure and the threat of a libel suit Katz was made to apologize to the Alexandroni Brigade's representatives (insignificant errors had been discovered in the transcript of a hundred hours of taped interviews), his acclaimed master's thesis was rejected, his academic degree revoked, and his life shattered. The official narrative of the events of 1948 was still heavily guarded. What was done then must not be allowed to cast a shadow over Israel's doings now, and in particular it should not be allowed to blur the line between the territories Israel had taken control of in the 1948–1949 war and which de facto had been recognized by the United Nations, and the territories Israel had taken control of in the 1967 war and which were considered illegally occupied and settled.

In a 2022 Israeli documentary, the al-Tantura massacre is recounted in excruciating detail.[1] Elderly eyewitnesses come forward, the witness tapes from Katz's work are replayed, repressed memories are brought to life. Some seem relieved to tell their stories late in life, others not.

"What good is remembering?"

I take the coastal road north from Tel Aviv toward Haifa. Since I last traveled here, the landscape has changed dramatically. Israel is growing by leaps and bounds, not least upward. Dense forests of high-rises are sprouting along the highway, which itself seems under constant expansion. I recall the misgivings of early Zionists that the land was too small to house the Jews of the world, and that Zionism should therefore find itself another aim. But the aim remained, and the founding principle of making room for all Jews who want to make Israel their home has transformed central Israel into a sprawling metropolitan region where towns and villages are growing together.

However, there is no escaping the fact that the country is still a narrow strip of land between the Jordan River and the Mediterranean Sea, and that it is home to two peoples (it is more complex than that, but for the sake of simplicity) totaling fifteen million, about half of whom are Israeli Jews and half Palestinian Arabs, but where the Israeli Jews have assumed full control of the land by the dislocation and suppression of the Palestinians. After 1948, this could be explained away as a consequence of a war triggered by the refusal of the Arabs to accept the State of Israel, but gradually it has become clear that Jewish control of the territory has been a central part of the Zionist project all along, while the idea of one land for two peoples has been a losing proposition from the very start. Even more losing, if possible, has been the idea that Israel should recognize the Palestinian disaster and its role in creating it, and in the best of worlds, initiate a process of truth and reconciliation.

There is an Israeli organization, Zochrot, dedicated to putting up signs in places where an Arab village had been eradicated. On the signs they write the name of the village and the date of its eradication.

On the beautiful beach in al-Tantura they put up a sign with the date May 23, 1948.

I missed the cutoff because it didn't say Tantura but Nahsholim, the name of the kibbutz established in the remnants of the village a few weeks after the massacre and the expulsion of the inhabitants. Tantura was a famously prosperous village with solid stone houses and marble-clad terraces facing the sea, and the incoming new residents, including a group of Holocaust survivors, were struck by its beauty and wealth. "We didn't have to do much to start a new life," one of them testified. "Everything was in abundance, the fields were ripe for harvest—and what a harvest, I'm not exaggerating when I say we were overwhelmed—the soil was fertile, life comfortable, the beach and the sea incomparable, the possibilities seemingly endless."[2]

In September 1950, the houses of Tantura were dismantled and the stones used for building new houses in an area just north of the village. In the early 1960s, the last remnants of Tantura were destroyed as part of a policy to erase any traces of previous Arab life. Foreign Minister Golda Meir wrote in a memorandum that "the ruins of Arab villages and Arab neighborhoods, or of Arab buildings empty since 1948, evoke unpleasant associations that can cause significant political damage."[3]

In 1958, plans were drawn up to turn the site into a holiday village, and it is the sign to Nahsholim Sea Side Resort I should be looking for if I want to revisit the place where I had bathed as a child. On a Saturday morning in May, I pull into the parking lot as it is rapidly filling up. I find an empty spot at the far end and try to find my way in a place that bears no resemblance to the Tantura of my memories. To the south of the parking lot there is a sea of igloo-shaped beach bungalows, to the north a gated resort hotel. Was this the place I had visited as a child? But as I approach the sea and walk onto the beach, the memories of Tantura resurface. The clear blue lagoon, the white sand between my toes, the excitement of having arrived. I don't remember fishing boats bobbing on the water, nor the arched stone house close to the water, but I have already learned that this is the only house left of Arab al-Tantura.

As I watch the Israeli documentary to better understand what Tantura had once looked like, I discover that my car had been parked on the exact spot where a mass grave had been dug in May 1948. An aerial photograph from 1949 shows traces of a freshly turned trench, thirty meters long and three meters wide.

A group of elderly settlers of Nahsholim are asked how they would react if the descendants of Tantura would want to erect a memorial on the site of the massacre.

"We would never allow that," says one. "It would mean that the memory is important to them. And if it is important to them, it threatens me. They want to remember what happened. I don't want that."

"If they can put up a memorial, it's like letting them put up a sign of ownership," says another. "And then it never ends."

Still, there is a memorial in Tantura. Just beyond the parking lot, there is a road sign pointing to "Alexandroni Battalion (The Fallen of Tantura)" and behind a closed gate, there is a white marble slab with thirteen names engraved under the inscription: "In memory of those who sacrificed their lives on this spot in the War of Liberation (May 23, 1948)." I cannot help but think that the day when next to it stands a memorial to the villagers who were massacred here on that same day, a process of truth and reconciliation will have commenced.

It should have commenced way back, of course, and I continue my journey north to rekindle the memory of an early wasted opportunity.

When I first met Sabri Jiryis, he was thirty-two years old and had just written a book in Hebrew that would later be published in English as *The Arabs in Israel*, which I translated into Swedish, deeply shaken by what it had to say about the legal status of the Arab minority in Israel (see page 231).

Jiryis belonged to a generation of Israeli Arab intellectuals who had hoped to organize a political movement against the ongoing confiscation of Arab lands, and the emergency laws and military rule that governed their lives, and ultimately against a state that regarded them as second-class citizens. But their movements and parties were outlawed, their newspapers banned or confiscated, and one by one they were imprisoned and/or driven into exile. In 1964, Jiryis had registered a political party under the name Al-Ard (The Land), calling for a Palestinian Arab state alongside Israel based on the 1947 partition plan, but Al-Ard was declared a threat to Israel's existence and the young Jiryis went in and out of Israeli house arrests and prison detentions, in good company with the leading poets, writers, and journalists of his Palestinian Arab generation.

Many of them went into exile, and so did Jiryis. On September 9, 1970, he and his wife, Hanneh, boarded a plane to Athens, and from there on to Beirut, where they joined a growing Palestinian community of refugees and exiles.

About what happened thereafter, Sabri's daughter, Fida, born in Beirut in 1973, has written a book that weaves together the fate of one Palestinian family with the Palestinian tragedy in its full dimension.[4] Here I learn that Sabri became the director of the PLO Palestine Research Center, where Hanneh also had worked. In June 1982, Israel invaded Lebanon, drove the PLO out of the country, and paved the way for the gruesome massacre in the Palestinian refugee camps of Sabra and Shatila in September 1982. It also paved the way for the car bomb that on February 5, 1983, detonated outside the Palestine Research Center, robbing nine-year-old Fida and her four-year-old brother, Mousa, of their mother.

Here I also learn that Sabri and his two children were among the few "Israeli Arabs" in exile who were allowed to return home in the political thaw following the 1993 Oslo Accords, and for a brief moment it seemed that Israeli-Palestinian reconciliation was in the making. In November 1994, after twenty-four years in exile, Jiryis was able to set foot again in Fassuta, his home village in the Galilee.

What then follows is Fida's story of hopes being extinguished, of doors closed, of the humiliation and harassment at the military checkpoints as she traveled back and forth from Fassuta to her work in the occupied West Bank city of Ramallah, and of the harrowing experience of being a stranger in your own country.

The Nakba has not ended, Fida concludes her story.

I had made contact with Fida a few years earlier, after reading an article by her in an English-language magazine,[5] and realizing that she was Sabri's daughter and that Sabri was still alive, I resolved to look them up as well.

I continue north on the coastal road from Tantura. In the town of Nahariya, less than a mile south of the Lebanese border, I turn right toward the interior of the Galilee. After a few kilometers, the GPS goes crazy and shows the airport in Beirut, which I had been warned about and therefore brought an old-fashioned map on paper. It is the Israeli military that has made the GPS go crazy so that Hezbollah's drones and missiles will have difficulty finding their targets. I have no trouble finding the gas station where Fida and Sabri are waiting in a red Volkswagen. We greet each other warmly, but with some apprehension. Who are we after all these years? Sabri is eighty-six years old and life has left its mark; his body is fragile and his cheeks sunken, but the eyes behind the tinted glasses are sharp and his intellectual acuity is that of a young man, which I discover as he resolutely gets into my car so that I won't get lost on the last winding road to Fassuta.

At a turn in the road there is a military roadblock.

"It's the entrance to Elkosh," says Sabri.

Elkosh is a moshav, a Jewish agricultural cooperative, established in 1949 on land confiscated from the Palestinian Arab villages of Dayr al-Qassi and Al-Mansura, which like most other villages in this part of the Galilee were emptied of their inhabitants and later destroyed. It had been a close call for Fassuta too. The military had planned to empty all Arab villages within a mile of the Lebanese border, but the plans were interrupted by the government, which decided to put the remaining Arab villages under military rule and allowed Fassuta to survive.

Fassuta is a predominantly Christian Arab village, and as we arrive Sabri wants to show me the church. He also wants to show me the beautifully mosaic-decorated square in front of it, and the stone-paved street leading up to it, and the solid stone houses lining it on both sides. An 1881 description of Fassuta notes the lush gardens of figs and olives and the surrounding fields of arable land. The majority of Fassuta residents belong to the Melkite Greek Catholic Church, which traces its origins to the earliest Christian congregations. The church is a branch of the Roman Catholic Church but the interior reflects a Byzantine Orthodox tradition, with saints and apostles in golden halos.

Sabri also wants to show me the view, and with surprising agility he leads us up rickety wooden stairs and ladders to the roof of the church. The border with Lebanon is only two kilometers away and we can see houses and villages on the other side. We could also have seen the neighboring Christian village of Ikrit, which is even closer, but of Ikrit there is nothing left to see but a restored church. On another day, we could have seen and heard the trails of missiles, drones, antiaircraft missiles, and fighter jets in the ongoing border war between Israel and Hezbollah, but on this day it is quiet. Many of the surrounding Jewish communities have been evacuated but, with one exception, no Arab village.

"To where would they evacuate us?" Fida asks with a touch of irony. "Besides, they don't believe that Hezbollah sees us as targets."

We continue our conversation in Sabri's study. Almost sixty years ago, he had hoped that a book in Hebrew would give voice to the Palestinian Arab cause in Jewish Israel, just as he had hoped that Jewish Israel would allow a democratic Palestinian Arab opposition to organize itself.

All these wars and disasters later, I cannot help but think what Sabri and his Palestinian Arab generation could have meant for the prospects of a reconciliation between Jews and Arabs in Israel-Palestine. Here was a democratic Israeli Arab opposition member in the making, not an armed guerrilla. What Israel could have become if Sabri's Palestinian generation had not been suppressed, banned, and driven into exile, we cannot know. We only know what Israel has become.

I notice that the shelves are filled with books in Hebrew and English, and that many of them deal with the topic of Zionism. And indeed, after a while Sabri tells me that he has just finished writing a history of Zionism, an "alternative history" he calls it, and that he is now writing the epilogue. The history after October 7, he clarifies. He has been writing in Arabic for a Palestinian readership, but Fida has translated the manuscript into English for a British publisher.

A few days later, Fida sends me her translation of Sabri's alternative Zionist history and I read it with great interest. Here is a Palestinian intellectual with bitter memories and experiences of the Zionist project, who has devoted years of his life to writing a carefully documented and factual description of the circumstances and ideas that shaped it. Almost sixty years ago, Sabri wanted to reach an Israeli Jewish audience with a book in Hebrew about the Palestinian Arabs they had learned to fear and hate. Now, he wanted to reach his own Palestinians with a book in Arabic about the ideology and movement they had learned to fear and hate—if possible even more so after October 7.

In the book's epilogue, written with Israel's genocidal war in Gaza on full display, the hope for a common Israeli-Palestinian future seems gone. Instead, there's the hope that Zionist Israel will come to an end, that new alliances of power will turn the tables on it, that the strong will become the weak and the weak will become the strong.

The Bible has much to say about the sometimes fatal consequences of being a people living on the narrow strip of land between the Jordan River and the Mediterranean Sea, of being wedged between much larger and more powerful and sometimes competing empires.

The biblical prophets, who witnessed the recurrent conquests and subjugations of their nations, thus came up with the historically groundbreaking idea of a society based not on the right of the mighty, but on the justice of the righteous.

"Woe to those who go down to Egypt for help, who rely on horses, who trust in the multitude of their chariots and in the great strength of their horsemen," the prophet Isaiah warned the kings of Jerusalem. "By righteousness shall Zion be redeemed, and by righteousness her penitents."

In a sense, Isaiah's prophecy came true. What remained after the small nations on the narrow strip of land had been repeatedly conquered and destroyed was a biblical people, Israel if you will, who in the "dispersion" or "Diaspora," could live on without relying on chariots and fighters. Even before the destruction of the Second Temple and the fall of Jerusalem, the majority of Jews lived elsewhere.

In the light of biblical history, chariots and horses have not been Israel's best weapon.

And perhaps not in the light of the history being written now.

Ein brera, no choice, is a Hebrew expression that has come to signify the state-founding myth that the forces of history and the realities of geopolitics have not given Israel the luxury of a choice. This is certainly not true; in the history of the State of Israel there have been choices not made and paths not explored. Where they might have led we do not know, of course. What we do know is that the choices made have led Israel into a dead end; its geopolitical vulnerability has increased, its security has weakened, and the prospects for a peaceful sharing of the land have been actively shattered. Thus, the most beautiful prophecy of Isaiah and the Hebrew Bible sounds more remote than ever:

> *For from Zion the law shall be proclaimed,*
> *from Jerusalem the word of the Lord.*
> *He shall judge between the nations,*
> *to execute justice among all peoples.*
> *They shall beat their swords into plowshares*
> *and their spears for vineyard knives.*
> *The nations shall not lift up sword against one another*
> *and never again shall they train for war.*

I end my revisit with a few days in Jerusalem. The city is preparing to celebrate Jerusalem Day on June 6, to commemorate Israel's conquest and annexation of East Jerusalem. On my visit in 1967, a month after the war's end, it was as if the city had never been divided. People were moving freely across demolished fences and desolate stretches of no-man's-land, and there were expectations on both sides of the former divide that reunification would bring the residents closer to each other.

But that was not to be. Soon the "Judaization" of Greater Jerusalem began, Arab neighborhoods were demolished, Jewish neighborhoods were built, and new borders were erected, both visible and invisible. East Jerusalem's Palestinian inhabitants were given the legally insecure status of "residents," which was a status that they risked losing at any time. Since then, thousands of Palestinians have lost their right to reside in Jerusalem. As I walk through neighborhoods where Palestinian families have been evicted from their homes and Jewish settlers have moved in, there can be no doubt that Jerusalem is a city where one people is consolidating its suppression of another.

Just around the corner from my hotel stands Orient House, the stately villa that in the wake of the Oslo Accords was allowed to serve as the PLO representation in Jerusalem, but which in 2001 was taken over by Israeli security forces and closed. One afternoon, I witness a dozen elderly gentlemen gathering in front of the sealed-off house to remember Faisal Husseini, the last Palestinian representative in Jerusalem, on the anniversary of his death in 2001. Posters with Faisal's portrait and the text (in Arabic) "Prince of Jerusalem" had been hung on the locked gate and on a sturdy security barrier in front. The memorial ceremony had not yet begun when a group of heavily armed police officers crossed from the other side of the street, tore down the posters, and brusquely dispersed the gathering.

Representatives of the same police force would stand with their arms crossed when, on Jerusalem Day, national-religious settler extremists stormed through the Arab neighborhoods of Old Jerusalem, chanting "Death to the Arabs," and attacking some of them along the way. Ideally, they would have liked to storm into the area that Jews call Har Habayit (the Temple Mount) and Muslims call Haram al-Sharif (the Noble Sanctuary), to provoke, with God's help, *Be'ezrat Ha'shem*, the apocalyptic war from which Solomon's Temple would rise anew on the ruins of Islam's third holiest site.

So that's what had become of my Israel, a state in which a horde of violent racist settlers were allowed to roam freely while a dozen Palestinian gentlemen gathered for a peaceful commemoration were not allowed to open their mouths.

This was not yet what Israel had become when I put the finishing touches on the first edition of this book in the spring of 1996. The Oslo Accords, with all their flaws, had created a climate for dreams of peace and reconciliation, which prompted me to end the book with a few lines from modern-day Israel's own Isaiah, the poet Yehuda Amichai.

In the place where we are right
No flowers will grow
In the Spring.
The place where we are right
is hard and trampled
like a courtyard
But doubt and love
Loosen the soil
like the mole, like the plow.
And where the ruined temple
once stood
a whisper shall be heard.

At the time, I added my hope that the whisper from the place where the ruined temple once stood would sound louder than the horn blasts from its reerected walls.

I hereby add it once more.

NOTES

PREFACE
1 Arthur Koestler, *The Invisible Writing: The Second Volume of an Autobiography, 1932–1940*, Danube edition (NY: Stein and Day, 1969), 19.

PART I: EXODUS

ASCENT
1 Arthur Koestler, "Judah at the Crossroads," in *The Trail of the Dinosaur* (Hutchinson, Danube edition, 1970).
2 Both my father and my mother were survivors of the Holocaust. I recount their fate in my childhood memoir *A Brief Stop on the Road from Auschwitz* (Other Press, 2015).

ARRIVAL
1 The Sicarii, after the Roman word for knife, *sica* (not far from the Hebrew *sakin*), were a radical Jewish sect who, at the time of the fall of the Second Temple, were dedicated to murdering suspected collaborators. They eventually became the model for a fascist-inspired movement in early 1930s Palestine. Its leader, Abba Ahimeir, wrote, among other things, a manifesto entitled *Megilat Sikarikin*, the scroll of the Sicarians.
2 Amos Elon, "Politics and Archeology," *The New York Review of Books*, September 22, 1994.
3 Howard M. Sachar, *A History of Israel: From the Rise of Zionism to Our Time*, vol. 1 (Alfred Knopf, 1991), 540.

TRANSFORMATION

1. Arthur Hertzberg, *The Zionist Idea* (Atheneum, 1959), 377.
2. Howard M. Sachar, *A History of Israel: From the Rise of Zionism to Our Time*, vol. 1 (Alfred Knopf, 1991), 73.
3. Amos Elon, *The Israelis: Founders and Sons* (Adam Publishers, 1981), 110.
4. Fredrik Böök, *Resa till Jerusalem våren 1925* (Bo Cavefors Bokförlag, 1977), 126.
5. Böök, 132.
6. Böök, 130–31.

EMANCIPATION

1. Karl Marx, "On *The Jewish Question*, II: 'The Capacity of Present-day Jews and Christians to Become Free,'" translator unknown, proofed and corrected by Andy Blunden, Matthew Grant, and Matthew Carmody, 2009. First published in German in 1844.
2. Arthur Hertzberg, *The Zionist Idea* (Atheneum, 1959), 22ff. The original Sanhedrin (from the Greek *synedrion* = *council*) was based in Jerusalem and operated in Palestine during the Roman Empire. It was dissolved with the fall of Jerusalem and the destruction of the Temple in 70 CE. A local Palestinian Jewish Sanhedrin, based in Yavneh, survived for nearly four hundred more years. Napoleon's Sanhedrin consisted of unrepresentative rabbis and Jewish personalities from France and Italy, all more or less ordered by the police to participate.
3. Hertzberg, 26.
4. Speech to the first Zionist Congress in Basel in 1897, in *Max Nordau's Zionistische Schriften* (Jüdischer Verlag, 1909), 46.
5. "Yes, a Judaizing Christianity would be the very disease we should inoculate ourselves against!" Jacob Katz, *Out of the Ghetto: The Social Background of Jewish Emancipation, 1770–1870* (Random House, 1988), 242; Fichte and Goethe quote, 100; see also Walter Laqueur, *A History of Zionism* (Weidenfeld and Nicolson, 1972), 20.
6. Moses Mendelssohn, *Phädon, oder über die Unsterblichkeit der Seele* (1767). This was certainly not the first attempt to link Jewish and Hellenic thought. Moses Maimonides, the medieval Spanish-Jewish philosopher and a key source of inspiration for

Mendelssohn, attempted to connect Judaism's belief in God with the Aristotelian philosophy of reason and logic. And more than a thousand years earlier, the Jewish thinker Philo of Alexandria had attempted to show that on a deeper allegorical level, Jewish texts wrestled with the same issues as the Neoplatonic philosophers. The attempt to create links between Jewish and non-Jewish thinking thus had a long tradition.

7 Charles Bonnet, *Untersuchung über die Beweise für das Christentum* (1787).
8 Marcus Ehrenpreis, *Skalder och siare som byggt Israel* (Bonniers, 1943), 144.

PART II: THE PROMISED LAND

A LAND LIKE ALL OTHERS

1 Howard M. Sachar, *A History of Israel: From the Rise of Zionism to Our Time*, vol. 1 (Alfred Knopf, 1991), 518.
2 Arthur Hertzberg, *The Zionist Idea* (Atheneum, 1959), 186.
3 Theodor Herzl, *The Diaries of Theodor Herzl* (Gollancz, 1956), 7.
4 Herzl, *The Diaries of Theodor Herzl*, 22.
5 Moshe Leib Lilienblum, *The Future of Our People* (1883), quoted in Hertzberg, 174.
6 *Beit Yaakov Lechu V'nelcha*.
7 Leo Pinsker, *Auto-Emancipation*, quoted in Hertzberg, 197.
8 Herzl, *The Diaries of Theodor Herzl*, 16.
9 Chaim Weizmann, *Trial and Error: The Autobiography of Chaim Weizmann* (Jewish Publication Society of America, 1949), 61.
10 Theodor Herzl, Marcus Ehrenpreis, ed., *Valda skrifter* (Herzlia, 1944), 25. See also my book *Another Zionism, Another Judaism: The Unrequited Love of Rabbi Marcus Ehrenpreis* (Other Press, 2025).
11 Herzl, *The Diaries of Theodor Herzl*, 33.
12 Zygmunt Bauman, *Modernity and Ambivalence* (Polity Press, 1991), 148.
13 Herzl, *The Diaries of Theodor Herzl*, 22.
14 John M. Efron, *Defenders of the Race: Jewish Doctors and Race Science in Fin-de-Siècle Europe* (Yale University Press, 1994), 98.
15 Efron, *Defenders of the Race*, 174.

16 Herzl, *Valda skrifter*, 168–69.
17 Bauman, *Modernity and Ambivalence*, 148.
18 Herzl, *Valda skrifter*, 149.
19 Hertzberg, 242.

A BETTER LAND

1 Arthur Hertzberg, *The Zionist Idea* (Atheneum, 1959), 276.
2 Ahad Ha'am, *The Jewish State and the Jewish Problem* (1897), quoted in Hertzberg, 268–69.
3 Ha'am, 267.
4 Ha'am, 80.
5 Ha'am, 79.
6 Ha'am, 80.
7 Ha'am, 82.
8 Shlomo Avineri, *The Making of Modern Zionism: The Intellectual Origins of the Jewish State* (Basic Books, 1981), 129.
9 Avineri, 130.
10 Avineri, 130–31.
11 Steven J. Zipperstein, *Elusive Prophet: Ahad Ha'am and the Origins of Zionism* (University of California Press, 1993), 320.
12 Arthur Ruppin, *Three Decades of Palestine: Speeches and Papers on the Upbuilding of the Jewish National Home* (Schocken, 1936), 135, from an article in *Die Jüdische Rundschau* in November 1924.
13 Ruppin, 199–200, from a speech to the World Zionist Congress in Zurich, July 1929.
14 Ruppin, 62, from an address before the 11th World Zionist Congress in Vienna, September 1913.
15 Ruppin, 116, from an address before the 13th World Zionist Congress in Basel, August 1923.
16 Ruppin, 197, 198–99.
17 Ruppin, 181.
18 Judah Leon Magnes, *Like All the Nations?*, pamphlet published in Jerusalem in 1930, quoted in Hertzberg, 447.
19 Judah L. Magnes, *Dissenter in Zion* (Harvard University Press, 1982), 186.
20 Magnes, *Dissenter in Zion*, 137, letter to Chaim Weizmann, May 25, 1913.

21 Magnes, *Dissenter in Zion*, 32, letter from Chaim Weizmann, December 15,1925.
22 Magnes, *Dissenter in Zion*, 312, letter to Arthur Ruppin, April 18, 1936.
23 Magnes, *Dissenter in Zion*, 276, letter to Chaim Weizmann, September 7, 1929.
24 Magnes, *Dissenter in Zion*, 210.
25 Magnes, *Dissenter in Zion*, 327, from *The New York Times*, July 18, 1937.
26 Magnes, *Dissenter in Zion*, 43.
27 Magnes, *Dissenter in Zion*, 393.
28 Magnes, *Dissenter in Zion*, 511ff. The plan was published in *Commentary* magazine in October 1948, entitled "For a Jewish-Arab Confederation," as a response to an article by Abba Eban against the idea of a confederation.
29 Magnes, *Dissenter in Zion*, 506, letter to Folke Bernadotte, August 10, 1948.
30 Magnes, *Dissenter in Zion*, 517, press statement of August 23, 1948.
31 Hannah Arendt, "The Mission of Bernadotte," *The New Leader*, October 23, 1948. See Magnes, *Dissenter in Zion*, 519, letter to Hannah Arendt, October 7, 1948.
32 Magnes, *Dissenter in Zion*, 519. The same diary entry also refers to what was probably Magnes's last protest, this time by resigning from the leadership of the American Jewish aid organization Joint Distribution Committee, which he had cofounded. The organization had not responded to his request for help for the Palestinian Arab refugees. "How can I continue to officially associate myself with an aid organization that can so seemingly effortlessly sidestep such a large and urgent refugee problem?"
33 Martin Buber, *On Judaism* (Schocken Books, 1967), 140.
34 Buber, "Hebrew Humanism," in Hertzberg, 459.
35 Buber, *On Judaism*, 1967, 135.
36 Buber, *On Judaism*, 78.

A STRONGER LAND

1 Vladimir Jabotinsky, "Betar's Idea," in Yonathan Shapiro, *The Road to Power: Herut Party in Israel* (SUNY Press, 1992), 17.

2. Jabotinsky, *The War and the Jew* (Altalena Press, 1987), 83.
3. Jabotinsky, *The War and the Jew*, 84.
4. Shlomo Avineri, *The Making of Modern Zionism: The Intellectual Origins of the Jewish State* (Basic Books, 1981), 172–73.
5. Betar is the Hebrew acronym for Brit Trumpeldor (the Covenant of Trumpeldor), after Joseph Trumpeldor, who in 1909 died defending Tel Hai, a Zionist outpost in northern Galilee.
6. Shapiro, 56.
7. Shapiro, 58.
8. Shapiro, 59–60.
9. Avineri, 170.
10. Jabotinsky, 86–87.
11. Jabotinsky, 75.
12. Mitchell Cohen, *Zion and State: Nation, Class and the Shaping of Modern Israel* (Columbia University Press, 1992), 165.
13. Alcázar was a military fortress that during the Spanish Civil War was besieged by Republican forces, who threatened to execute the captive son of a Franco commander if the fortress did not surrender, which it did not, and the son was executed in front of his father.
14. Uri Zvi Greenberg's poetry and journalism developed early on in a strongly anti-Arab and racist direction. As early as 1924–1925, he called for the removal of the mosques on the Temple Mount in Jerusalem. He began referring to Arabs as Canaanites, thus legitimizing the conquest of the country (it was the land of the Canaanites that God had given to Abraham), and he spoke openly about the need for violence. "Our nationalism is a historical *imperative* in the blood of the Hebrew race" was a characteristic statement. See Anita Shapira, *Land and Power: The Zionist Resort to Force, 1881–1948* (Oxford University Press, 1992), 148.
15. This line of reasoning was developed in Achimeir's 1926 pamphlet *Megilat Sikarikin*. Shapiro, 197.
16. The term "from the Nile to the Euphrates" is taken from Genesis 15:18, and was invoked by Stern in *18 Principles of Rebirth*, which led to the formation of Lehi.
17. Yitzhak Shamir, *Summing Up: An Autobiography* (Weidenfeld & Nicholson, 1994), 86–87.
18. Shapiro, 41.

19 Cohen, 158.
20 Emmanuel Neumann, an American Zionist leader, who in 1931 was mandated to negotiate a coalition with Jabotinsky on behalf of two "center parties": the General Zionists and the religious Mizrahi. Cohen, 151.
21 Menachem Begin, *The Revolt: Story of the Irgun* (Steimatzky's Agency Limited, 1952), 39.
22 "At our first attack we should have captured Ramleh...They needed only a few hundred rifles...or six per cent of the number loaded in the hold of the 'Altalena'." Begin, 154.
23 The party within Labor Zionism that historically represented a more expansionist stance on the territorial issue was Ahdut Ha-Avoda (Unity of Labor), whose ideology also permeated one of the three dominant kibbutz movements, Kibbutz Ha-Meuhad (the other two, Ihud Ha-Kibbutzim and Kibbutz Ha-Artzi, were affiliated with Ben-Gurion's Mapai and the occasionally Soviet-influenced Mapam, respectively). Ahdut Ha-Avoda argued that class was more important than state, that more collective farms were more important than fixed borders, that partition therefore was a bad thing, while the establishment of new kibbutzim throughout the Palestinian territory was an ideological imperative. After the June 1967 war, the Ahdut Ha-Avoda leader Yitzhak Tabenkin demanded immediate Jewish settlement in the occupied territories and advocated for national cooperation with Herut and the Revisionists. Shortly thereafter, the party merged with Mapai and Rafi, Ben-Gurion's breakaway party, including Moshe Dayan and Shimon Peres, to form a new labor party that thus included both ideological and pragmatic advocates for a greater Israel. Yigal Allon, the minister behind the first official Israeli settlement plan, came from Ahdut Ha-Avoda. See also Cohen, 264ff.

A LAND AT THE END OF TIME

1 Flavius Josephus, *Judarnas krig mot romarna* (Bokförlaget Rediviva, 1987), 240. An Egyptian who stirred up "four thousand knife men" and went out with them into the wilderness is also mentioned in Acts 21:38.
2 Moses Maimonides, *Mishne Torah*, chapters 11 and 12, quoted in Steven Schwarzschild, Menachem Kellner, ed., *The Pursuit*

of the Ideal: Jewish Writings of Steven Schwarzschild* (SUNY Press, 1990), 19, and Nathan Peter Levinson, *Der Messias* (Kreuz Verlag, 1994), 181.
3 From Habakkuk 2:3; in the Hebrew original: *achakeh lo bechol jom shejavo*.
4 Gershom Scholem, *Den judiska mystiken* (Brutus Östling Bokförlag Symposion, 1992), 325.
5 Levinson, 79.
6 Levinson, 79–80.
7 Levinson, 83.

PART III: THE LAND IN THE SHADOWS

THE CHILDREN OF THE HOLOCAUST

1 The German historian Eberhard Jäckel in his contribution to the collection *Historikerstreit*, quoted in Saul Friedlander, *Memory, History, and the Extermination of the Jews of Europe* (Indiana University Press, 1993), 50.
2 Tom Segev, *The Seventh Million: The Israelis and the Holocaust* (Hill and Wang, 1993), 86.
3 Ben-Gurion before the Mapai Central Committee in 1949, quoted in Segev, 179.
4 Primo Levi, *Moments of Reprieve* (Summit Books, 1986), 11.
5 Amos Elon, "The Politics of Memory," *The New York Review of Books*, October 7, 1993.
6 The story unfolded in the Hebrew press in August 1995 that on October 29, 1956, a parachute battalion under the command of Raful Eitan, later the architect of the Lebanon war and commander in chief, landed in the midst of a group of civilian Egyptian road workers. When the battalion was ordered to leave two days later, it did not take the prisoners with it but took them to a nearby quarry and shot them dead. The order was given by Eitan and executed by Biro. In an article published on August 8, 1995, in the Hebrew newspaper *Maariv*, Biro described what happened: "There were exactly 49 people, not 20 or 30... We tied their hands and led them to the quarry. They were scared and shaking. Raful did not give us an explicit order and I did not ask for one. Only an idiot would ask his commander for permission

to do what had to be done anyway. Anyway, I can say that Eitan did not mourn the bodies of the laborers we killed. Nor did he punish whoever did the job. They were a burden, a nuisance, a stick up our arse, and until we got rid of them, we couldn't do anything else."

7 Sarit Fuchs, "I Am Ariye Biro," interview in *Maariv*, October 3, 1995.
8 Segev, 260.
9 All quotations Segev, 208.
10 Segev, 226.
11 Steven Schwarzschild, Menachem Kellner, ed., *The Pursuit of the Ideal: Jewish Writings of Steven Schwarzschild* (SUNY Press, 1990), 94.
12 Schwarzschild, 96.
13 The theme is developed in an article by David Shakham in *Davar*, March 11, 1994: "Anyone who believes that the only choice is between being an executioner and being a victim, and who is prepared to become an executioner in order not to become a victim, can also become a Nazi."
14 Hannah Arendt, *Eichmann in Jerusalem: A Report on the Banality of Evil* (Penguin Books, 1977), 10.
15 Arendt, 225.
16 Segev, 356.
17 Segev, 362.
18 Richard L. Rubenstein, *After Auschwitz: History, Theology, and Contemporary Judaism* (Johns Hopkins University Press, 1992), 152.
19 Interview in the Hebrew weekly newspaper *Yerushalayim*, April 28, 1995.
20 Op-ed piece by Uzi Ornan in *Yedioth Ahronoth*, April 1994.

UNTO THE THIRD GENERATION

1 Adin Steinsaltz, *Teshuvah* (The Free Press, 1987), 10–11.
2 "Hanokmim jotzim mi'ha'aron," *Haaretz*, June 26, 1992.
3 Levi Arieh Sarid, "The Revenge Organization: Its History, Image, and Deeds," *Yalkut Moreshet* 52 (April 1992): 85.
4 Sarid, 45.
5 Sarid, 46.

6 Testimony of Yaakov Ronen, who took care of the bag and disposed of it. Sarid, 67.
7 Sarid, 39–40.
8 Nathan Alterman, "Songs of the Plagues of Egypt," quoted in Sarid, 37. My translation. The quotes from the contemporary debate in Palestine are taken from Segev, 149–51 and ibid., 37–39.
9 Hannah Arendt, *The Human Condition* (University of Chicago Press, 1958), 241. "The alternative to forgiveness, but by no means its opposite, is punishment, and both have in common that they attempt to put an end to something that without external interference, could go on endlessly. It is therefore quite significant, a structural element in the realm of human affairs, that men are unable to forgive what they cannot punish, and that they are unable to punish what has turned out to be unforgivable. This is the true hallmark of those offenses which, since Kant, we call 'radical evil' and about whose nature so little is known, even to us who have been exposed to one of their rare outbursts experienced on the public scene."

IV. THE LOST LAND

THE LAND UNDER THE STONES

1 David Grossman, *Sleeping on a Wire: Conversations with Palestinians in Israel* (Farrar, Straus & Giroux, 1992), 103.
2 Emile Habibi, *The Secret Life of Saeed: The Pessoptimist* (Interlink Books, 2001), 22.
3 Anita Shapira, *Land and Power: The Zionist Resort to Force, 1881–1948* (Oxford University Press, 1992), 283.
4 Robert John and Sami Hadawi, *The Palestine Diary: 1945–1948*, vol. 2 (Palestine Research Center, 1970), 271.
5 Neil Asher Silberman, *A Prophet from Amongst You: The Life of Yigael Yadin: Soldier, Scholar, and Mythmaker of Modern Israel* (Addison Wesley, 1993), 102ff. Silberman gives a detailed account of Plan Dalet, its creation and implementation.
6 Silberman, 103.
7 The Deir Yassin massacre is very well documented as it took place in the open. An eyewitness was Meir Pa'il, at the time a commander of the Palmach, an official armed wing of the

Zionist movement, later an Israeli army general, member of parliament, and military historian. In a testimony given the day after the massacre and published twenty-four years later in the newspaper *Yediot Ahronot* on April 4, 1972 (also reproduced in David Hirst's book *The Gun and the Olive Branch*), he said: "It was midday when the fighting and shooting stopped. All was quiet, but the village had not yet given up. The Irgun and Lehi irregulars left their hiding places and started cleaning up the houses. They fired with everything they had and threw grenades into the houses. They shot everyone they encountered in the houses, including women and children—indeed the commanders did not even attempt to stop the shameful slaughter. I myself and some of the villagers appealed to the commanders to order their men to stop shooting, but without success. In the meantime, twenty-five men had been taken out of the houses; they were loaded onto waiting trucks and taken to a 'victory parade,' in a kind of Roman triumphal procession, through the Mahaneh Yehuda and Zichron Yosef neighborhoods [in Jerusalem]. After the parade, they were driven to a quarry between Giv'at Shaul and Deir Yassin where they were shot in cold blood. The women and children who were still alive were loaded onto a lorry and left at the Mandelbaum Gate." Deir Yassin was by far the worst but not the only assault on Arab villages. In 1948, Battalion 89 of the official Israeli army, Tzahal, entered al-Duwayma, a large Palestinian village less than two miles west of Hebron, and killed eighty to a hundred of the inhabitants, including women and children. "Cultivated and well-mannered commanders...were turned into simple murderers, not in the heat of battle or out of blind passion, but because of a system based on displacement and annihilation. The fewer Arabs left the better..." (Eyal Kafkafi in the Labor Party newspaper *Davar*, on June 9, 1979). Israel Eldad, a later leading advocate of Jewish annexation of the West Bank, has written: "Had it not been for Deir Yassin, half a million more Arabs would have lived in the State of Israel [1948]." See Uri Davis, *Israel: An Apartheid State* (Zed Books, 1987), 8.

8. A critical summary of the military operations in the spring of 1948 can be found in Walid Khalidi, "Plan Dalet: Master Plan for

the Conquest of Palestine," *Middle East Forum*, November 1961. See also John and Hadawi, 325–49.

9 Walid Khalidi, *Sefer HaPalmach (The Book of the Palmach)*, vol. 2 (Kibbutz HaMeuchad, 1953), 286. It is not clear what Allon means by the phrase "Western Israel," but he probably means Palestine west of the Jordan River, since the revisionist branch of the Zionist movement openly claimed the area east of the river as well.

10 Quotes after Silberman, 150ff. The existence of the attack plan was later confirmed by Shaul Ramati, a deputy brigade commander in the Israeli army, also an Israeli delegate at the armistice negotiations in Rhodes in March 1949, in an article in *Haaretz* on April 18, 1994. He also testified that Ben-Gurion wanted to use the threat of a conquest of the West Bank as a means of diplomatic pressure in the negotiations. The attack plan in September 1948, however, was genuine. Ben-Gurion and Allon had planned to present the Israeli government with a fait accompli with the fabricated reference to an imminent Jordanian attack. The assassination of Bernadotte allowed the plan to be leaked and it had to be presented to a cabinet meeting, where it was rejected by a majority vote after a heated debate. Most government members feared that the UN would not quietly accept that Israel had so blatantly broken the existing cease-fire and conquered so much territory beyond the partition plan, at least in the days and weeks after Jewish terrorists murdered an already martyred UN mediator.

11 *Nochachim nifkadim* is also the Hebrew title of David Grossman's 1991 book, *Sleeping on a Wire*.

12 Sabri Jiryis, *Araberna i Israel* (PAN/Norstedts, 1970), 12–13; see also David Kretzmer, *The Legal Status of the Arabs in Israel* (Westview Special Studies on the Middle East, 1990), 141ff, and Menachem Hofnung, *Israel: Security Needs vs the Rule of Law, 1948–1991* (Nevo, 1991), 50ff. Another sharp critic was Dr. Bernard Joseph, then legal expert of the Jewish Agency and later, under the name Dov Joseph, the Israeli minister of justice, who in 1946 characterized the laws as follows: "There is no guarantee that a citizen will not spend his entire life in prison without trial. There is nothing to guarantee the freedom of the individual. There

is no opportunity to appeal against the actions of the ruler, no opportunity to appeal to a Supreme Court... The authorities have unlimited freedom to expel a citizen at any time. It is not necessary to have committed a crime... The principle of collective responsibility has been driven to absurdity. All the Hebrew inhabitants (600,000 in total) could well be hanged for a crime committed by a single person in this country. A citizen cannot be asked to put his trust in the arbitrary behavior of a public official. We cannot put our lives and property at stake... The citizen cannot be made to respect a law that makes him completely lawless." From Joseph's statement at the conference of the Jewish-Palestinian Bar Association in Tel Aviv on February 7, 1946, reproduced in the journal *Haparklit*, February 1946, quoted in Jiryis, 12.

13 Kretzmer, 58–59. The Land Acquisition (Validation of Acts and Compensation) Law of 1953 gave Israel's minister of finance discretionary power to issue certificates validating the new use of the land without consulting the landowner.

14 There were further cases where Supreme Court rulings in favor of the right of return of evacuated Arabs were ignored or countered by retroactive legislation. The inhabitants of the village of Rabsiye were expelled from their houses during the 1948 war but returned in the spring of 1949. In January 1950 they were expelled again by order of the military commander without any legal sanction. Only in August 1951 was the area declared closed under Article 125 of the Emergency Regulations, but the decision was not publicized in the prescribed manner. In September 1951, some of the villagers tried to enter the village but were expelled by the military. They appealed to the Supreme Court, which ruled that the emergency decree had no legal force. The minister of defense then used the emergency laws to retroactively sanction the military decisions. Shortly afterward, on November 30, 1951, a new closure order was issued. After another appeal by the villagers to the Supreme Court, the Knesset enacted a law retroactively authorizing the emergency decree without prior publication. The Supreme Court questioned the entire military action and its security-based motives, but in the judgment only a few of the villagers were allowed to return. This did not matter anyway, as the village was leveled shortly afterward. See Hofnung,

63–64. Several Jewish agricultural collectives were established or expanded in violation of Supreme Court rulings, including Kibbutz Lahavot Haviva (on land belonging to the village of Hirbat Jalame), according to the article "Ha'shomer Ha'tzair's Dark Secrets," *Haaretz*, September 24, 1993.

15 The only newspaper in Israel that published Kenan's letter (originally not intended for publication) was the organ of the small left-wing organization *Matzpen*, with which I had close contacts during these years.

16 The Allon Plan envisaged that Israel would militarily control a strip along the western bank of the Jordan River where Jewish security settlements could be established, but that the rest of the densely populated West Bank would be returned to Jordanian jurisdiction. The Allon Plan was never accepted by King Hussein as a basis for negotiations, and would in any case have given Israel jurisdiction over a quarter of the West Bank territory, including the expanded and annexed East Jerusalem. Nevertheless, the settlement in Hebron was already established in April 1968, and the settlement in Kiryat Arba in 1970, and between 1969 and 1973 the Israeli labor government of Levi Eshkol and Golda Meir spent more than $10 million on water, electricity, and sewage to these initially illegally established settlements. Howard M. Sachar, *A History of Israel: From the Aftermath of the Yom Kippur War*, vol. 2 (Oxford University Press, 1987), 12ff, and Robert I. Friedman, *Zealots for Zion: Inside Israel's West Bank Settlement Movement* (Random House, 1992), 15ff.

17 Kretzmer, 136.

18 Kretzmer, 57.

19 Don Peretz, *Israel and the Palestine Arabs* (The Middle East Institute, 1958), 142ff.

ON THE BARRICADES

1 One of the PFLP leaders I met in Amman was Bassam Abu-Sharif, who would later become one of Yasser Arafat's closest advisers and played an instrumental role in bringing about the PLO's recognition of Israel in 1989. Bassam later gave his own version of the event in the book *The Best of Enemies: Memoirs of Bassam Abu-Sharif and Uzi Mahnaimi* (Little Brown, 1995).

2. The articles were published in the English-language publication *Fateh* on November 20, 1969, and January 1 and 19, 1970.
3. The statement was made in an Israeli television interview in August 1973: "It was not that there was a Palestinian people in Palestine who called themselves that, and that we drove them away to take their place. It did not exist!"
4. *Fateh*, August 21, 1970.
5. There is every indication that in February 1971, Egypt's new president Anwar Sadat was prepared to negotiate peace and territorial recognition. An initiative by the UN mediator Gunnar Jarring to this effect on February 8, 1971, was immediately met with Sadat's unreserved yes—but the Israeli government voted an unreserved no. Not even the representatives of the left-wing Zionist party Mapam voted in favor.
6. Meir's statement in New York in October 1969, quoted in *Hadashot*, September 24, 1993, special issue on the twentieth anniversary of the Yom Kippur War in 1973.
7. Howard M. Sachar, *A History of Israel: From the Aftermath of the Yom Kippur War*, vol. 2 (Oxford University Press, 1987), 28.

BLOOD AND SOIL

1. The biblical source for the extent of the Land of Israel is Genesis 15:18–21: "On that day the Lord made a covenant with Abram [he had not yet become Abraham], saying, 'To your descendants I give this land, from the Wadi of Egypt to the great river, the Euphrates, the land of the Kenites, Kenizzites, Kadmonites, Hittites, Perizzites, Rephaites, Amorites, Canaanites, Girgashites, and Jebusites.'"
2. Ehud Sprinzak, *The Ascendance of Israel's Radical Right* (Oxford University Press, 1991), 114.
3. The movement was also supported by leading Labor Zionist veterans and cultural figures, among them the poet Nathan Alterman and Rachel Ben-Zvi, the widow of Israel's second president. Israeli newspapers and *The New York Times* published full-page ads with the headline "The establishment of Jewish settlements in the liberated territories is the highest priority... The mountains of Judea and Samaria, now returned to us, have never ceased to be the object of our hopes and dreams."

4 Sprinzak, 38.
5 Sprinzak, 39.
6 "Yes, where is our Hebron—have we forgotten it? And where is our Shechem, and our Jericho, where—will we forget them?! And all of Transjordan—it's all ours, every single clod of earth, each little bit, every part of the country is part of the land of God—is it in our power to surrender even one millimeter of it?" Richard L. Rubenstein, *After Auschwitz: History, Theology, and Contemporary Judaism* (Johns Hopkins University Press, 1992), 212.
7 Zvi Yaron, *The Philosophy of Rabbi Kook* (Torah Education Department of the World Zionist Organization, 1991), 72.
8 Yaron, 240. In the halachic tradition, dispersion, Galut, was not an inexplicable contingency but a divine punishment, the cancellation of which signaled the third redemption.
9 Yaron, 241.
10 Yaron, 236.
11 Yaron, 212.
12 In May 1990, Levinger was sentenced by an Israeli court to the symbolic penalty of five months' imprisonment, but at a specially convened meeting, hundreds of assembled rabbis expressed their support for Levinger's actions and interpretation of the law. See Sprinzak, 344n.
13 Robert I. Friedman, *Zealots for Zion: Inside Israel's West Bank Settlement Movement* (Random House, 1992), 29.
14 The pamphlet ("blessed" in Hebrew is *baruch*), which was printed in a thousand copies and sold out immediately, was written by the settler rabbis Yitzhak Ginsburg and Israel Ariel, and the five good principles realized by the massacre were the sanctification of the holy name, the saving of Jewish lives, revenge, the eradication of evil (Amalek), and war. *Haaretz*, September 4, 1994.
15 Friedman, 126; Sprinzak, 279.
16 For some Christian evangelical movements, mainly in the United States, the return of the Jews to the Holy Land is a prelude to Armageddon, the great battle between evil and good, God and Satan, which foreshadows the Last Days, the Day of Judgment, the final conversion of the Jews to Christ, and the return of Christ to the earth (Revelation 16:16). In the 1980s, under Ronald Reagan, Christian fundamentalism and the notion of Armageddon

had a strong influence in American politics. Reagan even said that Israel's recapture of the Temple Mount might be a sign that the battle of Armageddon was imminent; see Lou Cannon, *Reagan* (G. P. Putnam and Sons, 1982). Other statements suggest that he interpreted the struggle between America and the Soviet "evil empire" in similar apocalyptic terms; see, for example, Paul D. Erickson, *Reagan Speaks* (New York University Press, 1985), 83–85. During the 1980s, Christian fundamentalism in the United States provided both political and financial support to the messianic settler movement. Despite protests from liberal and democratic Jewish circles, a curious alliance was established between right-wing, antisemitic evangelists like Pat Robertson and right-wing Jewish organizations; see Friedman, 142–52.

17 Yehuda Etzion expressed his ideas in articles and essays during and after his imprisonment (he was released in 1988). He persistently denied the jurisdiction of the State of Israel over Jews submitting to a higher authority than the Knesset. Secular Israel was "an irrelevant system of rules and regulations whose purpose is to organize our daily life with no relation to the Torah of Israel and its heritage, with no interest in the redemption of Israel, and with no ability of carrying or serving it." Quoted in Sprinzak, 260.

18 Friedman, 127–28.

19 In August 1989, the Israeli Chief Rabbinate gave permission to implant "red" European embryos into Israeli cows for the breeding of animals for cultic purposes.

20 David Levy, the housing minister in the right-wing government of Itzhak Shamir, later revealed that the Israeli government had supported the house purchases of Ateret Cohanim through a subsidiary of the Jewish National Fund. The Ministry of Housing had in fact been supporting Ateret Cohanim's purchases of Arab real estate since at least 1986. See Friedman, 100.

21 In one article, Ne'eman compared Zionism to the metabolism of the human body. "People eat, breathe, excrete, and sweat. All the agents change and nevertheless there is an identical completeness—until the harmony is broken, the mechanism of metabolism deteriorates, and the system stops and dies. Zionism is a similar system. If it stops, it ceases. It can only exist as a process. The process changes its form; new actors enter; but the

whole remains the same and alive." In *Haaretz*, September 28, 1981, quoted in Sprinzak, 195.

22 Article by Aviva Sha'abi and Tzvi Gilat in *Yediot Ahronot*, March 18, 1994.

23 Ibid. See also Sprinzak, 269ff.

24 Sprinzak, 123; Amos Elon, "Israel's Demons," *The New York Review of Books*, December 21, 1995. The commandment of Amalek is based on Exodus 17:14 and Deuteronomy 25:17. It is perhaps superfluous to add that the commandment of Amalek has given rise to a much different and, until the rise of Messianic Zionism, fully dominant Jewish interpretative tradition.

25 And was evoked again in a statement by Prime Minister Benjamin Netanyahu on October 28, 2023. "'Remember what Amalek did to you' (Deuteronomy 25:17). We remember and we fight."

26 Yeshayahu Leibowitz, *Judaism, Human Values, and the Jewish State* (Harvard University Press, 1992), 243, 247.

27 Leibowitz, 236; Leibowitz is referring to Ezekiel 33:23–26.

28 Howard M. Sachar, *A History of Israel: From the Aftermath of the Yom Kippur War*, vol. 2 (Oxford University Press, 1987), 93–94.

29 Friedman, 210; ibid., 96ff.

30 Land ownership was in many cases, for historical reasons, poorly documented. Under successive Ottoman, British, and Jordanian regimes, many landowners tried to have as little to do with the authorities as possible for fiscal and bureaucratic reasons. Now, when the Israeli government demanded documents, they were faced with having to pay for expensive land surveys or, with the help of a lawyer, trying to find old bills of sale and documents in the archives in Amman or Istanbul. Most were at a loss.

31 Sachar, 98.

32 Sachar, 94, and Friedman, 73.

33 The Karp Committee, named after its chairman, the Israeli deputy attorney general Yehudit Karp, was established in April 1981 on the initiative of leading lawyers and legal experts, following reports of growing private police activity in the occupied territories. The committee examined fifteen randomly selected legal cases, ranging from the uprooting of olive trees to murder, which were found to have been poorly investigated or not investigated

at all. The committee recommended a radical overhaul of the settlers' access to and right to use weapons. The Karp Report was finalized in May 1982, but was not published until February 1984 (after the Lebanon fiasco), and only after Karp had resigned in protest of the cover-up.

34 In a study of Jewish fundamentalism in the occupied territories, *For the Land and the Lord* (Council on Foreign Relations, 1988), Ian S. Lustick writes: "Once settled in the occupied territories [...] these non-ideological Israelis were thrown into conditions that strongly encouraged them to adopt the views, attitudes and ideals of the Israeli right."

35 This section is based on a review of the French edition of Pinto's book *Journal de Judée*, in the Swedish daily *Svenska Dagbladet*, December 8, 1989.

36 Chava Alberstein's recording of "Chad Gadia" is on the album *London* (CBS 465470-2).

37 The radio incident was recounted by Nathan Shachar in an article in the Swedish daily *Dagens Nyheter*, December 7, 1989.

38 Sprinzak, 205.

39 *Anachnu kan, hem sham, ve'shalom al Israel.*

40 Sprinzak, 174.

41 "It Can Happen Here Too," *Haaretz*, January 21, 1994.

42 *Maariv*, November 7, 1995.

43 *Maariv*, November 10, 1995.

44 *Jerusalem Report*, February 8, 1996.

PART V: THE LAND REVISITED

2006: A FUNERAL

1 In Kielce, forty Jewish inhabitants (out of the two hundred returning after the war) were killed by an antisemitic mob. They were clubbed, stoned, kicked, and shot to death. In a subsequent wave of pogrom violence, Jews were killed all over Poland. See Jan T. Gross, *Fear: Anti-Semitism in Poland after Auschwitz* (Princeton University Press, 2006).

2 Already in 1946 Hannah Arendt warned of the development of a suicidal mentality in the nascent Jewish state: "Some of the Zionist leaders pretend to believe that the Jews can maintain

themselves in Palestine against the whole world and that they themselves can persevere in claiming everything or nothing against everybody and everything. However, behind this spurious optimism lurks a despair of everything and a genuine readiness for suicide that can become extremely dangerous should they grow to be the mood and atmosphere of Palestinian politics." Hannah Arendt, "The Jewish State," in *Hannah Arendt: The Jewish Writings*, eds. Jerome Kohn and Ron H. Feldman (New York: Schocken Books, 2007), 386–387.
3 In Hebrew, *Lenatzeah et Hitler* (Yedioth Ahronoth, 2007).
4 Ari Shavit interview with Avraham Burg, "Leaving the Zionist Ghetto," *Haaretz*, June 7, 2007.

2024: TANTURA
1 *Tantura*, directed by Alon Schwarz (Reel Peak Films, 2022).
2 Alon Confino, "The Warm Sand of the Coast of Tantura: History and Memory in Israel After 1948," *History & Memory* 27, no. 1 (2015): 58.
3 Confino, 71.
4 Fida Jiryis, *Stranger in My Own Land: Palestine, Israel, and One Family's Story of Home* (Hurst & Company, 2023).
5 Fida Jiryis, "Arabs of Inside," *London Review of Books* 39, no. 9 (May 4, 2017).

BIBLIOGRAPHY

Abu-Sharif, Bassam, and Uzi Mahnaimi. *Min vän, min fiende.* Ordfront, 1996.
Ahad, Ha'am. *Essays, Letters, Memoirs.* East West Library, 1946.
Arendt, Hannah. *Eichmann in Jerusalem: A Report on the Banality of Evil.* Penguin Books, 1977.
Arvidsson, Rolf, *Fredrik Böök och det judiska problemet,* Lund, 1977. Excerpted in Fredrik Böök, *Resa till Jerusalem våren 1925.* Norstedt, 1925.
Avineri, Shlomo. *The Making of Modern Zionism: The Intellectual Origins of the Jewish State.* Basic Books, 1981.
———. *Moses Hess: Prophet of Communism and Zionism.* New York University Press, 1985.
Bauman, Zygmunt. *Modernity and Ambivalence.* Polity Press, 1991.
———. *Postmodern Ethics.* Blackwell, 1993.
Begin, Menachem. *The Revolt: Story of the Irgun.* Steimatzky's Agency Limited, 1952.
Bentwich, Norman. *Judah L. Magnes: A Biography of the First Chancellor and First President of the Hebrew University of Jerusalem.* East and West Library, 1955.
Buber, Martin. *On Judaism.* Schocken Books, 1967.
———. *On the Bible.* Schocken Books, 1968.
Böök, Fredrik. *Resa till Jerusalem våren 1925.* Bo Cavefors Bokförlag, 1977.
Cohen, Mitchell. *Zion and State: Nation, Class and the Shaping of Modern Israel.* Columbia University Press, 1992.
Confino, Alon. "The Warm Sand of the Coast of Tantura: History

and Memory in Israel After 1948." *History & Memory* 27, no. 1 (Spring/Summer 2015): 43–82.

Davis, John H. *The Evasive Peace: A Study of the Zionist-Arab Problem.* John Murray, 1968.

Davis, Uri. *Israel: An Apartheid State.* Zed Books, 1987.

Dayan, Moshe. *Story of My Life.* Da Capo Press, 1992.

Efron, John M. *Defenders of the Race: Jewish Doctors and Race Science in Fin-de-Siècle Europe.* Yale University Press, 1994.

Ehrenpreis, Marcus. *Skalder och siare som byggt Israel.* Bonniers, 1943.

Eisenstadt, S. N. *Jewish Civilization: The Jewish Historical Experience in a Comparative Perspective.* SUNY Press, 1992.

———. *The Transformation of Israeli Society.* Weidenfelt and Nicholson, 1985.

Elazar, David J. *Israel: Building a New Society.* Indiana University Press, 1986.

Elon, Amos. *The Israelis: Founders and Sons.* Adam Publishers, 1981.

Friedlander, Saul. *Memory, History, and the Extermination of the Jews of Europe.* Indiana University Press, 1993.

Friedman, Robert I. *Zealots for Zion: Inside Israel's West Bank Settlement Movement.* Random House, 1992.

Gilman, Sander L. *Jewish Self-Hatred: Anti-Semitism and the Hidden Language of the Jews.* Johns Hopkins University Press, 1986.

Gitelman, Zvi. *The Quest for Utopia: Jewish Political Ideas and Institutions Through the Ages.* M. E. Sharpe Inc., 1992.

Goldberg, Michael. *Why Should Jews Survive?: Looking Past the Holocaust Toward a Jewish Future.* Oxford University Press, 1995.

Gordon, A. D. *Selected Essays.* New York: Arno Press, 1973.

Green, Arthur. *Tormented Master: The Life and Spiritual Quest of Rabbi Nahman of Bratslav.* Jewish Lights Publishing, 1979, 1992.

Grossman, David. *Sleeping on a Wire: Conversations with Palestinians in Israel.* Farrar, Straus & Giroux, 1992.

Habibi, Emile. *The Secret Life of Saeed: The Pessoptimist.* Interlink Books, 2001.

Halevi, Ilan. *A History of the Jews.* Zed Books, 1987.

Halevi, Judah. *The Kuzari: An Argument for the Faith of Israel.* Schocken Books, 1964.

Hamrin, Agne. *Murslev och svärd*. Bonniers, 1955.
Hedin, Sven. *Till Jerusalem*. Bonniers, 1917.
Hertzberg, Arthur. *The Zionist Idea*. Atheneum, 1959.
Herzl, Theodor. *The Diaries of Theodor Herzl*. Gollancz, 1956.
———. *The Jewish State*. Dover Publications, 1988.
Herzl, Theodor. Marcus Ehrenpreis, ed. *Valda skrifter*. Herzlia, 1944.
Hofnung, Menachem. *Israel: Security Needs vs the Rule of Law, 1948–1991*. Nevo, 1991.
Ilan, Amitzur. *Bernadotte in Palestine, 1948*. St Martin's Press, 1989.
Jabotinsky, Ze'ev. *The War and the Jew*. Altalena Press, 1987.
Jiryis, Fida. "Arabs of Inside." *London Review of Books* 39, no. 9 (April 2017).
———. *Stranger in My Own Land: Palestine, Israel and One Family's Story of Home*. Hurst & Company, 2023.
Jiryis, Sabri. *Araberna i Israel*. Göran Rosenberg, trans. PAN/Norstedts, 1970.
John, Robert, and Sami Hadawi. *The Palestine Diary: 1914–1945*. Vol. 1. Palestine Research Center, 1970.
Johnson, Paul. *A History of the Jews*. Harper & Row, 1987.
Josephus, Flavius. *Judarnas krig mot romarna*. Bokförlaget Rediviva, 1987.
Kats, Madeleine. *Taggig frukt—att leva i Israel*. Bonniers, 1965.
Katz, Jacob. *Out of the Ghetto: The Social Background of Jewish Emancipation, 1770–1870*. Random House, 1988.
Koestler, Arthur. *Promise and Fulfilment: Palestine 1917–1949*. Macmillan & Co., 1983.
Kretzmer, David. *The Legal Status of the Arabs in Israel*. Westview Special Studies on the Middle East, 1990.
Laqueur, Walter. *A History of Zionism*. Weidenfeld and Nicolson, 1972.
Laqueur, Walter, and Barry Rubin Barry. *The Israel-Arab Reader: A Documentary History of the Middle East Conflict*. Penguin 1976.
Leibowitz, Yeshayahu. *Judaism, Human Values, and the Jewish State*. Harvard University Press, 1992.
Levinas, Emmanuel. *Beyond the Verse: Talmudic Readings and Lectures*. Indiana University Press, 1994.
———. *Difficult Freedom: Essays on Judaism*. Johns Hopkins University Press, 1990.

Levinson, Nathan Peter. *Der Messias*. Kreuz Verlag, 1994.
Lundkvist, Artur. *Hägringar i handen*. Tidens Bokklubb, 1964.
Magnes, Judah L. *Dissenter in Zion*. Harvard University Press, 1982.
Maimonides, Moses. *The Guide for the Perplexed*. Dover Publications, 1956.
Mansour, Atallah. *Waiting for the Dawn*. Secker & Warburg, 1975.
Morris, Benny. *1948 and After: Israel and the Palestinians*. Clarendon Press 1993.
Mosse, George L. *The Nationalization of the Masses: Political Symbolism and Mass Movements in Germany from the Napoleonic Wars Through the Third Reich*. Fertig, 1975.
Netanyahu, Benjamin. *A Place Among the Nations: Israel and the World*. Bantam Books, 1993.
Nordau, Max. *To His People: A Summons and a Challenge*. Scopus Publishing Company for Nordau Zionist Society, 1941.
Oz, Amos. *In the Land of Israel*. Flamingo, London 1983.
Peres Shimon, *The New Middle East*. Henry Holt & Company, 1993.
Peretz, Don. *Israel and the Palestine Arabs*. The Middle East Institute, 1958.
Peters, Joan. *From Time Immemorial: The Origins of the Arab-Jewish Conflict over Palestine*. Harper & Row, 1984.
Pinsker, Leon. *Auto-Emancipation*. Association of Young Zionist Societies, 1932.
Rabinowicz, Harry. *Hasidism and the State of Israel*. Fairleigh Dickinson University Press, 1982.
Ravitzky, Aviezer. *Haketz hamegule vemedinat ha yehudim: Mashichiut, tsionut veradikalizm dati beisrael*. Am Oved, 1993.
Regev, Menachem. "The Arab Problem in Israel Children's Books." *Journal on Zionism and the Jewish World* 9 (1969): 84–110.
Rubenstein, Richard L. *After Auschwitz: History, Theology, and Contemporary Judaism*. Johns Hopkins University Press, 1992.
Ruppin, Arthur. *Three Decades of Palestine: Speeches and Papers on the Upbuilding of the Jewish National Home*. Schocken, 1936.
Sachar, Howard M. *A History of Israel: From the Aftermath of the Yom Kippur War*. Vol. 2. Oxford University Press, 1987.
———. *A History of Israel: From the Rise of Zionism to Our Time*. Vol. 1. Alfred Knopf, 1991.
Sarid, Levi Arieh. "The Revenge Organization: Its History, Image, and Deeds." *Yalkut Moreshet* 52 (April 1992): 35–106.

Scholem, Gershom. *Den judiska mystiken*. Brutus Östling Bokförlag Symposion, 1992.
———. *Jewish Gnosticism, Merkabah Mysticism, and Talmudic Tradition*. Jewish Theological Seminary of America, 1960.
———. *The Messianic Idea in Judaism and Other Essays on Jewish Spirituality*. Schocken Books, 1971.
———. *On Jews and Judaism in Crisis*. Schocken Books, 1976.
———. *Sabbatai Sevi: The Mystical Messiah, 1626–1676*. Princeton University Press, 1973.
Schwarzschild, Steven. Menachem Kellner, ed. *The Pursuit of the Ideal: Jewish Writings of Steven Schwarzschild*. SUNY Press, 1990.
Segev, Tom. *The Seventh Million: The Israelis and the Holocaust*. Hill and Wang, 1993.
Shahak, Israel. *Jewish History, Jewish Religion*. Pluto Press, London 1994.
Shalev, Meir. *The Blue Mountain*. HarperCollins, 1991.
Shamir, Yitzhak. *Summing Up: An Autobiography*. Weidenfeld & Nicholson, 1994.
Shapira, Anita. *Land and Power: The Zionist Resort to Force, 1881–1948*. Oxford University Press, 1992.
Shapiro, Leon. *The History of ORT: A Jewish Movement for Social Change*. Shocken Books, 1980.
Shapiro, Yonathan. *The Road to Power: Herut Party in Israel*. SUNY Press, 1992.
Sharett, Moshe. *Yoman Medini 1936*. Am Oved, 1968.
Shipler, David K. *Arab and Jew: Wounded Spirits in a Promised Land*. Penguin, 1987.
Shohat, Ella. *Israeli Cinema: East/West and the Politics of Representation*. University of Texas Press, 1987.
Silberman, Neil Asher. *A Prophet from Amongst You: The Life of Yigael Yadin: Soldier, Scholar, and Mythmaker of Modern Israel*. Addison Wesley, 1993.
Silberstein, Laurence J. *Jewish Fundamentalism in Comparative Perspective*. New York University Press, 1993.
Sprinzak, Ehud. *The Ascendance of Israel's Radical Right*. Oxford University Press, 1991.
Steinsaltz, Adin. *The Tales of Rabbi Nachman of Bratslav*. Jason Aronson, Inc., 1993.

———. *Teshuvah.* The Free Press, 1987.
Sternhell, Zeev. *Binyan ha'uma o tikkun ha'hevra?* Am Oved, 1995.
———. *The Birth of Fascist Ideology.* Princeton University Press, 1994.
Sykes, Christopher. *Crossroads to Israel: Palestine from Balfour to Bevin.* Collins, 1965.
Tingsten, Herbert. *Det hotade Israel.* Wahlström & Widstrand, 1957.
———. *Min politiska horisont.* Norstedts, 1969.
Vital, David. *The Future of the Jews: A People at the Crossroads?* Harvard University Press, 1990.
———. *The Origins of Zionism.* Oxford University Press, 1975.
———. *Zionism: The Formative Years.* Clarendon Press, 1982.
Walzer, Michael. *Exodus and Revolution.* Basic Books, 1985.
Weinstock, Nathan. *Le Sionisme contre Israël.* Maspero, 1969.
Weizmann, Chaim. *Trial and Error: The Autobiography of Chaim Weizmann.* Jewish Publication Society of America, 1949.
Weizmann, Chaim. Barnett Litvinoff, ed. *The Essential Chaim Weizmann.* Weidenfeld & Nicholson, 1982.
Yaron, Zvi. *The Philosophy of Rabbi Kook.* Torah Education Department of the World Zionist Organization, 1991.
Zipperstein, Steven J. *Elusive Prophet: Ahad Ha'am and the Origins of Zionism.* University of California Press, 1993.

ONE-WAY STREET AND OTHER WRITINGS

Walter Benjamin

Walter Benjamin – philosopher, essayist, literary and cultural theorist – was one of the most original writers and thinkers of the twentieth century. This new selection brings together Benjamin's major works, including 'One-Way Street', his dreamlike, aphoristic observations of urban life in Weimar Germany; 'Unpacking My Library', a delightful meditation on book-collecting; the confessional 'Hashish in Marseille'; and 'The Work of Art in the Age of Mechanical Reproduction', his seminal essay on how technology changes the way we appreciate art. Also including writings on subjects ranging from Proust to Kafka, violence to surrealism, this is the essential volume on one of the most prescient critical voices of the modern age.

'There has been no more original, no more serious, critic and reader in our time' George Steiner

THE WRETCHED OF THE EARTH

Frantz Fanon

Written at the height of the Algerian war for independence, Frantz Fanon's classic text has provided inspiration for anticolonial movements ever since. With power and anger, Fanon makes clear the economic and psychological degradation inflicted by imperialism. It was Fanon, himself a psychotherapist, who exposed the connection between colonial war and mental disease, who showed how the fight for freedom must be combined with building a national culture, and who showed the way ahead, through revolutionary violence, to socialism. Many of the great calls to arms from the era of decolonization are now purely of historical interest, yet this passionate analysis of the relations between the great powers and the Third World is just as illuminating about the world we live in today.

'In clear language, in words that can only have been written in the cool heat of rage, he showed us the internal theatre of racism'
Independent

CHERNOBYL PRAYER

Svetlana Alexievich

On 26 April 1986 the worst nuclear reactor accident in history occured in Chernobyl and contaminated as much as three quarters of Europe. While the official Soviet narrative downplayed the accident's impact, Svetlana Alexievich wanted to know how people understood it. She recorded hundreds of interviews with workers at the nuclear plant, refugees and resettlers, scientists and bureaucrats, crafting their monologues into a stunning oral history of the nuclear disaster. What their stories reveal is the fear, anger and uncertainty with which they still live but also a dark humour and desire to see the beauty of everyday life, including that of Chernobyl's new landscape. A chronicle of the past and a warning for our nuclear future, *Chernobyl Prayer* is a haunting masterpiece.

'A searing mix of eloquence and wordlessness . . . From her interviewees' monologues she creates history that the reader, at whatever distance from the events, can actually touch' Julian Evans, *The Telegraph*

THE ORIGINS OF TOTALITARIANISM

Hannah Arendt

Hannah Arendt's chilling analysis of the conditions that led to the Nazi and Soviet totalitarian regimes is a warning from history about the fragility of freedom, exploring how propaganda, scapegoats, terror and political isolation all aided the slide towards total domination.

'Perhaps Arendt's most profound legacy is in establishing that one has to consider oneself political as part of the human condition. What are your political acts, and what politics do they serve?' *Guardian*